Knowledge and Special Libraries

Resources for the Knowledge-Based Economy

Knowledge and Special Libraries

Edited by
James M. Matarazzo
Suzanne D. Connolly

Routledge
Taylor & Francis Group

LONDON AND NEW YORK

First published by Butterworth-Heinemann

This edition published 2011 by Routledge
2 Park Square, Milton Park, Abingdon, Oxon OX14 4RN
711 Third Avenue, New York, NY 10017, USA

Routledge is an imprint of the Taylor & Francis Group, an informa business

Copyright © 1999 by Taylor & Francis

Library of Congress Cataloging-in-Publication Data
Knowledge and special libraries / edited by James M. Marazzo,
  Suzanne D. Connolly.
    p. cm.—(Resources for the knowledge-based economy)
    Includes bibliographical references and index.

    1. Corporate libraries—United States. 2. Knowledge management—
United States. I. Matarazzo, James M., 1941– . II. Connolly,
Suzanne D. III. Series.
Z675.C778K58 1998
027.6'9—dc21   98–40687
                                                                    CIP

British Library Cataloguing-in-Publication Data
A catalogue record for this book is available from the British Library.
ISBN - 978 0 7506 7084 5

Contents

Introduction

OUR PROFESSION

Libraries have always existed with the sole purpose of serving patrons and providing information. Librarians have always been considered the experts at navigating through countless information sources and finding the correct answer to a request. By possessing these skills, we have always maintained a certain degree of control over our end-users. Librarians understand and know how to use cryptic reference books and complicated on-line databases. We have taken on the role of internal consultants to our clients when they sought specific information. For a very long time, librarians held the key to using these sources, which provided us great job security. This is evidenced in a 1990 study by Prusak and Matarazzo (*Valuing Corporate Libraries: A Survey of Senior Managers*, published by the Special Libraries Association, 1990) where 80 percent of the end-users surveyed said electronic database searching was the most important service provided by the library. But with the dramatic increase in target-marketing and sales of on-line products and services directly to end-users, we are losing many of our clients. In a follow-up 1995 survey (*The Value of Corporate Libraries: Findings from a 1995 Survey of Senior Management—A Follow-up Survey*, published by the Special Libraries Association, 1995), only 48 percent surveyed end-users cited electronic database searching as the most important service provided by the library. End-users feel confident enough to fulfill their own information requests.

What does all this mean? With the growth of all this computing power, end-users feel empowered to sign on and search. This has become increasingly evident through the growth of the World Wide Web. The explosion of the Web has provided everyone with a modem access to the world. Because some end-users are bypassing the library and fulfilling their own information requests, the future of libraries have come into question. Librarians are no longer needed to act as intermediaries between end-users and information. It is no small wonder that so much of the literature focuses around the changes taking place in libraries today. Much of the literature focuses around the creation of new operating models for libraries. Some argue that technology will replace librarians, and others debate that the human component of our work is necessary.

Whatever the outcome of the debate may be, librarians have a critical skill set that can be applied to new environments. All one has to do is look at the phenomenal growth of companies like Yahoo! that have applied traditional library practices such as indexing and classification to Web pages to make navigating the Web easier. We can only benefit from all the dramatic changes taking place. Within this chaotic workplace is opportunity for us to change our traditional mindset and master new skills, which can be added to our existing set. This should not be viewed as a disadvantage but as a liberation from some of our more mundane tasks. Providing information is our most important contribution to the field. When we discuss information, this includes not only third party vendor information but also internal company information. This includes understanding our company and identifying the most important activity it performs, which can be as simple as reading our company's mission statement or having a conversation with coworkers. It's building networks and leveraging them when necessary to provide our end-users the critical, much needed information. It includes making our libraries the crossroads within our corporations. End-users will look to us as liaisons between different parts of the organization.

How we deliver information is changing, but it is our opportunity to do more with information than just passively send it along to our end-users. Who knows better how to manipulate and deliver information than librarians? We have seen the growth of the information technology (IT) function within firms, and although they focus solely on the electronic component, they very often dismiss the relevance of the human element. When someone needs an answer to a question, the fastest, most efficient way is to ask someone not to try to manipulate some database.

REASON FOR THIS READER

The purpose of this reader is to provide my colleagues a well-thought-out and organized selection of articles about our profession. Currently, much of the literature focuses solely on the management of libraries but not on the environment in which libraries operate.

ARTICLE SELECTION

The articles selected for this compendium are drawn from the fields of information and library science and business management. Since most special libraries are corporate libraries, the selections are taken from these different disciplines to provide perspectives from both a business standpoint and an information management one. The first part focuses on the necessity of information within organizations. It highlights how information is critical to a firm's success. Although information is recognized as a vital commodity, many political implications surround its delivery. More is involved than understanding how to deliver information, such as to whom to deliver it to have an impact. This part brings to light many challenges that librarians face in a corporate environment.

The second part focuses on the positive contributions libraries have made to their firms. Librarians often are not given enough credit for their achievements. Because what we do is so difficult to measure, we are not recognized as valuable contributors. The last part focuses on the future of our profession.

The selections contain many different predictions about libraries and librarians of the future. They focus on new roles and highlight the importance of our profession. We definitely have a strong place on our firm's organization charts, and we must seize the opportunity. With the rapid growth of technology, end-users are being inundated with choices. They need expert advice from experienced practitioners.

INFORMATION AS A STRATEGIC WEAPON FOR THE ORGANIZATION

Librarians have always viewed themselves as separate. We tend to think of ourselves as islands within a firm. We need to step back and look at the big picture. In the first part, the selected five articles focus on the importance of information within a firm.

The first selection by Blaise Cronin and Elisabeth Davenport, "Competitive Edge," reviews how firms maintain a competitive advantage in the marketplace. Companies compete on many different levels such as time, cost, price, product differentiation, quality, and image. Information plays a major role in these different areas. If decisions makers have the correct information they can make the critical decisions. Thus, they can determine whether their firm is a leader or a follower. But senior management can not make good decisions if it receives bad or, worse, "late" information. Often times, management has good information at its fingertips but the challenge lies in the delivery of it. The second selection "Information Politics" by Thomas H. Davenport, Robert G. Eccles, and Laurence Prusak, highlights that firms are very political. People become possessive of what they know and are not willing to share information for fear it will diminish their power base. Sometimes bad information can be given to deter certain power plays in motion. Understanding how a firm operates and its culture often is as important as knowing how to use information. In "Powers of Information" by William Davidow and Michael Malone, the authors emphasize the importance of providing *correct* and *timely* information. So often, decisions are made based on bad information. which produces disastrous results.

To provide a perspective from the field of library science, an article is included stressing the importance of a special library's role within a corporation. Because the use of information cannot be measured, people tend to think of it in the abstract. It doesn't always provide immediate value. In "The Importance of Information Services for Productivity 'Under-recognized' and Under-invested," Micheal Koenig stresses this problem which libraries constantly face. Libraries are synonymous with information but when downsizing comes into effect, the library's budget is first to be cut because people think of information services as a luxury instead of a necessity.

Another important aspect of information management includes the IT function. Traditionally, these groups are very systems oriented, and most information needs can be fulfilled through technology. The selection by Michael E. Porter and Victor Millar, "How Information Gives You Competitive Advantage," contrasts with many of the other selections. It provides the perspective from an IT point of view. The emphasis is focused more on the IT function within firms, but there is the same belief regarding the necessity of information. To survive in the 1990s, firms need to make a commitment to the development of their IT functions. Like libraries, IT departments have been treated as a support service within firms and often experience downsizing during times of recession. Although the delivery of information is very different between librarians and systems groups, the goals are ultimately the same. Both stress the importance of the firm understanding the broad effects and implications of information and how it can create substantial and sustainable competitive advantage.

THE SPECIAL LIBRARY AS A BUSINESS ASSET

Special libraries are important within an organization. They provide services to end-users, which help them to perform more effectively in their work. In "Toward a Better Understanding of New Special Libraries," by Elin Christianson and Janet L. Anrensfeld, the authors discuss the growth of special libraries within many different organizations. Some of the reasons for this growth include management relations, management attitudes, economics, and user commitment. Also this growth can be attributed to the special libraries ability to market themselves better.

Even with all the changes taking place today, the library's mission is still the same to serve and inform. Although D. N. Handy's article "The Library as a Business Asset" is over eighty years old, it still reflects on the necessity of maintaining libraries. The value of a library is not reflected in the size of its collection but on its use. The library is a tool to foster efficiency and enlighten the masses. The challenge lies in shared agreement of this concept to management. Because financial statements only reflect the cost of maintaining a library, it is difficult to see its contribution. It is becoming more difficult to see the value of corporate libraries as time progresses. Some of the changes in the profession are exemplified in two studies done by James Matarazzo and Laurence Prusak. The studies focus on the value of corporate libraries within organizations. The first was completed in 1990 and a follow-up one done in 1995. Both reflect the changes that have taken place in our profession over the last five years. The 1995 study highlights a disturbing decrease in the number of librarians in corporate libraries. In the 1990 study, 11 percent of the libraries reported a staff of 20 employees or more. By 1995, only 6 percent reported staffs of 20 or more. Some of the changes are attributed to the growth of computing power and the expansion of network capabilities, growth of on-line services and products available to end-users and corporate downsizing and reengineering.

The next selection draws on the writings of Patrick Wilson, a major contributor in the field of library science. His piece, "The Librarian as Information Source," reviews the librarian's role as an intricate part of the library process. Librarians offer not only a wealth of information in terms of navigating through bibliographic sources but also can prove immensely valuable as a sort of corporate memory. They can act as a liaison between the different business units by bringing people together. This can happen, providing librarians continue to be well-informed. As Lynda Woodman points out in her piece "Information Management in Large Organisations," certain factors constrain the development of information management in most firms, such as open communication.

A NEW MODEL FOR SPECIAL LIBRARIES

Having outlined the information environment in the first part and the impact of special libraries within the existing information environment, the last part focuses on the evolution of special libraries. It is clear that libraries cannot remain staid within their organizations. The old model no longer works. The value does not come from our collections but from *us*. Librarians offer so much, and it is time for us to get out of the stacks. This section contains selections that speculate about the future of libraries and librarians within society.

Stephen Abram's article "Post Information Age Positioning for Special Librarians: Is Knowledge Management the Answer?" looks at increased focus on managing knowledge within firms. He contends that since librarians are the experts at managing information; this is the next venue for us to explore. "Future Librarians" by Robert C. Berrings examines our shift from a print society to a virtual one. The selection explores the librarian's role in this new culture. It attempts to answer the questions where we fit and how will we operate in our new environment.

The next selection, "Blow up the Corporate Library," challenges librarians to do away with traditional conventions. It is no secret that libraries play a marginal role in today's corporation, which is frustrating to librarians because we are living in the "information age." Prusak and Davenport believe that the problem is that librarians are operating under the wrong conceptual model of what an information service should be in the 1990s. The authors offer some alternative operating models that will help librarians achieve more recognition with their firms.

Although Prusak and Davenport promote new ways for librarians to succeed within their firms, Betty Eddison, the author of "Our Profession Is Changing," looks at the issue of library services being outsourced. Firms have been moving toward this model with the belief that it is better to bring in services from the outside to achieve quality services than to do everything on their own.

The next selection "Special Libraries at Work: The Library Manager as Part of the Organization Team" advises librarians to take on more of a proactive role. Librarians should manage their departments as a business unit. This includes setting objectives and goals and defining its purpose within the organization. Also, it is necessary to measure achievements at the end of the year and be accountable for successes and failures. The last piece, "Information Management: A Process Review," addresses the human element necessary when managing information. Valuable information often resides in people's briefcases, files, or heads. To leverage this information, it is important for information managers to be familiar with the complex world of information sources, human or otherwise. Since information management is cross-functional, the expertise of others in an organization may be necessary to produce new and more effective approaches and mechanisms to manage information.

SUMMARY

Formerly, a library was viewed as a place for information storage, and information was viewed as simply bits of data. Furthermore, many wielded information as a tool of power, in that those who had more information had more authority. It is becoming increasingly clear that shared collective knowledge of an organization is of far greater value than that of each individual's privately held data. In view of our changing profession, it has become clear that we are being charged with the mission to explore and implement new and innovative methods to encourage sharing and to better manage information.

Part One

Information as a Strategic Weapon for the Organization

Part One

Information as a Strategic Weapon for the Organization

1

Competitive Edge

Blaise Cronin and Elisabeth Davenport

WHERE TO COMPETE

Where do you compete? In a biological sense, by being smart, by being strong, by being attractive (in terms of the criteria of the moment). In a business sense, by being a leader, not a laggard (smart), by being predator rather than prey (strong), by dominating markets (attractive). These areas of competition can be broken into specifics:

- you compete in time
- you compete on cost
- you compete on price
- you compete on product differentiation
- you compete on quality
- you compete on image

What information do you need in order to compete on each of these dimensions? Take cost, for example. Obviously you need to know the cost structure of the industry and how you compare with competitors. What are typical unit costs? Where are cheap sources of raw materials? Where do your competitors source their materials? What are the delivered and installed costs of a substitute product? What are the associated capital costs if the substitute product is to be matched? The information you need to answer these questions will be drawn from a spectrum of in-house experts (accountants, production managers, bench scientists, procurement specialists) and outsiders (sectoral analysts, suppliers, distributors, industry insiders, dealers, ex-employees, consultants), using both publicly available and private sources. Figure 1-1 maps the terrain and players.

What can you do about quality, short of industrial espionage? You can *listen* to suppliers, reverse-engineer products, track the trade press to identify state-of-

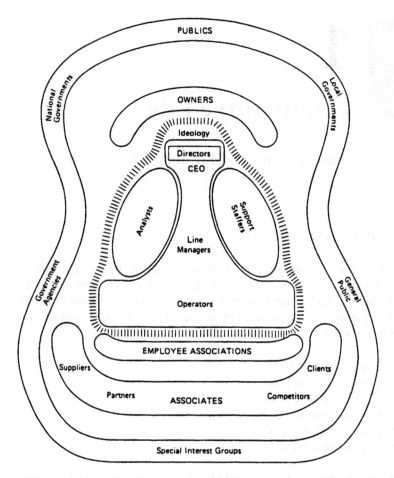

FIGURE 1-1   Reprinted with permission of The Free Press, a Division of Macmillan, Inc., from *Mintzberg on management: inside our strange world of organizations*, by Henry Mintzberg. Copyright © 1989 by Henry Mintzberg.

the-art technologies and services, and, most importantly, *talk* to buyers (wholesalers, retailers, final customers). You can also *look,* by visiting trade fairs, competitor plants and specialist demonstrations. As before, your source mix is heterogeneous; formal, informal, eyes, ears, hands.

How do you reverse-engineer an image? What information do you need to compete successfully where the market is dominated by established brands? How do you compete against exclusivity (the Cartier, Gucci, Ferrari, or Bollinger *marques*)? Paloma Picasso has entered the fragrance sector: like other vendors, she is selling pheromones (chemical attractants) and she is selling virtual social mobility (the fantasy of participation in the Picasso *milieu*). Like her competitors, she can to some extent ensure success by deploying a team of market researchers, with a battery of market research techniques for in-depth demographic and psy-chographic modeling. But the real value of the Paloma brand name is exclusivity: she is selling herself (her face and signature dominate the advertisements). A com-petitor in this case can carry out equally sophisticated consumer research, but must find a name of comparable *cachet* to front the product.

And how do you compete on innovation? By scanning formal sources (tech-nical journals, databases, product announcements), by using futurologists and by tracking the work of those at the research front. A primary formal source is patent literature. Patents and trademarks exist to protect ideas. In a highly competitive industry like pharmaceutics, where innovation tends to drive profitability, knowl-edge of the prior art is crucially important. The ability to access historic or archi-val information can thus be as important as the inputs from industrial "spies." The services of informers (a generic for those who gather informal information) will also be of use; moles, and deep throats who work under cover, or scouts (pro-fessional barflies) who gather information by osmosis in public places.

SOURCES OF ADVANTAGE

Good coordination is the *sine qua non* of successful competition. Many of our elements of competition will be managed by specialists (accountants know about costs and prices, production managers handle timing and scheduling); their working environment (in terms of structure and technology) must allow them to connect. Generic sources of competitive advantage also include superior strength, nerve and fitness; experience and depth of knowledge; insight into your rival's strengths and weaknesses; inside track on a competitor's intentions; gamesman-ship; alliances. These apply as much in business as in sport, or arenas where physi-cal prowess is important.

The athlete's superior strength and fitness translate into manufacturing ca-pacity and reputation, strong market share and cash flow; expertise and depth of knowledge (how to conserve energy; judge conditions) are the equivalents of know-how and proprietary technology; gamesmanship (elbowing or swerving in front of a rival) can be equated with industrial espionage, aggressive advertising ("knocking copy"), or poaching key personnel; alliances (using a pace setter in a middle-distance race; partners in tag wrestling) translate into joint ventures in re-search and development, marketing, manufacture or distribution, or the creation of a buying group.

Checking the form and track record of a competitor is analogous to carrying out a S.W.O.T. (strengths, weaknesses, opportunities, threats) analysis of industry competitors, while having an inside track on a competitor's intentions (in a take-over bid, for example) means deciphering a barrage of official press releases, com-pany reports and public pronouncements and assessing their reliability. There is, as we said [earlier], a difference between public posture and corporate body lan-guage: on occasions, the former will be used to conceal actual strategic intentions. Camouflage counts in battle and in business. The role of information technology (heavy artillery, to sustain the military analogy) in leveraging competitive advantage is widely acknowledged: "As labour, in the traditional sense, evaporates in most industries, and capital becomes a globally purchasable commodity, IT will become the tool for building competitive organisational behaviour—along with investments in management. Indeed, the computer industry reflects this with direct labour typically representing only 4% or so of sales."[1]

As we have already said, competitive advantage is achieved on the back of differentiation. A firm can differentiate itself from its rivals using a range of strategies, from reducing costs, through focusing (on a particular market segment), to broadening its scope (offering bundled products or services to its customers). A fuller list is given in Figure 1-2.

The Oil Mix

Where you are competing on all or many of these fronts, information management is a major issue. In a large multi-national, intelligence may be as strategically important as it is in the military environment. The logistics are similar: coordinating a complex of sources, channels, feeds and outputs; optimizing the technology platform, and using both activities to establish a competitive edge over your adversaries.

Sources of Differentiation

* COST (aim for cost leadership)

* EXCLUSIVITY (superior product quality)

* FOCUS (on a clearly defined market, or market segment)

* SCOPE (offer bundled service/product; vertical integration)

* CUSTOMIZATION (tailor product to expressed market demand)

* DISTRIBUTION (convenience; choice of mode; global reach)

* INNOVATION (stay one step ahead of rivals)

FIGURE 1-2   Sources of Differentiation

In the oil industry, for example, internal information systems are a critical resource as the processes of exploration, extraction, fractionation, and distribution depend on detailed and accurate reporting and coordination. Information intensity is a feature of any company operating in this sector. Competitive edge, therefore, may not depend on external monitoring with a view to knocking out the competition, or securing a geographical niche (unless there is a state monopoly sustained by protectionist legislation), but on prowess in-house (R&D, perfecting a new process, producing a new synthetic material).

It may be linked to quality factors like performing each stage of the production process better, prospecting with fewer misses, extracting with fewer disasters, processing with less pollution, distributing with fewer spills: a strong health and safety record improves street and political credibility. Or (another internal factor) a company may choose to compete on issue management, or the major public concerns of the day (lead pollution; protection of species).

The sector is fiercely competitive and no company can rest on its laurels: since 1980, eleven of the twenty-five U.S. majors have been acquired, merged or sold off. No matter how well a company competes on the factors we have mentioned, forces outside its control can make or break an operation. Oil is a highly volatile commodity, and survival may depend less on cost containment or technological supremacy than on the ability to cope with macro-environmental turbulence (slump in market demand resulting in slashed prices for crude).

In this situation there is a limited number of courses which might put a particular producer at an advantage. A company may choose to enter a cartel, but the advantages here are shared, and may be limited by regulation. What else can a player do? Monitoring of commodity fluctuations can offset the worst of surprises, or a company may choose to lobby at the level of national energy policy (political action committees). Alternatively, producers may choose to invest in macro-level smear campaigns targeted at alternative sources of energy; or they may attempt to boost demand in alternative markets like plastics or animal feeds (diversification strategy).

Whether quality or issue management is the primary focus of competitive activity, detailed and wide-ranging intelligence will be required, what may be called total information, based on systems which can analyze input from wildly disparate sources and global locations. At one end of the spectrum, a company may use lugworms (a common marine species) to detect gas bubbles or leakage; at the other end, expert systems are used as aids to prospecting and fault diagnosis.

Total quality is best assured by integration and interaction. Geographic information systems (GIS), for example, allow major companies to process ever-changing lease maps, to identify optimum locations for gas stations, to create 3-D geological models; these may link with EIS (executive information systems) which can analyze market data, key business indicators, time series data and competitor intelligence (of the non-worm, non-barfly sort). These in turn may integrate with engineering and operations information to ensure that the right spare parts are delivered, or welds accurately performed.

Such capabilities are in place in many companies. Why, in that case, the tanker spillages (Exxon Valdez, Torrey Canyon), the oil platform infernos (Piper

Alpha), the refinery explosions (Whiddy Refinery)? Tolerated because infrequent? Or because they don't happen all at once to the same company? Or because intelligence isn't quite total enough? Reports from Piper Alpha that employees reported tell-tale warning signs two days before the disaster suggest that systems are perhaps not optimally participative, or that at the well-head, they are not heeded. Is human resource intelligence all it should be at this level? Do companies know sufficient (in a non-prurient sense) about employee lifestyles, personality traits, skills and motivations for both the company and employees to develop optimally?[2]

A hot issue at the beginning of the nineties is the greening of oil, as much a question of hearts and minds as of health and safety. What sort of intelligence is needed to ensure that *issues* are managed for competitive advantage? The thermoclines of public opinion must be mapped at consumer level; this is as important as tracking and lobbying those who regulate the industry, but, of course, such intelligence may be gathered by competitors. Differentiating the company by acts of philanthropy may be effective: the public may warm to gestures like British Petroleum's endowment of an ecology gallery in the Natural History Museum in London. A detailed knowledge of how consumers' attitudes to issues differ is important. The values which drive environmental concern vary across geographical regions; in the U.K., for example, the Greens worry about health, a sense of duty drives the Germans, the main concern of the Italians is aesthetics. . . .[3] Case presentation and advertising must pick up such nuances. In some cases, however, psychometry is irrelevant; the critical differentiator is location of a gas station, where convenience ensures brand loyalty.

STRATEGIC INFORMATION

Competition, then, may be grounded in specifics. In the previous chapter [from which this article was taken], we explored ways in which the value of information could be quantified in terms of these specifics (time saved; cost reduction). We stressed throughout, however, that many of the benefits of information investment are intangible, and can only be expressed in terms of open-ended variables, like increased market share, whose full value will only be realized after the event. We address such soft variables in this chapter, what might be called the macro elements of competition which affect overall strategy.

The specifics, or micro elements, may be configured to create advantage where it matters most. The *strategic gameboard* [see Figure 1-3] can focus your thinking. The specifics may also be seen as weapons in a war, or pieces in a game. Judicious investment in information and information systems impacts each of these micro elements, but investment, as we have already stressed, will only be effective when linked to business objectives. Given this perspective, the manager's concerns will not be saving dimes and adding bells and whistles, but major issues, like

- the shape of the market
- optimizing intelligence
- competitive posture
- playing the system
- trading risks against rewards.

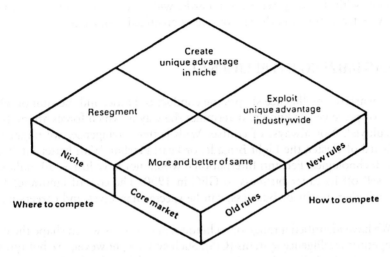

FIGURE 1-3 Reproduced from L. Bergsma, From market research to business research. *McKinsey Quarterly,* Autumn 1984, 50–62. Reprinted by permission of McKinsey & Company.

THE SHAPE OF THE MARKET

In economic terms a market is an exchange mechanism, which is shaped by the information available to the participants. In an ideal market, the consumer is assumed to make a rational choice on the basis of perfect information. This, in reality, is impossible to achieve, though some systems approximate to the ideal more closely than others. The types of information which shape perceptions and behavior in markets are what we have labeled the micro elements of competition, cost, differentiation, quality.

Price, for example, is a key determinant of propensity to purchase; in a complex and fractionated market, it is unlikely that the consumer can even approximate to full information. A manager, in contrast, who has greater knowledge of overall price structure than both the consumer and rival producers, may be able to compete effectively on this basis.

A classic example is the use of customer reservation systems in the airline industry, where computerization has produced intense competition on price. In the short run this has benefited the air traveler (predatory pricing resulting in huge discounts; the introduction of frequent flyer schemes), but the pressure on operating costs is such that airlines with tight margins, if not forced to the wall (Braniff, People Express, Laker Airways), will tend to cut back on safety levels (bend or flout Federal Aviation Administration [FAA] rules) and defer investment in replacement planes.

The deregulation of the U.S. airline industry illustrates this scenario: the early euphoria which greeted bargain basement pricing was followed by a wave of discontent with declining service standards, widespread labor unrest, protracted industry restructuring and the emergence of an effective oligarchy.

OPTIMIZING INTELLIGENCE

In warfare, intelligence shapes the conduct of battle, and the sum of what is known, or perceived as known, determines the way in which forces are mobilized and deployed. Not always, of course. With better intelligence, we might never have heard of Custer, the Light Brigade, or Pearl Harbor. With better intelligence on ISC Technologies, Ferranti International would not have lost $350 million *and* had to sell off its radar business to GEC in 1990. The cost of ignorance (blind spots), whether in war or business, can be spectacular. Lives and careers may be lost.

We have identified a range of techniques and sources which shape the design of competitor intelligence systems (CIS). Such systems, however, are but one facet of an organization's IS (information systems) portfolio. Herein lies the paradox: intelligence shapes business strategy which in turn determines IS investment priorities, yet the funding case for CIS invariably has to be argued along with all other systems proposals.

Intelligence has two main purposes: warning about enemy intentions, and long-term assessment of the enemy's capabilities. The sources of intelligence vary. Some may be covert (and fuel campaigns of subversion or destablization); some may be overt (hard evidence, by direct or remote observation of the adversary's real intentions). Intelligence involves both present perception, and prediction.

Present perceptions may be distorted for a variety of reasons. Preconceptions act as filters of what may be essential information (the "impossibility" of *glasnost* in the U.S.S.R. resulted in disregard of early signs of such a development). Distortion of perception may occur because of what is known as action-reaction interference: "The more absorbed intelligence becomes in understanding the uniqueness of its target, the more it may forget how far the target is responding to its own perceptions of the other side."[4]

In other words, the observer inevitably influences the situation observed. There is a potential dissonance between the intelligence agents and policy-makers; if relations are too distant, the first group will have little credibility in the eyes of the second; if they work too closely together, the second group may bias investigation. Many intelligence operators favor interpretation in terms of worse case scenarios, which may encourage unreasonable pessimism or paranoia. Commercial paranoia, in contrast, may be not only healthy, but necessary (the consequences are less devastating than those of military paranoia).

A crucial component of intelligence is self-awareness or the capacity to see ourselves as others see us, a blind spot in many organizations. Where an enemy's movements are a response to their perception of your own stance, they may take action that is labeled by you "irrational" or "aggressive." In their terms, however, they have made a rational defensive move. In the business field, the capability for self-awareness has been labeled defensive competitor intelligence, that is monitoring and evaluating your business activities as your competitors might perceive them.[5] Routine scanning of standard sources for competitor intelligence on one's own company, and analysis on the same terms as information on rivals, may provide unexpected and important insights.

Self-awareness is now part of standard management training, yet is rarely discussed in the context of business strategy. Figure 1-4 is a simple tool which

	Known to self	**Unknown to self**
Known to others	*Public Arena*	*Blind Spot*
Unknown to others	*Private Life*	*Unknown Area*

4 quadrants ... 4 intelligence objectives

Public arena = optimization
Private life = concealment
Unknown area = penetration
Blind spot = minimization

FIGURE 1-4 Johari Window. Reproduced from J. Luft, *Of human interaction.* Palo Alto, CA: Mayfield, 1969. Reprinted by permission of the author.

helps to identify blind spots. Where can you get reliable information on how the world sees you, given the prevalence of sycophancy or telling people what they want to hear? Potential sources include press clippings, salesforce gossip, feedback from user groups, customer complaints, employee suggestions, analysts' advice to investors and stockholders, shareholder comments at the company's annual general meetings.

If realistic assessment of the existing competitor environment is difficult, prediction is more so. Past actions may have been intentionally misleading, intended to feed a false profile. Current statements of intent may be equally devious.

THE JAPANESE WAY

Japan has had minimal defense obligations since 1945, and the country's resources have been concentrated on commercial, not military, superiority. The Japanese approach to competitors is pragmatic, immediate and grounded in detail; it resembles the body search, rather than large-scale reconnaissance (an analogue of the activity which characterizes many intelligence or long-range planning units in Western corporations, where the military model is considered exemplary). The story of Honda's entry into the U.S. biking sector is one of marketing's classic folktales: when their initial model failed (a sure seller in Japan, because its handlebars resembled the eyebrows of the Buddha), the pioneer salesforce camped on the street, and observed the habits and the machines of their clientele . . . the rest is history.

Factory visits and trade fairs are primary hunting grounds, rather than the conference or seminar circuit favored by many marketing units in the U.S. or U.K., and focus on detail is complemented by wide diffusion of observations, with iterative and flexible discussion, role playing and interpretation. Strategy formulation admits many degrees of freedom and multiple perspectives are held to be a source of strength, not confusion. The same questions will be asked over and over again, or with different questioners and respondents to catch every nuance and shift in perspective. These methods harvest information on rivals, and on how other groups see the company (suppliers or distributors for example).

SOCIAL INTELLIGENCE

The approaches outlined in this chapter can be also be applied at the level of the state. Take the case of a developing nation, trying to sustain its commodity exports, build up indigenous manufacturing capability, identify alternative sources of energy, or attract foreign direct investment. Where does it turn for reliable information, trend data, intelligence and technological know-how? What kinds of information systems and intelligence effort will be needed?

The problems facing these nations are orders of magnitude greater than those facing industrialized (or newly industrialized) countries. As a bloc, developing countries account for more than 70 percent of world population, 20 percent of trade, 11 percent of industrial production, 7 percent of the global telecommunications infrastructure, less than 6 percent of the world's computers, 5 percent of published scientific output, and 3 percent of R&D expenditures.[6] The gap between first and third worlds can be measured using a variety of indicators such as productivity rates, output levels, capital formation, average income, morbidity and mortality statistics, quality of life factors, and so on. But the divide between the two worlds is also a function of the massive cognitive and social intelligence gaps which exist on almost every conceivable dimension.[7]

At this level, the game is multi-form: it includes aid negotiation, commodity trading, mega-marketing, foreign direct investment, dumping, debt restructuring, price fixing. There is a motley cast of players: transnational corporations (TNCs), non-governmental agencies (NGOs), donor nations, trading partners, creditor banks, lobbyists, peripatetic consultants. The rules are complex, and prone to flux (price taking, debt rescheduling, trans-border data flow, local content levels, nationalization, sequestration). It is a game in which the long-term stakes are high.

Knowledge of the rules and sanctions is important; so too, insights into the strategic thinking and intentions of competitors. In this game, intelligence quality is the difference between losing and losing hopelessly. A panoptic model of a development-orientated intelligence effort is shown in Figure 1-5. The scope ranges

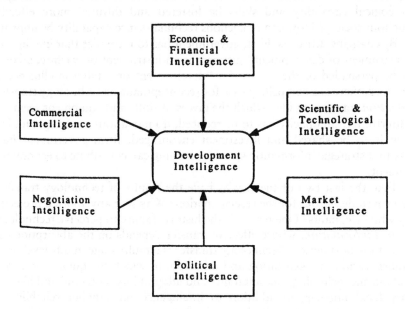

FIGURE 1-5 Components of a Development-Orientated Intelligence Effort. Reproduced from N. Jequier and S. Dedijier, Information, knowledge and intelligence: a general overview. In: S. Dedijier and J. Jequier (eds.), *Intelligence for economic development: an inquiry in the role of the knowledge industry.* Oxford. Berg, 1987, p.12. Reprinted by permission of the publisher.

from intelligence on multinationals (track record; intentions; commitment; sensitivity to local conditions; unionization; screwdriver plants or local R&D) through information on science and technology (emergent technologies; "hot spots"; technology licensing opportunities; standards; patenting trends) to market intelligence (shifts in consumer behavior; niche markets; low-cost suppliers).

Systems can be set up to track and store information under each of these headings, but crucial insights or leads will often depend on links being made between disparate elements (the compound value factor we discussed earlier). The results of current research in advanced materials science, for example, should not be stored in a vacuum: new ideas and methods emerging from research laboratories impact on a country's technological and industrial base, and should ultimately translate into marketable products (ranging from consumer goods to the aerospace sector). Intelligence implies connectivity: facts and figures culled from discipline-specific databases should be married to rumors picked up by overseas trade attachés, the results of sectoral studies and other relevant information.

The dice are loaded against third world players, and unless they can change the rules of the game or outflank the competition (powerful and possibly exploitative inward investors), the development gap will widen.[8] How can such countries improve access to knowledge and ideas produced in industrialized nations? How can they hope to penetrate the charmed circle? How can appropriate technologies and processes be identified and successfully transferred? How can home-grown technological capability and skills be fostered and diffused more effectively throughout society? How can indigenous reconnaissance capability be improved?

By changing attitudes. First, government has to recognize that intelligence is "an instrument of development" just as it is an instrument of warfare; second, it must be persuaded of the need for a "development orientated intelligence policy";[9] third, there is a compelling case for reconceptualizing technology transfer as *information* transfer, an idea which the givers of skills and equipment seem to resist; fourth, terrain opacity has to be reduced, if innovations are to spread, information is to be shared and investment encouraged; fifth, government has to realize that strategic information systems planning can contribute to economic development.

Take the last two of these: why have the results of technology transfer so often proved disastrous for the receiver nation? Why so many aborted projects, so many white elephants? One reason is the historic failure to perceive technology as *embodied information,* whose effective transfer depends on the absorption capabilities of the host nation. Technology transfer is a multi-stage, multi-level process of domestication, indigenization and diffusion, in which the quality of information about the technology, its suitability and adaptability, potential and likely secondary local impacts, in addition to intelligence on supplier reliability and motivation, are crucial to smooth transfer.[10]

Secondly, why is it that the great majority of strategic information management systems (SIMS) have been implemented in (a) the private sector and (b) developed economies? By shifting the focus from profit to the promotion of economic health, the fundamentals of SIMS for competitive advantage can be applied in a developing country context. Palvia,[11] in fact, has adapted the ideas of Porter and others to construct a conceptual model for SISEDs (strategic information systems for economic development). In addition to the three forces of suppliers, buyers and rivals, government and logistics have been factored into the matrix to take account of third world realities. The result is a set of tools for identifying competitive advantage opportunities, one of which, a scanning grid, is reproduced as Figure 1-6.

Strategic Information Systems for Competitive Advantage
Scanning Grid

- For Developing Countries -

	Suppliers	Customers	Competitors	Government	Logistics
Differentiation					
Cost					
Focus					
Innovation					
Growth					
Alliance					

FIGURE 1-6 Strategic Information Systems for Competitive Advantage. Scanning Grid—for Developing Countries. Reproduced from P. Palvia, S. Palvia, and R. M. Zigli, Models and requirements for using strategic information systems in developing countries. *International Journal of Information Management* 10(2), 1990, 117–126. Reprinted by permission of Butterworth Scientific Ltd.

HARVESTING INTELLIGENCE

How do you harvest intelligence? We list some techniques and sources (formal and informal) in Figure 1-7. Any of these can be applied to the elements of competition (cost, quality, new products, etc.) to gain specific advantage; combined, they are a strategic information base, which can be tapped and sliced, to profile and project potential competitor behaviors.

TECHNIQUES	FORMAL SOURCES	INFORMAL SOURCES
Observation	Media	Moles
Eavesdropping	Press (localised)	Scouts/fleas
Reconnaissance	Gov. documents	Journalists
Market research	Speeches	Trade fairs
Reverse engineering	Analysts' reports	PR events
Issue analysis	Patents	Conferences
Planting	Directories	Former employees
Trend analysis	Court records	Old boy network
Empirical testing	Credit information	Dealers/suppliers
Asking questions	Statistics	Customers
Literature search	Consultants	User groups

FIGURE 1-7   Intelligence Harvesting

A technology platform which supports such activity must be

- flexible
- hospitable
- portable
- distributed
- comfortable

as it must admit input from a cast of players (with disparate experience) dispersed across several stages. Beer[12] has achieved macro-level systems which meet such specifications in Chile and Venezuela [see Figure 1-8]. These were conceived a decade ago, since when the technology of connective adaptivity has quantum leaped, though costs and unfamiliarity have constrained uptake.

COMPETITIVE POSTURE

The language of posture is important. The Maori war dance performed by the New Zealand All Blacks before their rugby matches is designed to unnerve the opposition. Just as animals inflate or raise their hackles, so companies may choose to band together to strengthen their competitive position (the Microelectronics

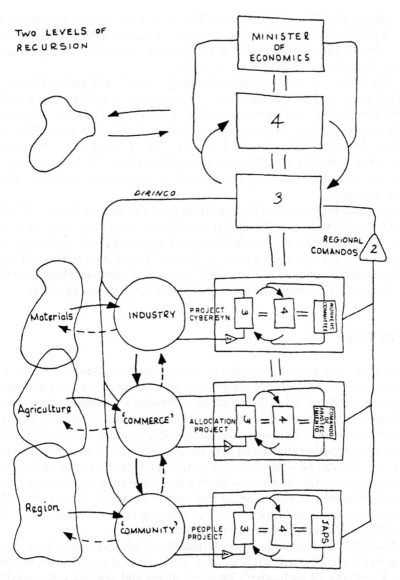

TWO LEVELS OF RECURSION

FIGURE 1-8   Reproduced from S. Beer, *Brain of the firm,* 2nd ed. Chichester [England]: Wiley, 1981, p. 325. Reprinted by permission of John Wiley & Sons, Ltd.

nd Computer Technology Corporation [MCC] emerged as a cooperative re- ponse to the Japanese Fifth Generation Project). Business also has its overt pos- ures or ritual dances. An illustration of the former is block buying of shares in a arget company, a way of unsettling sitting management. Courtship strategies eeking a white knight in the face of a hostile bid) are a form of ritual dance. An entrepreneur may choose to cast himself as a latter day Napoleon (Robert Maxwell) or find himself cast as a rapacious opportunist (James Goldsmith in his raid on Goodyear). Faced with a predator, a corporation will take every opportunity to portray the bidder as a self-seeking aggressor.

Harder to deal with are hidden hands, games of bluff, political feints: "the grim jockeying for position, the ceaseless trading, the deliberate use of words not for communication but to screen intention. In short, a splendidly exciting game for those who play it." (a paraphrasing of Gore Vidal on politics). This is the world of the casino table: good poker players give nothing away. *They* may be bluffing; *you* cannot be sure. The assets they hold in their hand may be no greater than yours, but their gambling skills give them competitive advantage in tense bidding situations.

Complex business deals have much in common with card games. Hard negotiators are likened to professional poker players, using every piece of information to assess the odds: in a hostile take-over, bargaining positions change as new information is fed into the negotiating process, and as both public and institutional shareholder opinion is manipulated by fresh disclosures (about the raider's downsizing plans or excessive bureaucracy in the target company's HQ).

ROLES

Competition implies other players. Except with a monopoly, business presupposes rivalry. The degree of competition will, however, vary enormously: in a mature, consolidated industry, competition between established players may be muted, or sublimated into a cartel (peaceful co-existence). Where a company has a *de facto* monopoly, or an unassailable leadership position, the quest for competition may instead be internalized (like the sprinter who chooses to race against the clock). This can be achieved in one of two ways: (a) by setting (and regularly ratcheting up) exacting quality standards which force company personnel to stay alert and responsive to technological and market changes (a feature of the Japanese consumer goods industry); or (b) by operating an internal market, in which each SBU or LOB competes for central resources.

Each SBU or LOB will consist of individuals who work as a team. On the playing field successful teams rely on impeccable physical coordination and on intimate knowledge of each other's likely initiatives and responses. Knowledge of the opposition may be less intuitive, but nonetheless reasonably detailed (via prematch analysis sessions).

Your rivals may be of long-standing, or they may be hiding in the wings, unseen or unrecognized as such. Given the volatility of the business environment, roles must not be taken for granted, as the script can change rapidly. It may be imprudent to dismiss potential players on the grounds that they are nominally located in a different business sector: in this jungle, leopards *can* change their spots (AT&T's entry into the computer and information services business is a case in point). Tomorrow's rivals may have little in common with today's. Knowing how to identify new entrants and potential competitors is critically important as a pre-emptive strike may be needed against rivals in search of extra *Lebensraum*.

Reconfiguration of territories may result from political dictat (the formation of a united Europe by 1992, the creation of a value-added network market by means of deregulation).

So scanning of the political environment (infrastructural intelligence) is essential, and knowledge of individual decision-makers (the basis of successful courting strategy) as important as understanding competitors.

Competition occurs at different levels: individual; intra-group; inter-group; international. Alignments and axes are volatile. Individuals compete head-to-head in fencing matches, piano competitions, and televised political debate. In business, competition of this kind routinely takes place: between members of the salesforce ("highest over quota"), public service staff ("receptionist of the month"), inventors (numbers of patents logged), and researchers in corporate laboratories (greatest number of discoveries, breakthroughs, patents, or publications). There is also intra-organizational competition: in the drug industry it is not uncommon for a number of research divisions or candidate research programs to lobby and compete internally for central funds. In the context of a holding company, each SBU may be treated as an independent profit center and forced to compete against other groups in the portfolio (domestic Darwinism).

But the competition is perhaps most obvious between firms (Redskins vs. Bears): slugging it out in the commodity PC market; battling for market share at the luxury end of the automobile market; price discounting in the package holiday industry. And just as we have sporting competitions between nations (the Olympics or World Cup), there is a continuous struggle between nations, whether at the level of a specific commodity (coffee), technology (customized chips), industry sector (biotechnology), or at the level of overall trade (U.S. vs. Japan). Competition, of course, can also be analyzed in terms of other economic perspectives, multi-nationals, and geopolitical blocs.

RULES

Competition usually takes place within a framework of rules. The rules define the parameters of acceptable action (no punching below the belt; bishop moves diagonally) and a serious or persistent breach of a rule may lead to disqualification. Some rules are straightforward and can be divined from observation (quoits); others not (cricket). Many, however, are clearly codified (Queensbury rules; rules of Monopoly™), and such rule sets are the basis of formal business refereeing. In many cases, however, rules are unspoken or opaque, and work as prescriptions for etiquette, which can only be learned by participation in the required social milieu.

In the business context, the appropriate cues can be picked up via surrogates; by observation (who power-breakfasts with whom? what is the correct handshaking/shoulder clasping/hugging ritual to conclude a deal in a particular culture?) or by consulting published intelligence (trade directories, almanacs, gaz-etteers, "Who's who's"), but such sources can only offer primary orientation; of more use is conversation with industry insiders (journalists, mentors, consultants, deep throats). Once inside the charmed circle, a player can choose to adopt a low or high profile.

Interpretations of the rules may differ (exactly how and where to replace a golf ball during the course of play; whether to permit use of a dictionary during a formal written examination; the implications of the U.K. Copyright Act for soft-ware vendors) or the rules may be inexact (what is the precise definition of insider trading? how should goodwill be valued in accounting terms?), or barely under-stood (running the bulls of Pamplona). In grey areas, knowledge of precedent or informal norms will be especially valuable.

Ignorance of the law is not be accepted as a defense plea in court, nor will it be in the boardroom. The rules governing the addition of artificial sweeteners to German white wine are clearly laid down. If a spot check reveals excessive saccha-rine additives, a hefty fine will follow, with the attendant damaging publicity. So too in athletics; anabolic steroids may bring Olympic gold, but the risks are great. If a U.S. computer manufacturer knowingly or unwittingly exports (or facilitates the export of) products (or components) to a "hostile" nation, the consequences can be calamitous, in terms of fines, blacklisting, and lost contracts.

REFEREES

In other cases, the game is transparent: both sides agree to participate ac-cording to stated rules. Observance of the rules may be monitored by referees whose remits may include sending players to the sin bin (in ice hockey), sectoral regulation (in financial services we have the Securities and Exchange Commission in the U.S. or the Securities and Investments Board in the U.K.), national anti-trust legislation, inter-governmental or global agreements (the Common Agricultural Policy of the European Community or the General Agreement on Trade and Tar-iffs). Generally speaking, referees can function in developed and transparent in-formation environments where adequate reporting and enforcement mechanisms can be sustained.

The authority of the referee's decision varies across contexts. Cricket has its umpires whose word is law, but the regulation of American rules football is sup-ported by real-time, slow motion action replay which double checks the human decision. Where wording is ambiguous, or the contexts in which the *ur*-set was conceived have little in common with the prevailing environment, the application of regulations may be hotly disputed (*vide* copyright legislation; *Humanae Vitae*). In such cases, interpretation and arbitration may be necessary, or settlement may be by *fiat* (a high court ruling is laid down; the Pontiff pronounces *ex cathedra*).

Sometimes the rules of the game are set down in a broad-brush manner, with the intention of defining a dynamic, regulatory framework rather than the minu-tiae of each rule and the detailed conditions under which it might or might not be invoked. This kind of approach has been favored in the telecommunications arena by both the U.S. and U.K. governments in the wake of divestiture and deregulation, with the role of Solomon being played, respectively, by Judge Harold Greene and Professor Bryan Carsberg, backed by the FCC (Federal Communications Commission) and Oftel (Office of Telecommunications). Reading the rules is insufficient in this case: it is necessary to read between the lines and to second guess your competitor's responses to legislators.

Wilmot's following summary of company objectives (italics added) shows how the game metaphor is embedded in the literature of business: "The sense that an organization's key mission is to *compete,* and to *win,* which of course means *beating* someone, is spreading across the entire economy—and is a direct result of *global competition.* No longer is 'better than last year' an acceptable performance. Nor is peddling faster in the same tired and proven way, because *changing the rules of the game* is increasingly the only available route for gaining *competitive advantage.* . . . *Innovation,* the capacity to do things differently, to change the rules of the game, is a premium."[13]

STRATAGEMS

Games, as we have pointed out, need rules, players, and in some cases a referee, though this function may be assumed by the participants provided they agree to abide by the rules. In some cases there may be no objective or documented set of rules, and players may not even be aware that they are participating (it doesn't take two to tango). The rules are opaque, and action is defined as a game simply because one player has a set of undivulged strategies to take advantage of the others. Until victims realise they are being taken for a ride, they may unwittingly collude (we looked at this in more detail in the section on social intelligence, where the players are multi-nationals and developing countries).

At what level of complexity and engagement do stratagems become games and games become war? The absence of rules is one feature which distinguishes war (the Geneva Convention is probably more honored in the breach than observance); this in turn implies a higher degree of complexity, as rules limit a player's degrees of freedom. The size of the stake and the scale of participation are other distinguishing features. War implies loss, devastation, suffering *on both sides,* and is not undertaken lightly. It may be just, or unjust, but the cost remains the same. Compulsion is also a feature. Participants may not have agreed to take part: war is declared, not negotiated, and often fought by conscripts.

It can be fought on surrogate grounds, psychological, economic, trade, diplomatic, and cultural ("the battle for hearts and minds"). War is normally overt: tanks roll over borders; bombs fall from the sky, but you can also have hidden war conducted through espionage, counterespionage, and code breaking.

Much of the language of warfare and battle management has worked its way into the vernacular of business. Companies elaborate defensive strategies (buying back shares), knock out competitors, battle for and capture market share;

advanced information systems are the basis for launching a first strike on competitors (ATM technology in banking); price wars are a regular feature of commodity markets (pocket calculators, PCs); advertising campaigns are launched (the Pepsi/Coke ad wars); companies adopt flanking strategies, unveil secret weapons, invade one another's territories, and occupy niche markets.

The phrase "niche market" is part of another pervasive metaphor for struggle in the literature of business, ecology. The Victorian vision of "Nature red in tooth and claw" no longer holds. Competitors in current terms are simply seen as "players" seeking a niche in a common territory: their awareness of rivals, and consequent strategy, need not be constructed in terms of direct aggression. Strategies for survival, as we have indicated, may be instinctive or embodied, rather than calculated. In the animal kingdom, spots and stripes are not accessories of strife (like warpaint or camouflage), but in-bred survival and defense mechanisms. In the case of the manager, this may appear as intuition.[14]

Embodied survival kits will be most effective in a local environment which tends to stability, reinforced by recognized roles and rituals. There are predators and prey, for example, but each knows who the other is, and how they behave. Survival information is acquired by routine and constant scanning: signals are obvious; messages are clear; dirty tricks, black propaganda, and misinformation are not required. Evolutionary change is incremental, and paced at a manageable rate.

Business evolution to some extent parallels ecological succession where a maturing environment produces characteristic patterns of consumption (energy inputs, packaged in different forms; what is known as biomass) and diversity (in terms of niches and occupying species). The overall business equivalent of a mature ecology is a well-established marketing environment. The energy or input which drives consumption is information, and diversity appears in a range of products or players or clients. In a mature niche, a long food chain (where a complex and highly developed organism feeds on an organism which feeds on an organism at successively lower levels of development) may be compared to the value chain in a complex organization.

In times of turbulence, generalists (who can tolerate change) or higher-level strategists can survive, but organisms which are over-specialized die out. A similar phenomenon can often be observed in business: "The railroads did not stop growing because the need for passenger and freight transportation declined . . . [t]he reason they defined their industry wrong was because they were railroad-oriented instead of transportation-oriented."[15]

SIZING UP THE ODDS

Risk involves trade-off: a choice between alternatives. It may be the risk of failing, pure and simple (loss of face or *amour propre*); or the risking of life and limb (ski jumping; pistol dueling), or investment risk (putting your savings into a venture capital company or *premier cru* clarets). How can you hedge against risk? The racing track *habitué* can lay off bets (a form of damage limitation, or risk aversion) while the speculator can hedge by spreading his investments over a range of stocks (from blue chip to high risk). Back-ups and diversification might be business equivalents. Another tactic is to ensure that adequate compensation is paid: ski jumpers would be advised to take out a life insurance policy (though the premium will be prohibitive and in the event of a claim it is the next of kin who will be the beneficiaries); the business analogy might be the penalty clause for non-completion or non-delivery, or the quality guarantee. Or a risk taker can minimize impact: duelists could resort to protective clothing (a bullet-proof vest), through this might increase the risk of loss of reputation.

The risks associated with Formula 1 racing extend beyond the obvious danger to life (the risk faced by the drivers, and to some extent the spectators). Financial risks are taken by the various constructors and backers, as well as the advertisers who lay out millions to have their brand names emblazoned across car bodies and drivers' apparel. The rewards associated with the international *grand prix* circuit are great: so too the risks. However, the cost of entry is prohibitive: in making the decision to compete, consortia have to assess both entry costs (what it takes to assemble and support a traveling circus) and exit barriers (the cost of disassembling or decommissioning a team and disposing of a highly specialized plant). The same is true of leading-edge, high-cost information systems investment projects.

Subjective expected utility theory may help you reach an investment decision. Intuitively, we make decisions of this kind every day. On occasion we are more systematic, and identify options on the basis of the probabilities we attach to different outcomes which we fashion into a pay-off matrix. Even fairly systematic probability models, however, are ruffled by surprises. Chaos theory accommodates such perturbations: chaologists have joined the phalanx of analysts available to business strategists.

Risk-taking can be clean (above board) or dirty (of dubious legality). As American as apple pie is the entrepreneur who second-mortgages the family home to generate start-up capital. Less acceptable is the case of the employee with his finger in the pie (insider trading; computer fraud).

People take risks for a variety of reasons. The rewards need not be tangible. Beating the system may be sufficient in itself (the case with most hackers), or the thrill of risk-taking (running a red light). The rewards may be symbolic (a cup, blue riband, or plaque), or derive from prestige (claim staking in science, first past the winning post, belle of the ball, *primus inter pares* status). Of course, they may also be monetary. All of these apply in business: improved ROI; profits and stockholder dividends; enlarged remuneration packages and bonuses; cover story status and the hagiography it engenders.

The stakes have escalated in recent years: golden hellos and golden parachutes, stock option schemes and performance-related pay have inflated executive salaries. But as rewards have grown, so too have the risks: hostile raids, greenmailing, LBOs (leveraged buy-outs), downsizing and restructuring have become daily features of corporate life and sharpened the competitive pressures on companies large and small. In the business jungle (to use a hackneyed metaphor) predators and prey need be to alert to all that is going on around them: the quality of an organization's intelligence gathering (the bush telegraph) and analysis capability are increasingly vital to survival.[16]

TOOLS

What tools are available to make you a better player, a better warrior, or a more skilled survivalist? Porter[17] offers an analytic schema for market reconnoiter or analyzing the competitive structure of any given industry. The five forces (potential entrants, buyer power, supplier power, substitute threat, internal rivalry) shown in Figure 1-9 are the generic drivers of competition, though their relative influence will vary from industry to industry, and from moment to moment. His model is an all-in-one orientation tool, combining the attributes of a map and compass: it tells you about the lie of the land, your position and direction you are heading. Its utility, however, depends almost wholly on the quality of the information gathered on each of the five dimensions. Although intended as an analytic for use in commercial contexts, the schema can be applied usefully to public sector organizations, provided you make some minor adjustments to the nomenclature.

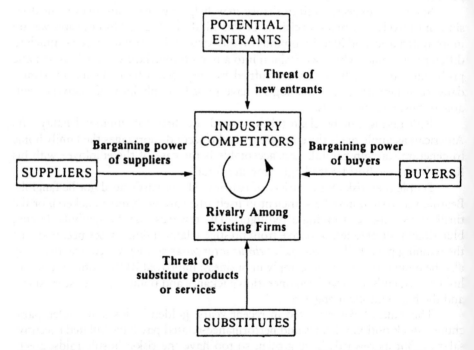

FIGURE 1-9 Reprinted with permission of The Free Press, a Division of Macmillan, Inc., from *Competitive strategy: techniques for analyzing industries and competitors*, by Michael E. Porter. Copyright © 1980 by The Free Press.

The model can be used to answer a wide range of strategic questions:

- What are the strengths and weaknesses of the other players in our industry?
- Where are our core LOBs vulnerable, in terms of next generation or successor products?
- Where might potential new entrants emerge from outside the existing set of players?
- What are potential sources of differentiation (new focus, market re-segmentation, predatory pricing, innovation, improved scope)?
- What is known about the structural dynamics of the industry?
- What strategies are likely to yield positive results?

How can Porter's model be linked to the tactics described in this chapter? In a gaming sense, we might want to know what the consequences of moving from one position to another (rook to king four) might be. In manufacturing industry, for example, an option might be forward or backward integration (moving further into territory occupied by an existing supplier of raw materials or upstream into the domain of a buyer of semi-processed or finished goods) or strategically relocating a company's headquarter operations.

Blocking strategy (a defensive line-up in gridiron) could be a viable alternative: a company prevents a potential new competitor from moving into the arena by raising the entry level barriers (by upgrading the bedrock technology, thus raising the minimum level of investment required to play the game). A variant on the blocking move might be to form a strategic alliance with other established players (cartelization; joint venturing) to deter would-be interlopers.

Competitive edge can also be gained by changing the pace of the game, an extension of competing in time which forces all players on the field to break new barriers. Some will fail to cope: they will be run off their feet. In industry terms, time ramping may translate into accelerated research or a foreshortening of the product development cycle.

In terms of warfare, backward integration is the equivalent of securing your supply lines; making sure that the front line troops (in production and processing) have the ammunition and materials to carry on the manufacturing struggle. Forward integration is akin to launching an offensive, seeking to knock out the enemy immediately ahead. Gathering information on the threat of a substitute product and reacting accordingly (upgrading or bundling your existing offerings) is a maneuver to protect your flank. Reconnaissance or scouting in military terms equates with information gathering on potential new entrants.

Porter's model allows you to determine the level of stability within your operating environment (the degree of inter-firm rivalry), and the scope for populating new niches. New entrants may be equated with the arrival of a potentially superior species, or genus, capable of disturbing the prevailing harmony. Links between buyers and suppliers in an industry recall the food chain: one firm feeding off and nurturing another to ensure survival of the system, as we have mentioned.

The launch of a radically new product by a major competitor, the introduction of regulatory controls, price discounting or the advent of new players on the scene are the equivalents of turbulence. The result may be that weaker or overspecialized species (companies with lackluster products or narrowly defined markets) may be eliminated.

PORTFOLIO PLANNING MATRICES

The original 2 x 2 portfolio matrix produced by the Boston Consulting Group (BCG) has spawned useful variations, many of which have been reviewed by Ward.[18] The matrix was developed to show how a portfolio of businesses or products might be managed most effectively in a competitive environment. It is now frequently applied in IS/IT assessments within organizations: the matrices show you which way to leap (in terms of product design or information investment).

Organizational information systems can be classified in terms of their strategic significance. Not all are of equal importance: some have tactical, others strategic value. Some have high current utility, others future potential. A second tool is Ward's matrix [see Figure 1-10] which can be used to group systems into one of four cells, strategic, turnaround, support, and factory, in terms of whether their

	High		
High	Strategic Applications that are critical for future success	Turnaround (or high potential) Applications that may be of future strategic importance	Strategic impact of future IS
	Factory Applications that are critical to sustaining existing business	Support Applications that improve management and performance but are not critical to the business	
Low	High	Low	

Strategic importance of existing operational systems

FIGURE 1-10 Reproduced from J. M. Ward, Information systems and technology application portfolio management—an assessment of matrix-based analyses. *Journal of Information Technology,* 3 (3), 1988, 205–214. Reprinted by permission of Chapman & Hall, Publishers.

resource consumption (vertical axis) and strategic significance (horizontal axis) are high or low. Calibration and weighting do not feature in this exercise: subjective assessment is all that is required.

The labeling is not definitive: today's factory system may be tomorrow's support system, or last year's problem child (turnaround) may be tomorrow's rising star (strategic). As IS innovations become widely imitated and competitive parity is restored, strategic may be downgraded to factory. In theory, an information system could rotate through each of the four quadrants in the course of its life cycle.

Nor will the classification be the same for all firms in a particular sector; location on the matrix will be a function of an organization's maturity and its relative systems sophistication. Systems are not in themselves strategic; they acquire the appellation through association. If a business activity is of strategic significance to an organization, the information systems which underpin that function inherit the classification. In another similar company, however, such activities (and the associated systems) might have much lower status.

Ward's matrix relates the value of information systems to both current expenditure and future investment levels. It can be used to review your IS arsenal and to highlight anomalies (where funding is high but IS value is low, or vice versa). It can also be used to plot high- and low-yield information resource entities (where a meaningful distinction can be made between an IS and an IRE).

We conclude with a version of the BCG matrix which links information intensity/propensity with key competitive variables. Ginman's[19] model based on detailed interviews with chief executive officers (CEOs) of SMEs (small- and medium-sized enterprises) and large corporations suggests a link between information investment and some variables commonly associated with competitive edge [see Figure 1-11]. Strassmann's caveats[20] on the dangers of facile association must, however, be remembered.

Degree of interest in information,
Relative market share. Rate of feedback.

	High	Low
Interest in external matters, market growth rate. Risk-taking	**B** Intense interest in information Revival phase Bet your company culture 'STAR' product	**A** Casual attitude to information Development phase Tough guy/macho culture 'QUESTION MARK' products
	C Stable interest in information Maturity phase Work hard/play hard culture 'CASH COW' products	**D** Hostile attitude to information Decline phase Progress culture 'DOGS' products

FIGURE 1-11 Reproduced by permission of the Oxford University Press, from M. Ginman, Information culture and business performance. *Iatul Quarterly*, 2 (2), 1998, 93–106.

REFERENCES

1. Wilmot, R. W. *Organisational issues and I.T.* A management briefing prepared from a presentation to the IBM CUA Conference, 21 April 1988. London: Oasis, 1988.

2. See: *The Independent,* 28 October 1989 and *Financial Times,* 28 October 1989.

3. Derived from the RISC International/ACE (Anticipating Change in Europe) System.

4. Herman, M. British and American concepts of intelligence: barriers or aids to cooperation? Paper presented at BISA/ISA Conference, 1989.

5. Ohmae, K. *The mind of the strategist: business planning for competitive advantage.* Harmondsworth, Eng.: Penguin, 1982.

6. Jequier, N. and Dedijer, S. Information, knowledge and intelligence: a general overview. In Dedijer, S. and Jequier, N. (eds.). *Intelligence for economic development: an inquiry into the role of the knowledge industry.* Oxford, Eng.: Berg, 1987, 1–23.

7. Cronin, B. Blind spots and opaque terrains. In Cronin, B. and Tudor-Silovic, N. (eds.). *The knowledge industries: levers of economic and social development in the 1990s.* London: Aslib, 1990, 1–3.

8. Salinas, R. Forget the NWICO . . . and start all over again. *Information Development,* 2(3), 1986, 154–158.

9. Jequier and Dedijer, *op. cit.*

10. Onyango, R. The knowledge industries: aid to technological and industrial development in Africa. In Cronin, B. and Tudor-Silovic, N. (eds.). *The knowledge industries: levers of economic and social development in the 1990s.* London: Aslib, 1990, 5–29.

11. Palvia, P., Pava, S., and Zigli, R. M. Models and requirements for using strategic information systems in developing countries. *International Journal of Information Management,* 10(2), 1990, 117–126.

12. Beer, S. *Brain of the firm.* Chichester: Wiley, 1981. 2nd ed.

13. Wilmot, *op. cit.*

14. Agor, W. H. (ed.). *Intuition in organizations: leading and managing productively.* Beverly Hills: Sage, 1989.

15. Levitt, T. Marketing myopia. *Harvard Business Review,* July–August 1960, 45–56.

16. Cronin, B. New horizons for the information profession: strategic intelligence and competitive advantage. In Dyer, H. and Tseng, G. (eds.). *New horizons for the information profession: meeting the challenge of change.* London: Taylor Graham, 1988, 3–22.

17. Porter, M. E. *Competitive strategy: techniques for analyzing industries and competitors.* New York: Free Press, 1980.

18. Ward, J. M. Information systems and technology application portfolio management—an assessment of matrix-based analyses. *Journal of Information Technology,* 3(3), 1988, 205–214.

19. Ginman, M. Information culture and business performance. *Iatul Quarterly,* 2(2), 1988, 93–106.

20. For a discussion of Strassmann's research see: Huggins, T. Bad managers made worse. *Informatics,* July 1984, 18–19.

2

Information Politics

Thomas H. Davenport, Robert G. Eccles, and Laurence Prusak

Information technology was supposed to stimulate information flow and eliminate hierarchy. It has had just the opposite effect, argue the authors. As information has become the key organizational "currency," it has become too valuable for most managers to just give away. In order to make information-based organizations successful, companies need to harness the power of politics—that is, allow people to negotiate the use and definition of information, just as we negotiate the exchange of other currencies. The authors describe five models of information politics and discuss how companies can move from the less effective models, like feudalism and technocratic utopianism, and toward the more effective ones, like monarchy and federalism.

> *"Information is not innocent."*
>
> —James March[1]

During the past decade, many firms have concluded that information is one of their most critical business resources and that broadening information access and usage and enhancing its quality are key to improving business performance. The "information-based organization," the "knowledge-based enterprise," and the "learning organization," forecasted by management experts, all require a free flow of information around the firm.[2] The computers and communications networks that manipulate and transmit information become more powerful each year. Yet the rhetoric and technology of information management have far out-

Reprinted from "Information Politics" by Thomas H. Davenport, Robert G. Eccles, and Laurence Prusak. *Sloan Management Review* 34, no. 1 (Fall 1992), pp. 53–65, by permission of publisher. © 1992 by Sloan Management Review Association. All rights reserved. Thomas H. Davenport is a partner and director of research at Ernst & Young's Center for Information Technology and Strategy in Boston. Robert G. Eccles is professor of business administration at the Harvard Business School. Laurence Prusak is a principal, also at the Center for Information Technology and Strategy.

paced the ability of people to understand and agree on what information they need and then to share it.

Today, in fact, the information-based organization is largely a fantasy. All of the writers on information-based organizations must speak hypothetically, in the abstract, or in the future tense. Despite forty years of the Information Revolution in business, most managers still tell us that they cannot get the information they need to run their own units or functions. As a recent article by the CEO of a shoe company put it: "On one of my first days on the job, I asked for a copy of every report used in management. The next day, twenty-three of them appeared on my desk. I didn't understand them. . . . Each area's reports were Greek to the other areas, and all of them were Greek to me."[3] A more accurate metaphor might be that these reports each came from a different city-state—Athens, Sparta, Corinth, Thebes, and Peloponnesus—each part of the organization but a separate political domain with its own culture, leaders, and even vocabulary.

We have studied information management approaches in more than twenty-five companies over the past two years. Many of their efforts to create information-based organizations—or even to implement significant information management initiatives—have failed or are on the path to failure. The primary reason is that the companies did not manage the politics of information. Either the initiative was inappropriate for the firm's overall political culture, or politics were treated as peripheral rather than integral to the initiative. Only when information politics are viewed as a natural aspect of organizational life and consciously managed will true information-based organizations emerge.

Furthermore, a good argument can be made—and there is increasing evidence for it—that as information becomes the basis for organizational structure and function, politics will increasingly come into play. In the most information-oriented companies we studied, people were least likely to share information freely, as perceived by these companies' managers. As people's jobs and roles become defined by the unique information they hold, they may be less likely to share that information—viewing it as a source of power and indispensability—rather than more so. When information is the primary unit of organizational currency, we should not expect its owners to give it away.[4]

This assertion directly contradicts several academic and popular concepts about how widespread information and information technology will affect organizations. These thinkers have hypothesized that as organizations make widespread use of information technology, information will flow freely and quickly eliminate hierarchy. Mention is rarely made in such accounts of the specter of information politics.[5] Although this optimistic view has widespread appeal, it is not what we see today in companies.

When owners of key information resist sharing it either outright or, more commonly, through bureaucratic maneuvers, they are often dismissed as unfair or opportunistic. Yet they may have quite legitimate reasons for withholding the information. Political behavior regarding information should be viewed not as irrational or inappropriate but as a normal response to certain organizational situations. Valid differences in interpretation of information, for example, may lead to apparently intransigent behavior. At an electronics company we once worked with, the marketing organizations for direct and indirect channels could never agree on what constituted a sale. Getting the product to the end-customer was direct marketing's sale; getting it to the distributor, even though it might return eventually, was how the indirect group wanted to measure its success. When the indirect channel was the dominant one for the company, this group's view of sales prevailed. Later, as more product moved directly to buyers, end-customer sales became the official definition. In information politics, might makes right. As a result of losing influence, however, the indirect group wanted to create its own sales databases and reports. Political disputes of this type will often arise when there is no consensus around the business's information needs.

One reason the stakes are so high in information politics is that more than information is at stake. In order to arrive at a common definition of information requirements, organizations must often address not just the information they use, but the business practices and processes that generate the information. Most firms have not recognized the linkage between processes and information, but there are a few exceptions. At a fast-growing specialty manufacturer, CEO-appointed information "czars" are responsible for ensuring consistency in the information-generating activities of their areas. For example, the order-processing czar mandated common companywide practices for assigning customer and product numbers, recognizing revenue, and determining contract prices. At IBM, eighteen key business processes (e.g., "customer fulfillment") are being redesigned to build a new information infrastructure. Out of each new process will come information on its performance—how long it takes, how much it costs, how satisfied the customer is with it—as well as the more traditional results-oriented information such as sales and profitability. At Dow Chemical, managers believe there must be common financial processes around the world in order to create common measures of financial performance.

The overall organizational climate is also a powerful influence on information politics.[6] Unfortunately, the very factors that make free information flow most desirable and necessary also make it less likely. An organization that is highly unstable and operating in an uncertain business, in which employees are uncertain about their job security and place in the hierarchy, needs as much information as possible about the environment and its own performance. Yet this type of organization is most likely to engender information politics that inhibit sharing.

Our purpose is to help companies understand information politics and manage them. In the next section, we classify the major models of information politics we have seen in client companies and firms we have studied. Following that, we present a set of approaches to managing information politics at both a strategic and a day-to-day level.

MODELS OF INFORMATION POLITICS

We have identified five information models (or, to continue the political metaphor, "states") that are representative of the practices we have observed (see Table 2-1). Three of these, technocratic utopianism, anarchy, and feudalism, are

TABLE 2-1   Models of Information Politics

Technocratic Utopianism	A heavily technical approach to information management stressing categorization and modeling of an organization's full information assets, with heavy reliance on emerging technologies.
Anarchy	The absence of any overall information management policy, leaving individuals to obtain and manage their own information.
Feudalism	The management of information by individual business units or functions, which define their own information needs and report only limited information to the overall corporation.
Monarchy	The definition of information categories and reporting structures by the firm's leaders, who may or may not share the information willingly after collecting it.
Federalism	An approach to information management based on consensus and negotiation on the organization's key information elements and reporting structures.

less effective than the other two, monarchy and federalism.[7] After we define each model, we will evaluate their relative effectiveness along the dimensions of information quality, efficiency, commonality, and access.

Any organization is likely to have proponents for more than one of these models. Sometimes the models conflict, and sometimes one model predominates. Table 2-2 shows the distribution of models among the companies we studied. The first step in managing information more effectively and realistically is explicitly recognizing these existing models and then choosing a single desired state. Maintaining multiple models is confusing and consumes scarce resources. Once a model has been selected, an organization can manage the daily politics of information, just as an alderman manages a ward.

TECHNOCRATIC UTOPIANISM

Many companies have a strong bias toward approaching information management from a technological perspective. This approach eschews information politics, assuming that politics are an aberrant form of behavior. It is usually driven by a firm's information systems (IS) professionals, who see themselves as the custodians, if not the owners, of the firms information. Their technological efforts to alleviate information problems often involve a considerable amount of detailed planning and revolve around modeling and efficient use of corporate data. Their goal is to plan a technology infrastructure that can deliver information to each individual's desktop and then to build databases with the correct structure to

TABLE 2-2 Models Observed in Research Sites

25 Companies Studied	Federalism	Monarchy	Technocratic Utopianism	Anarchy	Feudalism
Chemicals					
Company A			✓		✓
Company B	✓	✓			
Company C	✓		✓		
Computers					
Company A	✓			✓	✓
Company B	✓		✓		
Consumer Goods					
Company A			✓		✓
Company B					✓
Direct Marketing		✓			
Electronics					
Company A					✓
Company B					✓
Entertainment					✓
Financial Services		✓		✓	✓
Gas Transmission		✓			
Information Services					
Company A			✓		
Company B	✓				✓
Insurance					
Company A		✓	✓		
Company B	✓				✓
Company C					✓
Medical Supplies					
Company A			✓		
Company B	✓				✓
Office Products	✓		✓		
European Office Products			✓		
Software					
Company A		✓		✓	
Company B				✓	
Specialty Manufacturing		✓			
Total	8	7	9	4	12

store this information without redundancy. Some technical efforts around information management are reasonable; however, when the technological approach to information predominates, the company's model of information management can be described as technocratic utopianism.

Although neither the IS professionals nor the users may be consciously creating a technocratic utopia, there is an underlying assumption that technology will resolve all problems and that organizational and political issues are nonexistent or unmanageable. In fact, information itself—its content, use, and implications for managing—receives little attention in this model. The focus is instead on the technologies used to manipulate the information.

We found technocratic utopianism, either by itself or alongside another model, in almost a third of the firms we analyzed. The model usually coexists, however uneasily, with other models; in fact, the technocratic utopian model is often held by a small group of technologists supported by many technical journals, consultants, and technology vendors. While the technologists plan a utopia around the free flow of information, the senior executives for whom they work usually ignore, or are ignorant of, their efforts. Because these technical models are difficult for nontechnologists to understand, managers outside the IS function are rarely active participants. If a technocratic utopia is the only political model, it is probably because senior managers have abdicated their roles in selecting and managing information.

Technocratic utopians often have three factors in common: they focus heavily on information modeling and categorization; they highly value emerging hardware and software technologies; and they attempt to address an organization's entire information inventory.

A key emphasis in most technocratic utopias is information modeling and categorization. Once a unit of information is represented in an "entity-relationship model" or a "data-flow diagram," all problems in managing it have been solved, according to the extreme utopians. They consider such modeling and categorization a key aspect of the engineering of information (indeed, "information engineering" is an established discipline within the IS profession). In this ideal world, information flows like water, and the only task is to construct appropriate canals, aqueducts, and dams in order for information to flow freely to those who need it. Information sometimes feels as common in organizations as water; since it is so plentiful, there is a natural instinct to try to channel it rather than drown in it.

Information engineering is important, of course, but the political aspects cannot be neglected. Information may flow like water, but in the real world even water doesn't flow without political assistance. Those knowledgeable about the back-room politics involved in bringing water to Los Angeles or about Robert Moses's political steamrolling in New York's water management will understand the role of politics in managing a "natural" resource like information.[8]

Technologists also frequently assert that new forms of hardware and software are the keys to information success. Executives often hear that they will get the information they need "when our new relational database system is installed" or "when our new network is complete." The coming panacea for many organizations is object-oriented technologies, in which information is combined with application functions in reusable modules. Too often, however, when the silver bullet arrives it does not have the intended effect. No technology has yet been invented to convince unwilling managers to share information or even to use it. In fact, we would argue that technology vendors suffer from the same political forces as do data modelers. The failure of the "diskless workstation" to thrive in the marketplace may well be due to individuals' reluctance to lose control of their information.

Finally, utopians focus on all information throughout the corporation—at least all that can be captured by a computer. A common example is the creation of an "enterprise model"—a structured inventory and categorization of all data elements used throughout the firm. Such modeling exercises often take years and yield vast amounts of detail. Although their purpose is often to eliminate redundant data storage, they often yield little real business value. Several MIT researchers have chronicled their failure.[9] Like most utopias, they lead to nowhere (or, in Samuel Butler's famous utopian novel, Erewhon—nowhere almost backwards).

Technocratic utopians assume that managing information is an exercise without passion. Their rallying cry is an uninspiring, "Data is a corporate asset."

They believe, consciously or unconsciously, that information's value for business decisions is not only very high but also self-evident. They assume that employees who possess information useful to others will share it willingly. They assume that information itself is valueless, or at least that its value is the same to all organizational members. If they are conscious of the relationship between information access and hierarchy, they assume that those high in the hierarchy would not restrict the free flow of information for any reason other than corporate security. These assumptions resemble human behavior found only in utopias.

ANARCHY

Some firms have no prevailing political information model and exist in a state of anarchy. Rarely do organizations consciously choose this state, in which individuals fend for their own information needs. Information anarchy usually emerges when more centralized approaches to information management break down or when no key executive realizes the importance of common information. Information anarchy was made possible—and much more dangerous—by the introduction and rapid growth of the personal computer. Suddenly individuals and small departments could manage their own databases, tailoring their own reports to their own needs at any time and at minimal cost.

Although several firms we researched have allowed anarchy to survive, we found only one firm that had consciously chosen it. This software firm had previously tried to develop an overall information management structure by asking key managers what information they needed to run the business. When the firm could not achieve consensus, it determined that a bottom-up structured exchange of documents across its network, using a new software technology developed for this purpose, would yield all of the required information. Even here, however, an alternative information model flourished in some quarters; as one senior executive put it, "I get all the information I need in breakfast meetings with the CEO."

The long-term shortcomings of information anarchy are obvious. Technologists might worry that so much redundant information processing and storage is inefficient, but anarchy has more serious shortcomings. When everyone has his or her own database, the numbers for revenues, costs, customer order levels, and so on will diverge in databases throughout the company. Although anarchy is seldom chosen consciously, its effects are not uncommon; we know of several firms in which it was the source of late or inaccurate quarterly earnings reports. A firm cannot survive for long with such information discrepancies. The desire for information that leads to anarchy should quickly be harnessed into a more organized political model.

FEUDALISM

The political model we most often encountered was feudalism. In a feudal model, individual executives and their departments generally control information acquisition, storage, distribution, and analysis.[10] These powerful executives determine what information will be collected within their realms, how it will be interpreted, and in what format it will be reported to the "king" or CEO. They can also decide what measures are used to understand performance as well as what "language," by which we mean a common vocabulary, is used within the realm. Different realms often end up with different languages, and the subsequent fragmenting of information authority diminishes the power of the entire enterprise—just as the growth of powerful noblemen and their entourages inhibited the king's power in medieval times.

Feudal actions diminish the central authority's power to make informed decisions for the common good. Key measures of the enterprise's health often are not collected, reported, or even considered beyond roll-up of financial outcomes, further diminishing the central authority's power. Corporatewide performance is of interest only to those within corporate headquarters, and its indicators may poorly reflect what is actually happening around the firm.

Feudalism flourishes, of course, in environments of strong divisional autonomy. When divisions have their own strategies, products, and customers, it is almost inevitable that their information needs will differ. Furthermore, they may also be reluctant to fully disclose potentially negative information at the corporate level.

At a major consumer electronics firm's U.S. subsidiary, the feudalism was quite overt. The firm was organized along product lines; product division heads were informally referred to as "barons." Each had his or her own financial reporting system, with only the most limited amounts of data shared with the subsidiary head. The latter executive eventually brought in consultants to give a seminar on the value of common data and systems—all, the last we heard, to no avail.

At a large consumer goods firm organized by distribution channel, each channel had its own measures of performance that it thought were important. This information autonomy had prevailed for years and was tolerated because the firm had long been profitable using any set of measures. A new CEO arrived at a time when profits were down, and he felt he had no way to manage across the entire firm. He mandated the development of a common information architecture. Unfortunately, the IS group charged with this initiative began to create a technocratic utopia. We suspect that the feudal culture will eventually prevail.

We have also seen a few examples of functional feudalism, in which financial and operational functions have their own information architectures and cannot achieve consensus on what should be monitored and how. In one high-technology manufacturing firm, for example, the quality function head created an executive information system that reported on operational performance and quality data. The IS director, and the CFO to whom he reported, strenuously opposed the system, arguing that the firm's traditional financially oriented reporting approach should be the only one. The quality-oriented system was building adherents (and product quality) until the quality director left for a summer vacation. When he returned, he found that the IS head and CFO had enlisted sufficient support from other executives to shut down the system. The battle over which type of system will eventually predominate is still raging.

Despite these battles in feudal environments, some degree of cooperation can emerge. Powerful executives can create strategic alliances to share information or establish a common network or architecture, just as feudal lords banded together to build a road or common defense wall, go to war, or plan a marriage for mutual enrichment—although such communal efforts rarely include all of the lords. It is also possible that, as in Renaissance times, the proliferation of patrons will encourage innovation and creativity within each realm—for example, the development of a particularly useful quality information system by one division.

MONARCHY

The most practical solution to the problems inherent in the feudal model is to impose an information monarchy. The CEO, or someone empowered by the chief executive, dictates the rules for how information will be managed. Power is centralized, and departments and divisions have substantially less autonomy regarding information policies.

Much depends on the approach the "monarch" takes to managing the realm's information. A more benign monarch (or enlightened despot, as they were called in the eighteenth century) will tilt toward freer access and distribution of key information and may attempt to rationalize and standardize the parameters used to measure the state's health and wealth. This top-down model may be most appropriate for firms that have difficulty achieving consensus across business units.

The rapidly growing specialty manufacturer mentioned above is an example. The CEO, who felt that information flow was critical to developing a flexible organization, decreed a policy of "common information" to bring about access to consistent information by all who needed it. His appointment of czars to define and implement common information policies reflected his belief in the importance of information management issues. Currently efforts are underway to embed this decree into a set of business practices and a technical architecture. This top-down approach is an example of enlightened monarchy at its best, since the action was taken not in response to a specific crisis but as a well-considered response to a broad organizational objective.

A progressive further step is a constitutional monarchy. Constitutional monarchy can evolve directly from feudalism or from the more despotic forms of monarchy. It is established by a document that states the monarch's limitations, the subjects' rights, and the law's authority. As a model for information management, this means that dominion is established over what information is collected, in what form, by whom, and for what ends. The chart of accounts becomes the realm's Magna Carta ("great charter"), a document establishing rules that will be enforced by processes and enabled by an information technology platform. A common vocabulary is developed so that the information's meaning is consistent and has integrity throughout the firm. The financial functions at both Digital and Dow Chemical are establishing constitutional monarchies for financial information, with strong support from the CEOs.

We have seen several firms in which the installation of an executive information system (EIS) was the occasion for an attempt at constitutional monarchy. The CEO is usually considered the primary user of such a system, although some attempt is usually made to solicit the information requirements of other executives. The exercise of building consensus on the system's content can help to build a constitutional monarchy. However, the effort is not always successful. At one insurance company we studied, an EIS intended for the entire senior management team was never used seriously by anyone other than the CEO. Other executives were concerned about how their units would fare under close analysis, and they kept their own feudal information sources.

One drawback to any information monarchy is the simple fact of mortality. When a monarch dies or is overthrown, new governments can be imposed. Likewise, retirement or turnover of CEOs and senior executives can open the door to very different approaches to information, even in the most constitutional of monarchies. Cultures and traditions take years to solidify in an enterprise. In one high-tech manufacturing firm, the founder CEO's retirement led to information anarchy for many years; only now is the firm beginning to establish a more structured environment. The short reigns of most monarchs bodes poorly for the growth of persistent information traditions.

FEDERALISM

The final information state, federalism, also has a number of desirable features, and in today's business environment, it is the preferred model in most circumstances. Its distinguishing feature is the use of negotiation to bring potentially competing and noncooperating parties together. Federalism most explicitly recognizes the importance of politics, without casting it in pejorative terms. In contrast, technocratic utopianism ignores politics, anarchy is politics run amok, feudalism involves destructive politics, and monarchy attempts to eliminate politics through a strong central authority. Federalism treats politics as a necessary and legitimate activity by which people with different interests work out among themselves a collective purpose and means for achieving it.

Firms that adopt or evolve into this model typically have strong central leadership and a culture that encourages cooperation and learning. However, it takes tough negotiating and a politically astute information manager to make the federalist model work. Such an information manager needs to have the CEO's support (although not too much support, or a monarchy emerges) as well as the trust and support of the "lords and barons" who run the divisions. He or she needs to understand the value of information itself as well as of the technology that stores, manipulates, and distributes it. Such skills are not widely distributed throughout organizations, even (or perhaps especially) among IS executives.

An executive who has this perspective can then use cooperative information resources to create a shared information vision. Each realm contracts with the executive and with other realms to cede some of its information assets in return for helping to create a greater whole. This is a genuine leveraging of a firm's knowledge base.

At IBM, the former head of corporate information services, Larry Ford, concluded that the firm needed to manage information in a dramatically new way. Ford and his organization produced an information strategy that focused on the value that information can bring to all of IBM. The strategy was refined and ratified by all of the senior executives, and now Ford, his staff, and the divisional IS executives have gone out into the field to negotiate with senior managers about sharing their information with others in the company. "Would you share your product quality data with the service organization? How about sales?" Eventually all the important information will be in easy-to-access "data warehouses." Information management at IBM has become very personal politics, like the ward politician campaigning door to door.

Of course, the politician has only so much time to ring doorbells. A division may have hundreds of important data elements that need to be shared. IBM is finding that the time to educate and persuade information owners of their responsibilities is the biggest constraint to implementing a federalist model. Ford's departure from IBM to head a software firm may also place the federalist initiative at risk.

MANAGING INFORMATION POLITICS

Given these options for building an information polity, how do firms begin to effectively manage information? The first step is to select the preferred information model, as discussed in the next section. Following that, we present other principles of politically astute information management, including matching information politics to organizational culture, practicing technological realism, electing the right information politicians, and avoiding empire-building.

Select an Information State

The first step in managing information politics is figuring out which models people in the firm hold, which model currently predominates, which is most desirable, and how to achieve it. As we have noted, adopting multiple models will needlessly consume scarce resources and will confuse both information managers and users. Therefore, a firm should choose one model and move continually toward it, however long it takes.

We believe that there are only two viable choices among the five models: monarchy and federalism. In a business culture that celebrates empowerment and widespread participation, federalism is preferable, but it is harder to achieve and takes more time. Federalism requires managers to negotiate with each other in good faith while avoiding the temptation to use and withhold information destructively. Most firms we know of profess a desire to move toward a federalist model. But a firm that has difficulty getting consensus from its management team on other issues may find that federalism is impossible; a benevolent monarchy may be almost as effective and easier to implement.

Table 2-3 summarizes our assessments of the five political models along four dimensions: (1) commonality of vocabulary and meaning; (2) degree of access to important information; (3) quality of information—that is, its currency, relevance, and accuracy; and (4) efficiency of information management. These dimensions can be useful for evaluating a firm's current model and its effectiveness.

Commonality refers to having a set of terms, categories, and data elements that carry the same meaning throughout the enterprise. The desirability of common discourse may appear obvious, but in our experience it does not exist in many large firms. Even the definition of what a "sale" is can be variously interpreted by different divisions, to say nothing of more ambiguous terms such as "quality," "performance," and "improvement."[11]

The degree of information access is another good indicator of political culture. Many firms proclaim that all employees should have the information they need to do their work well. However, in making the choices about who actually needs what information, firms are making political decisions, whether or not they acknowledge it. The technocratic utopians focus less on what information is accessed by whom and more on the mechanisms of distribution.

In many ways the quality of information is the most important of these indicators. Information quality is achieved through detailed attention to its integrity, accuracy, currency, interpretability, and overall value. As with other types of products, the quality of information is best judged by its customers. Even companies that declare themselves as firmly in the Information Age, however, rarely have measures or assessments of their information's quality.

Efficiency is often the objective of technologists who wish to minimize redundant data storage. The incredible improvements in price-performance ratios for data storage technologies have reduced this issue's importance somewhat. However, there is still the human factor. Multiple measures of the same item take time to analyze and synthesize. Effective management requires focusing on a few key performance indicators. Computers and disk drives may be able to handle information overload, but people still suffer from it.

TABLE 2-3 Ranking Alternative Models of Information Politics

	Federalism	Monarchy	Technocratic Utopianism	Anarchy	Feudalism
Commonality of Vocabulary	5	5	3	1	1
Access to Information	5	2	3	4	1
Quality of Information	3	2	1	2	2
Efficiency of Information Management	3	5	3	1	3
Total	16	14	10	8	7

Key: 5=high   3=moderate   1=low

Federalism has the potential to be effective on all four dimensions of information management. A common vocabulary emerges through negotiations between levels and units. This makes possible the widespread access and distribution of meaningful information, which is then used for the benefit of the whole enterprise. Federalism strikes a balance between the unintegrated independence of the feudal baronies and the undifferentiated units under monarchy. Although satisfying all constituencies may require gathering more information than is absolutely necessary (hence decreasing efficiency), and the necessary compromises may reduce quality, federalism scores higher in the minds of the managers we interviewed than any other model.

Because federalism explicitly acknowledges the important positive role that information politics can play, it is apt to be the most effective model for companies that rely on individual initiative for generating collective action. This is most likely to be the case for companies operating in complex and rapidly changing competitive environments, which create a high level of uncertainty. The federalist approach supports both autonomy and coordination. Accomplishing it, of course, requires negotiating skills and the willingness of managers to take the time to negotiate. Not all companies have executives with the ability or the commitment to do this. The temptation always exists to look to a strong monarch to resolve the endless negotiations by fiat, to fall prey once more to the alluring utopian vision painted by the technologists, to fall back into a nasty and brutish condition of feudal conflict, or to dissolve into the chaos of anarchy. Firms may want to pursue alternative models, in case federalism fails. In fact, as Table 2-2 shows, many of the firms pursuing federalism were also pursuing other models, either consciously or implicitly as a backup strategy. Sooner or later it is obviously best to settle on one model, though most firms find this difficult.

An information monarchy solves some of the problems of managing information throughout the enterprise. A strong, top-down approach ensures that a common language—in both vocabulary and meaning—underlies the information generated. Little unnecessary information is collected or distributed, guaranteeing a high level of efficiency. The monarch and his or her ministers mandate and oversee the right processes to generate the right information to be used in the right way—all enhancing information quality, at least as they perceive it. These advantages, however, are often gained at the expense of information access. It is the rare monarch who has enough democratic ideals to make information as broadly available as in a federalist state.

Technocratic utopianism focuses on using information technology to dramatically improve data distribution. Efficiency is high, at least in terms of a lack of data redundancy. Information access is also relatively high, at least for technologically oriented users. Because technocratic utopians do not concern themselves with the processes that produce information, the quality of information remains low. Further, the quality of information usage is inhibited by technocratic efforts such as complex data modeling that are often not understood or appreciated by line managers. As a result, the information produced by computer systems and the information actually used to manage the company are decoupled. Although this model scores high in principle, many of these initiatives fail. Commonality, access, and efficiency in a failed utopian scheme may actually be as low as in feudalism or even lower.

Although few executives would consciously adopt anarchy, it is not the lowest-scoring model. Commonality and efficiency are the lowest possible, of course, but at least individuals have easy access to the data they need. The customer controls information, thus its quality is likely to be high—unless the customer is an executive trying to take an organizationwide perspective.

Feudalism is the least effective political model along these dimensions. The existence of strong, independent, and often warring fiefdoms prevents the development of a common vocabulary and shared meaning. The feudal lords restrict access to and distribution of information under their authority. Feudalism gets only middling marks for quality; it may be high for individual divisions, but it is low from the corporate perspective. Finally, because some information is duplicated around the organization, efficiency is also only moderate. Feudalism is the least desirable yet the most common state in the organizations we researched; when more difficult and effective models fail, it is easy to fall back into the feudal state.

The key in managing information politics is to know which political model is currently in ascendance within the firm and to which the organization should be moving. Most firms we know of profess a desire to move toward a federalist model, while currently operating in a feudal or technocratic utopian environment. But a firm that has difficulty getting consensus from its management team on other issues may find that information federalism is impossible; a benevolent monarchy may be almost as effective.

Match Information Politics to Your Organizational Culture

It is no accident that democracy emerged in eighteenth-century America, a sprawling continent with vast resources and an ethic of independence and self-sufficiency. Similarly, a firm's culture must be conducive to participative information management and free information flow before they will happen. Put another way, information flow does not make an organizational culture less hierarchical and more open; rather, democratic cultures make possible democratic information flows. When faxes were flying to and from pre-Tiananmen China, some observers argued that the free flow of information was leading to a more open society; now that the faxes and those who faxed are silent, we know that the causal relationship was in the other direction.

Information policies, we have found, are among the last things to change in an organization changing its culture. We have never seen increased information flow leading to elimination of a management layer or a greater willingness to share information. When these latter changes happen, they happen for reasons unrelated to information: restructurings, tighter cost control, external events (e.g., the 1970s oil shocks or the current banking crisis), and so forth. Several companies, however, state that their new organization could not have survived without new information policies. Phillips Petroleum, for example, radically reduced its management ranks after a raider-forced restructuring. A new information policy was the key to its functioning.[12]

We observed this relationship between organizational culture and information politics in two computer companies. One firm was a fast-growing personal computer (PC) manufacturer when we studied it; since then, its growth has slackened. The other firm was a large manufacturer of several types of computers that was experiencing financial problems when we visited it. Their cultures seemed similar at first glance; they both had tried to develop cultures in which information was shared freely throughout their organizations with little regard to level or function. However, two key aspects of their cultures—their organizational structures and their relative financial success—had led to radically different information politics.

The PC firm had a traditional functional structure. According to the executives and employees we interviewed, information flowed relatively freely in the company. The firm had an explicit ethic of open communications, stressing early notification of problems and a "don't shoot the messenger" response. As a key U.S. executive stated, "Someone in international can request any piece of data and ask us to explain it. Allowing others access to information requires a lot of trust, but that trust seems to exist here." However, the firm is beginning to face more difficult competitive conditions, as PCs increasingly become commoditized. In more difficult times, with new management, the open information environment may not persist.

The other firm had a "networked" organization, with ad hoc teams assembling to address specific tasks. This structure, which made the firm flexible and responsive, also seemed to hinder the flow of important information. Several managers we interviewed reported that hoarding of valuable information was common. The ad hoc teams often resisted sharing their unique information. The managers we interviewed speculated that this was because a team that shares its information fully may lose its reason to exist. This is particularly true during the economically difficult times now facing the company. If an organizational structure is defined by information nodes, then those who freely surrender information may lose their place in the structure. Put more broadly, in the information-based organization, information becomes the primary medium of value and exchange, and who would give it away for free?

How do you know when your culture is right for more democratic information politics? There are a number of indicators. We have noticed, for example, that companies that successfully implement quality programs have to deal with many of the same issues affecting information flow. They have to empower front-line workers to make decisions, work cross-functionally to improve processes, and remove as much as possible the use of fear as a motivator. Similarly, companies highly attuned to customer satisfaction must be able to deal with negative results in a positive fashion—a trait highly necessary in an information democracy.

Not surprisingly, in an era of mergers, acquisitions, and global management, most large organizations have multiple political cultures. A newly acquired firm may resist adopting the information-sharing norms of its acquirer (or even, as seen in *Barbarians at the Gate,* of its potential acquirers attempting to perform due diligence).[13] Poorly performing divisions will rarely be as enthusiastic about new information reporting initiatives as long-term strong performers. And geographic differences affecting the willingness to share information are legendary; how many times has it been uttered, "We're having problems getting data from our French subsidiary."

Practice Technological Realism

Although technology will not lead us to an information utopia, there are still important technological factors to consider. Information engineering should be highly focused, information should be in units that managers can understand and negotiate with, and technology platforms should be as common as possible.

Previously we pointed out the folly of trying to engineer an organization's entire information inventory. We (and other researchers) believe that focused, less ambitious information management objectives are more likely to succeed, given that the volume of information in corporations is too great to be rigorously categorized and engineered.[14] This is particularly true in a federalist environment, in which each key information element will require substantial negotiations. Information management efforts must be directed at only those information elements that are essential to implementing strategy and to running the business day to day. At IBM, for example, the firm's internal information strategy focuses primarily on customer and market information and secondarily on process quality information.[15] Although this approach includes a great deal of data, it also excludes a considerable amount.

It is also important to acknowledge that not all information will be managed through technological means, just as most of the water around us does not run through our water meters. Only about 5 percent to 10 percent of the information in most firms is in electronic form. According to a recent study of information use by managers, even computer-based data are often preceded by word-of-mouth renditions of the same information.[16] The verbal and visual information that informs all of us is not totally unmanageable, but it cannot be modeled and categorized through technological means.

Companies may also find it useful in negotiating on information to use a larger unit of information than the data element. Most managers do not think in such narrow terms; as one executive said, "Don't give me all the molecules; tell me the key compounds they can form." A more relevant unit of information may be the document—form, report, or memo. Technologists must concern themselves with the data elements that appear on documents, but managers will normally be happy not to delve below the document level in developing a common information language. Xerox, having designated itself "The Document Company," is beginning to explore how business processes can be supported through documents.[17]

A key aspect of making information more widely available, ineffective technocratic utopias to the contrary, is the nature of the information technology platform. Specifically, technology for widespread information use must be common, easily used, and interconnectible.[18] Technological realists recognize that their computers may not be best for all applications, but they meet basic needs. Common, standardized technology is essential if the same information is to be presented in the same way all around the company. Aetna Life & Casualty, American Airlines, Du Pont, IBM, and a large consumer products firm are all initiating efforts to build and operate a common platform for information distribution. This may seem obvious, but few companies can send a piece of data to all their workstations without considerable machinations to address different products, protocols, and other technical particulars. These companies are discovering that the same federalist approach required for achieving consensus on information meaning is also required to achieve consensus on a standard technology platform.[19]

Elect the Right Information Politicians

Along with having a suitable political culture and technology environment, companies desiring to change their information politics must elect (or otherwise get into office) the right information politicians. We find that the information politician role—not the owner of information but the manager with primary responsibility for facilitating its effective use—is still up for grabs in many companies, despite some pretenders to the throne. In one fast-growing software company, for example, problems with information flow were widespread, but no one below the CEO took any ownership of the problem.[20] One would assume that CIOs would own this domain, but until now they have not necessarily been the best choice.

Until recently, most CIOs were selected for technical acumen rather than political skills. Few would have embarked on initiatives to improve the way information—not just information technology—is used and managed. Only a few IS function heads have the political clout to persuade powerful barons to share their information for the good of the entire kingdom. Still, this is changing. At companies such as IBM, Xerox, Kodak, and Merrill Lynch, recent CIOs have been fast-track executives with records of managing important nontechnology aspects of the business. If these nontechnical managers can master the considerable technical challenges in creating an information infrastructure, they will likely have the skills and influence to bring about a political environment in which the information can be shared and used.

The CFO is another candidate for information politician. Most CFOs, however, are solely associated with financial information. In order to take on broader responsibility for information management, they must at a minimum convince operational executives of their ability to understand and manage operational performance information. We have found a few CFOs with the sincere desire to do this but have seen no examples of a CFO becoming a successful information politician.

The CEO is perhaps best positioned to lobby for a particular information environment; indeed, in an information monarchy, the CEO is the only politician who counts. In more democratic environments, such as federalism, the CEO must appreciate the importance of information and communicate it throughout the firm. The time demands of day-to-day information negotiation may require that the CEO delegate political authority to other managers.

Like real politicians, information politicians must be good at both charismatics and organization. They must be able to persuade both individuals and the masses of the importance of information management and the correctness of the chosen political model. They must also organize collections of "advance agents" and "ward heelers" to work every day at building coalitions, influencing opinion leaders, and swaying recalcitrant members of the electorate.

Avoid Building Information Empires

Because information is such a powerful tool, federalist organizations will inherently resist or distrust managers who try to build an empire by controlling information. Concentration of all responsibility for collecting, maintaining, and interpreting information in one person, regardless of position, is too much power in any organization with democratic leanings. In fact, the concept of information ownership is antithetical to federalist information management. Rather, companies should institute the concept of information stewardship—responsibility for ensuring data quality—with ownership by the corporation at large. Stewardship of information, again perhaps at the document level rather than for individual data elements, should be assigned widely throughout the organization.

The IS organization should be particularly careful to avoid building an information empire. It may already wield considerable power by virtue of its technical custody of information. We have observed organizations that cede control over information to this "independent" third party, assuming that it will not use information for political gain. But the IS function may have its own interests to advance, its own kingdom to build.

For example, at a major direct marketing firm, nontechnical executives were intimidated by technology, and control over the firm's sixty-million-name database was ceded to IS. As a result, access to the database had to be on terms acceptable to IS. This often meant denial and delay to managers wishing to exploit the database for valid business purposes. IS built a proprietary database management system, further reinforcing the walls around the database. When the CEO himself was denied a report, the IS head was deposed and replaced by a trusted nontechnical associate of the CEO. Yet because he could not understand the technology, he could not dismantle the walls around the data. A new IS vice president was brought in from outside the company with an explicit mandate to open up the empire.

CONCLUSION

Explicitly recognizing the politics of information and managing them constructively is a difficult, complex, and time-consuming task. It will not happen by itself, nor will the problem go away. Effectively managing information politics requires a shift in organizational culture; new technology and even new executives alone are not enough to make this happen. Information management must become something that all managers care about and most managers participate in. They must view information as important to their success and be willing to spend time and energy negotiating to meet their information needs. As in real democracies, democratic information models like federalism require informed participation of all organizational citizens.

Unless the politics of information are identified and managed, companies will not move into the Information Age. Information will not be shared freely nor used effectively by decision makers. No amount of data modeling, no number of relational databases, and no invocation of "the information-based organization" will bring about a new political order of information. Rather, it will take what politics always take: negotiation, influence-exercising, back-room deals, coalition-building, and occasionally even war. If information is truly to become the most valued commodity in the businesses of the future, we cannot expect to acquire it without an occasional struggle.

REFERENCES

1. J. G. March, *Decisions and Organizations* (Cambridge, Massachusetts: Basil Blackwell, 1988).

2. For example: M. S. Scott Morton, *The Corporation of the 1990s: Information Technology and Organizational Transformation* (New York: Oxford University Press, 1991); P. G. W. Keen, *Shaping the Future: Business Design through Information Technology* (Boston: Harvard Business School Press, 1991); and D. R. Vincent, *The Information-Based Corporation: Stakeholder Economics and the Technology Investment* (Homewood, Illinois: Dow Jones-Irwin, 1990).

3. J. Thorbeck, "The Turnaround Value of Values," *Harvard Business Review*, January–February 1991, pp. 52–62.

4. J. Pfeffer, *Power in Organizations* (New York: HarperBusiness, 1986).

5. See articles in W. G. McGowan, ed., *Revolution in Real-Time: Managing Information Technology in the 1990s* (Boston: Harvard Business School Press, 1991). A notable exception to the apolitical perspective is found in M. L. Markus, "Power, Politics, and MIS Implementation," *Communications of the ACM* 26:6 (June 1983): 434–444.

6. J. G. March, "The Business Firm as a Political Coalition," in J. G. March (1988).

7. A term similar to "technocratic utopianism" has been defined, without reference to information management, by Howard P. Segal. See: H. P. Segal, *Technological Utopianism in American Culture* (Chicago: University of Chicago Press, 1985).

8. See R. A. Caro, *The Power Broker: Robert Moses and the Fall of New York* (New York: Random House, 1975); and *Chinatown*, the film.

9. See D. L. Goodhue, J. A. Quillard, and J. F. Rockart, "Managing the Data Resource: A Contingency Perspective," *MIS Quarterly* (September 1988), 373–392; and D. L. Goodhue, L. Kirsch, J. A. Quillard, and M. Wybo, "Strategic Data Planning: Lessons from the Field" (Cambridge, Massachusetts: MIT Sloan School of Management, Center for Information Systems Research, Working Paper No. 215, October 1990).

10. Some interesting examples of feudalism, again largely outside the information management context, are described in: J. Pfeffer, *Managing with Power* (Boston: Harvard Business School Press, 1991).

11. Some of the reasons for these discrepancies are described in: S. M. McKinnon and W. J. Bruns, Jr., *The Information Mosaic* (Boston: Harvard Business School Press, 1992).

12. L. M. Applegate and C. S. Osborn, "Phillips 66 Company: Executive Information System," 9-189-006 (Boston: Harvard Business School, 1988).

13. B. Burrough and J. Helyar, *Barbarians at the Gate* (New York: Harper & Row, 1990).

14. See Goodhue et al. (1988) and Goodhue et al. (1990).

15. "Using Information Strategically: A Road Map for the 90s," Information and Telecommunications Systems, IBM Corporation, 15 November 1990.

16. McKinnon and Bruns (1992).

17. See the proceedings volume from the Xerox Document Symposium, March 10–11, 1992, Xerox Corporation, Stamford, Connecticut.

18. L. Sproull and S. Kiesler, *Connections: New Ways of Working in the Networked Organization* (Cambridge, Massachusetts: MIT Press, 1991).

19. See J. Linder and D. Stoddard, "Aetna Life & Casualty: Corporate Technology Planning," 9-187-037 (Boston: Harvard Business School, 1986).

20. J. Gladstone and N. Nohria, "Symantec," N9-491-010 (Boston: Harvard Business School, 1990, revised 4 February 1991).

3

Powers of Information

William H. Davidow and Michael S. Malone

The phrase "power of information" is used so frequently that it has become at best a cliché and at worst an advertising slogan. In the process, the phrase has been so inflated into science fiction—the omnipotent and dangerous supercomputer peering into our lives—that information seems some priceless and enslaving commodity.

The truth is, extraordinary advances in information processing will serve as the dynamo of the virtual corporation. Furthermore, in the years to come, incremental differences in companies' abilities to acquire, distribute, store, analyze, and invoke actions based on information will determine the winners and losers in the battle for customers.

For those unable to previously identify with the implications of the power of information, the events of the Persian Gulf War should have been a revelation. For it was a war in which information gave the Allies the power to win over the bulk of its enemy. After all, solely in terms of available manpower within the zone of combat, the Iraqis at the beginning of the campaign held a 20 percent edge. Most military texts of the last two hundred years have argued that to be successful an attacking force must be twice to three times the size of an entrenched defender. So, by all traditional measures, the Iraqis should have been able to put up a good fight.

Yet, the war itself, first over Baghdad and then on the ground in Kuwait, was among the most one-sided in history. The Allies lost fewer than 100 of their 450,000 troops in the war zone. As has been much remarked since, American troops were statistically safer on the front than they would have been on many city streets at home.

Why the rout? The answer was obvious to anyone watching television during the brief course of the war. The Allied troops had information on the Iraqis far superior to any information held by their enemy and then managed that information more effectively. In strategic command and control, the Allies used satellite and reconnaissance information to learn just about everything they needed to know about Iraq's static defenses. Tomahawk cruise missiles, using reconnaissance information stored in their memories, were so well programmed that they actually followed roads and streets to their targets. Further, because the Allies appreciated the importance of information, they also knew the value of denying it to the other side. They either destroyed or negated the ability of the Iraqis to deliver commands or identify attackers—a plan made unforgettable by the image of Baghdad antiaircraft fire filling the air long after a Stealth fighter had passed.

In battlefield tactics, the power of information was even more striking. While some Iraqi commanders were reduced to using runners to carry messages, Allied soldiers used hand-held digital devices to pick up satellite transmissions and locate themselves accurately within a few yards in the trackless desert. Minicomputers quickly calculated complex artillery trajectories, put shells dead on target, and wiped out the enemy before it could mount a counterstrike. M-1 Abrams tanks used their on-board computers to fire accurately on the fly and wreak devastating damage on Iraqi armor with only a handful of losses.

With the Persian Gulf War, the value of information reached a zenith—bytes became more important than bullets. The case was made, with brutal clarity, that information could become the foundation for devastating destruction.

If there were one piece of Allied hardware that captured and held the world's attention during the short course of the war, it would have to have been the Patriot antiballistic missile. For several days at the height of the air war, Israeli and Saudi Arabian cities were held hostage to Iraqi Scud missiles. Like the German V-2 before it, the Scud threatened the unstoppable horror of a ballistic missile aimed at a civilian population. The jury-rigged Patriot, though only partially effective, saved the day.

Historically, ground defense against airborne attack has always been exceedingly difficult, from antiaircraft fire over Berlin to SAM missiles launched over Hanoi. The intercept times are so short that any deviance in the path of the incoming object is usually enough to guarantee defensive failure. Drop a ballistic missile in from the stratosphere and the population is essentially left undefended and paralyzed in fear.

The Patriot changed that. In some instances, Allied satellites detected launch backfires as the Scuds left Iraq, then transmitted the data to ground stations in the United States and elsewhere, where it was processed and then relayed to Patriot batteries in Israel and Saudi Arabia. There, the surprise gone, the skies could be scanned by radar for the incoming missile, the lock-on information conveyed to the Patriot's own guidance system, and the missile launched. In flight, intercepting at a closing speed of several thousand miles per hour, the Patriot would make the final real-time trajectory adjustments to adapt to the flight path of the often-tumbling Scud. The result was seen in the skies over Tel Aviv and Riyadh.

What enabled the Patriot to accomplish this remarkable task was that it continuously changed its flight behavior to adapt to evolving circumstances. It did this by using sophisticated (though hardly state-of-the-art) computational equipment. But more important was the information this equipment processed, information that captured not only the nature of the attacking ordnance nor just its overall trajectory, but the second-by-second behavior of the Scud as it descended through the turbulent atmosphere.

In many ways, the ability to predict—whether it was the path of ballistic missiles or the movements of ground troops—and then quickly react was the decisive factor for the Allies in the Gulf War. In the process, time seemed to accelerate, such that the real ground war, expected by many experts to drag out for months, in the end essentially lasted only forty-eight hours. Because the Allies knew so much about the deployment and behavior of the enemy, they could encircle and destroy the Iraqi troops with certain knowledge that there would be no significant resistance.

GETTING THE INFORMATION RIGHT

One might argue that the power of information in battle is not the same as its strength in other scenarios, for war has its unique intensities and skills. Can information really be of comparable importance in business? The answer is a qualified yes.

Certainly, better information won't allow American Airlines to annihilate USAir overnight. Sears won't vanish tomorrow because Wal-Mart and Kmart use information more effectively. Motorola won't destroy its Japanese semiconductor competitors because it has a better information-gathering network. However, over time better information can translate into a decisive competitive advantage. It can be said with certainty that if two competitors are equal in other respects, the one making the best use of information will undoubtedly win—sometimes with stunning speed.

Consider how Toyota, the world's most successful automobile company, sells cars in Japan. Toyota has shown the competitive power that can be gained by adding electronics to an efficient, low-tech, information-reporting system. *The Machine That Changed the World* describes how Toyota also used computer intelligence to amplify an established information-reporting program in its distribution system.

Like many Japanese auto companies, Toyota long sold automobiles door-to-door, an unusual process outside Japan. But in doing so, Toyota has probably learned more about its buyers than has any U.S. or European car company. Such a sales technique has led to a tight relationship between company and customer:

> *Toyota was determined never to lose a former buyer and could minimize the chance of this happening by using the data in its consumer data base to predict what Toyota buyers would want next as their incomes, family size, driving patterns, and tastes changed. . . .*
>
> *[Sales] team members draw up a profile on every household within the geographic area around the dealership, then periodically visit each one, after*

first calling to make an appointment. During their visits the sales repre-
sentative updates the household profile: How many cars of what age does
each family have? What is the make and specifications? How much parking
space is available? How many children in the household and what use does
the family make of its cars? When does the family think it will need to re-
place its cars? The last response is particularly important to the product-
planning process; team members systematically feed this information back
to the development teams.[1]

In recent years, as door-to-door selling has grown too expensive, Toyota has
begun a gradual shift toward dealerships in Japan. But even these dealerships are
nothing like their U.S. counterparts. Because Japanese car makers are capable of
responding very quickly to changes in demand—automobiles can be custom ordered and delivered in a matter of days—dealerships are often little more than
storefronts, with a few sample cars.

Here is a typical experience for a Japanese automobile customer:

The first thing a consumer encounters on entering a Corolla dealership to-
day is an elaborate computer display. Each Corolla owner in the Corolla
family has a membership card that can be inserted in the display, just as one
would insert a card in a bank machine. The display then shows all the sys-
tem's information on that buyer's household and asks if anything has
changed. If it has, the machine invites the owner to enter new information.
The system then makes a suggestion about the models most appropriate to
the household's needs, including current prices. A sample of each model is
usually on display in the showroom immediately adjacent to the computer
display.[2]

That's not all. Using the same terminal, potential customers can also access
information on insurance, financing, even parking permits. They can also learn
about used cars, if they so wish.

Record keeping on processes inside the firm has been equally extensive.
There Toyota uses its famous production system, centered around *kanban*, a simple system of cards attached to part bins that track the progress of those parts
through the production process, serving as both a tracking tool and an order form
for new parts.[3] In the past, with *kanban*, Toyota could use information management to obviate the need for warehouses and high inventories, escape the roller
coaster of over- and underproduction by its suppliers, and implement the first
just-in-time production system—and do it all without computers.

When computers did come to the Toyota factories they were smoothly integrated into the process, because Toyota already understood the flow of information in its production areas. Just as important, Toyota workers were committed to
making both the *kanban* and automated information processing systems work.
Labor and management worked as a team. This second lesson was lost on many
companies, most famously General Motors, which rushed to install computers

and robotics before it fully understood the information-worker culture in its plants and the relationship between its factories and dealers.

Within the GM factories, the environment was poisonous to the notion of teamwork and shared information. Says Maryann Keller in *Rude Awakening,* "The workers wanted to do their jobs well, wanted to be competitive, but all too often they were fighting against unbeatable odds to get their jobs done. Every problem became a confrontation; since there was a basic mistrust between labor and management, it was hard to establish a cooperative environment where problems could be solved."[4] Fittingly, it took a joint venture with Toyota (the NUMMI plant in Fremont, California) to show GM how far it had fallen behind in the business it once dominated.

General Motors suffered a similar breakdown in information transfer in its relationship with dealerships. Like other U.S. car makers, GM expected its dealers to accept unsalable cars they didn't want, often by tying them in with delivery of more desirable models. In *The Machine That Changed the World,* the Big Three U.S. automakers are described in the following way:

> To make matters worse, coordination between the sales division and the product planners in the big mass-production companies is poor. While the product planners conduct endless focus groups and clinics at the beginning of the product-development process to gauge consumer reaction to their proposed new models, they haven't found a way to incorporate continuous feedback from the sales division and the dealers. In fact, the dealers have almost no link with the sales and marketing divisions, which are responsible for moving the metal. The dealer's skills lie in persuasion and negotiation, not in feeding back information to the product planners.
>
> It's sobering to remember that no one employed by a car company has to buy a car from a dealer (they buy in-house through the company instead, or even receive a free car as part of their compensation package). Thus, they have no direct link to either the buying experience or the customer. More-over, a dealer has little incentive to share any information on customers with the manufacturer. The dealer's attitude is, what happens in my showroom is my business.[5]

These weaknesses in information management may not be fatal for General Motors, but the resulting lack of understanding of the needs of the market has contributed greatly to the firm's loss of market share. The danger of this lack of information becomes even more obvious when one considers that the design cycle on Japanese cars is, on the average, more than a year faster than the five-year cycle of U.S. car makers.[6] This puts the Japanese manufacturers in a far better position to track changing market tastes and then quickly design new models to meet them.

The Toyota story shows that computer technology can be used to reinforce already-efficient manufacturing and direct-sales information systems. This access to information about the market in turn acts as an early warning system for the company about any sudden shifts in customer attitudes. As much as any company in the world, Toyota understands the power of information.

One U.S. company that does appreciate the implications of the Toyota story is Hewlett-Packard. When HP decided to bring computer power to the organization and control of its manufacturing, it chose this as its charter: "Getting the right information to the right people at the right time to achieve our business objectives."

What makes this statement remarkable is that Hewlett-Packard is one of the world's largest manufacturers of computers used in design, process control, and inventory management. Yet, there is no mention of computers in the statement, only of the efficient use of information. The implicit message is that any effective means of information transfer is acceptable. If handwritten notes can do the job, use them; if it means the fully networked data processing hierarchy known as computer-integrated manufacturing, use that—as long as it gets the right information to the right people at the right time to achieve Hewlett-Packard's business objectives.

BOLTS OF INFORMATION

Another example of the way information can transform a business, this time in distribution, is the quick response (QR) movement in the U.S. textiles industry. QR has been driven by fabric giants Milliken and Du Pont and by such retailers as J. C. Penney, Kmart, and Wal-Mart.[7] For instance, Milliken, challenged by offshore competition, set out to obtain the maximum advantage from its proximity to U.S. customers by bringing technology to bear to slash the time between the appearance of a new fashion and its arrival in volume at retailer sites.

A model for these firms was the Italian company Benetton, which had tripled sales to $1.7 billion in just seven years by delivering knitted goods in the hottest new colors seemingly overnight. One way Benetton did this was to invert the traditional method for manufacturing sweaters. Instead of dying the yarn and knitting the sweaters, it knitted sweaters with a neutral yarn and then dyed them to meet market demand. That way, should the market go from blue to green overnight, not only could Benetton respond quickly but it didn't have to be stuck with obsolete inventory. Benetton further accelerated the process by putting into place fast and sophisticated retailer reporting systems.[8]

A study of the U.S. garment industry determined that it took an average of sixty-six weeks to complete the process of converting raw materials to textiles to apparel and then moving it through the distribution channel to the retail consumer. In the fast-moving world of fashion this was slow enough to cost the industry an estimated $25 billion per year in lost potential business. Most of this damage occurred at the retail end, where an estimated $16 billion was lost each year from markdowns, lost potential sales on out-of-stock items, and excess inventory.

The problem resulted in part from a breakdown in the means for passing newly obtained information backwards through the supply chain. Information about a decline in sales of a particular style would slowly worm its way back from the cash register to the buyer, then to the garment manufacturer, and from there to the textile firm and then on to the fiber producer. As orders were canceled at each point along the supply chain, valueless inventory would pile up.

The obvious solution—that of simply hustling the goods through the system faster—turned out to be inadequate for the situation. There would still be too much waste. Instead, a two-way system was needed: in one direction speeding the apparel down the distribution channels and in the other direction feeding back results to each upstream participant.

To see if the theory of a two-way system was right, a research firm set up three pilot runs. The results were staggering. One quick response chain involving Belk and Haggar (jackets and slacks) saw sales jump 25 percent, gross profits 25 percent, and inventory turns 67 percent. A pilot QR chain in tailored clothing involving J. C. Penney, Oxford, and Burlington not only saw sales up 59 percent and inventory turns climb 90 percent, but cut forecasting errors by more than half. Similar results were seen by Wal-Mart, Seminole, and Milliken in tests with slacks.[9]

The QR system, with its overlapping feedback loops of information, had proven itself. Just as important, the participants in the program had learned to trust one another with what was once proprietary information, such as sales, orders, and inventories. Reports Joseph D. Blackburn of Vanderbilt University:

> *The first step in a quick response program is to find willing partners. As in other industries, finding partners is challenging because, as an industry spokesman states, "In your traditional relationships, what's out there today is lack of trust. Nobody trusts anybody. Breaking down those barriers is not easy, but that is the key to quick response. There's got to be a lot more communication. In quick response programs or any other program where change must be made, it is harder than the old way of doing business. A lot harder."*[10]

Blackburn adds, "Adversarial relationships block communication and inhibit the unfettered flow of information needed for effective supply chains." As with Toyota, only when the informational and cultural systems were in place could electronics be inserted into the program to amplify its strengths.

The key technologies of QR proved to be computer networks, bar code systems, and scanners. Wal-Mart alone invested half a billion dollars in QR point-of-sale equipment.[11] Now a retailer could scan the bar code on a given item being sold and instantly pass the information on that sale all the way back through the chain to the textile maker. Not only was the style of the product recorded, but also information on color and size, and that information served as the underpinning of a fast just-in-time inventory system along the distribution chain.

By the end of the 1980s the QR system had become so efficient—and the level of trust among its participants had become so high—that different players began to use additional technology to tighten the system even further, and in the process approached delivering the virtual product. One such example is described by Blackburn:

> *In this case, Milliken supplied the finished product, an oriental rug-design area rug, to a major retailer. Milliken made the following offer to the retailer: "You send us the daily orders that you get from the consumer, we will manufacture the rugs and ship UPS directly to the consumer's home." This meant that the retailer could eliminate not only his entire distribution center for that product, but all of his inventory except for display items in the showroom. The retailer responded, "That will work only on regular sales, but commercial sales are such a spike [in demand] in our sales pattern that we've got to carry inventory to cover the spikes." Milliken responded by asking, "What percent are the spikes?" It turned out that two-thirds of their sales were promotional. If they guessed wrong on those two-thirds of their sales, they had excess inventory. Milliken then said, "It's all or nothing. It's either quick response or it's not quick response; we will satisfy your orders. Now you have to tell us when these big spikes are coming. We have got to share that kind of information." The retailer agreed and now Milliken is taking orders on a daily basis and shipping directly to the consumer. The system responds much faster than through the traditional [distribution center] channel and with a fraction of the inventory. Moreover, the retailer's costs were slashed by 13 percent.*[12]

COORDINATION AND CONTROL

The pivotal role of information management in the corporation is something that has occurred within our lifetimes. In *The Visible Hand,* Chandler argues that the modern corporation was built on intensiveness of capital, management, and energy (and with it, material).[13] High-speed information processing will soon have to be added to that list.

The success of a virtual corporation will depend on its ability to gather and integrate a massive flow of information throughout its organizational components and intelligently act upon that information. The very vigor of this process will result in a less capital-, management-, and energy-intensiveness, one of the fundamental advantages of the virtual corporation over contemporary business enterprises. The virtual corporation will significantly alter the traditional internal balance of individual businesses and of the economy as a whole.

It is Chandler who noted that the first management hierarchies appeared in the railroad industry in the 1850s in response to a need to provide and analyze the information that was necessary to run these complex enterprises:

No other business enterprise, or for that matter few other non-business insti-
tutions, had ever required the coordination and control of so many different
types of units carrying out so great a variety of tasks that demanded such
close scheduling. None handled so many different types of goods or required
the recording of so many different financial transactions.[14]

As corporations in other industries began to experience the same complexity
of size and scope in their businesses, they too moved to adopt multiple-level hierarchies of management. General Motors in its heyday boasted of nearly twenty
levels of management, as did IBM and General Electric.

As these and other companies have struggled to boost efficiency and become
ever more market responsive, they have stripped out layers of management and
broadened the remaining span of managers' control. For example, in June 1991
GM restructured its giant Chevrolet-Pontiac-Canada Group, by itself one of the
twenty largest businesses in North America. It turned three engine groups into one
and cut thirteen freestanding parts-making operations to just eight, in the process
"pruning away several vice presidencies" and expanding the responsibilities of the
rest.[15]

Today the trend in management is to delegate ever more decision making
and control to the employees doing the actual work. Computers now gather and
supply the information that was once provided by management hierarchies. In the
process, training has had to be substituted for supervision. The modern employee
is expected to use the information gathered by computer networks and know
what to do instead of having to be told. One proven way of doing this has been
through the use of quality circles, groups of employees that regularly meet to discuss how to improve product quality and workplace productivity. Such programs
teach employees how to analyze and solve quality problems with minimal management supervision.

In some cases, the lines between worker and middle manager essentially dis-
appear. Rosabeth Moss Kanter, editor of the *Harvard Business Review,* has written that

> *as work units become more participative and team oriented, and as profes-*
> *sionals and knowledge workers become more prominent, the distinction be-*
> *tween manager and non-manager begins to erode. . . . Position, title, and*
> *authority are no longer adequate tools, not in a world that encourages sub-*
> *ordinates to think for themselves and where managers have to work syner-*
> *gistically with other departments and even other companies.*[16]

T. J. Rodgers, CEO of Cypress Semiconductor, has taken a technological approach to the challenge of removing layers of bureaucracy. Starting Cypress with
the goal of maintaining a flexible, adaptive organization no matter how large the
company grew, Rodgers from the beginning refused to allow a middle management to form. Instead, he installed a computer system to track the daily objectives
of every company employee. Such a system, wrote Brian Dumaine in *Fortune,*

allows him to stay abreast of every employee and team in his fast-moving or-
ganization. Each employee maintains a list of ten to 15 goals like "Meet
with marketing for new product launch," or "Make sure to check with Cus-
tomer X." Noted next to each goal is when it was agreed upon, when it's
due to be finished and whether it's finished yet or not.

This way, it doesn't take layers of expensive bureaucracy to check
who's doing what, whether someone has got a light enough workload to be
put on a new team, and who's having trouble. Rodgers says he can review
the goals of all 1,500 employees in about four hours, which he does each
week. He looks only for those falling behind, and then calls not to scold but
to ask if there's anything he can do to help them get the job done. On the
surface the system may seem bureaucratic, but it takes only about a half-
hour a week for employees to review and update their lists.[17]

At one manufacturing company after another, middle management—the
most populous of industrial professions a quarter-century ago—is fast becoming
an endangered species. Some executives have even grown vehement in their desire
to root out what they see as an impediment to success. *Industry Week* quotes
Richard C. Miller, founder and vice president of Aries Technology, as assigning
middle managers much of the blame for American industry not adapting quickly
enough to new technology. Says Miller: "I'm not real impressed with middle managers. Many are [just] hiding out until they retire.

There are times when I would like to take middle managers by the necks,
bang them against the wall and ask: 'Don't you realize the company is going to be
out of business in five to ten years if you take that attitude?'"[18]

Similar opinions can be heard these days in services as well, such as banking,
accounting, and government. Not surprisingly, given this attitude, business is becoming less and less management intensive and increasingly dependent on competence at the worker level. The role of management in the business of the future is
bound to decline as computers gather and provide the information that was at one
time the product of middle management and as employees become better trained
and empowered to make decisions. Information and the power it provides will
flow to the worker.

As for the energy intensity of business that Chandler identified as one of the
cornerstones of the modern corporation, evidence of its decline is no farther away
than your Sony Walkman. The value of the products we purchase is determined
increasingly by their sophistication and information content and less by their material and energy content. Nowadays, more powerful products don't necessarily
weigh more, they just do more. Their value is a function of their information
processing features.

For example, the items that boost the price on today's automobiles include
sophisticated audio systems; antilock brakes; electronic controls for fuel, ride adjustment, traction, air bags, and transmissions; and automatic controls for temperature adjustment and seat and mirror position. All are highly prized features
and important profit makers for car companies. All are also highly information
dependent and add little to the material content of the car.

Home electronic equipment has become better in performance and capability and lighter in weight than ever before. The nineteen-inch, remote-controlled, eighty-two-channel stereo color TV of today weighs only twenty pounds, compared with its sixty-pound, black-and-white, thirteen-channel-dial, monaural predecessor of 1960. Today's midsize color TV sells for about $20 per pound. A 386-type laptop computer weighs only about twelve pounds and sells for about $200 per pound. This compares with just $5 or $10 per pound for an automobile like the Ford Escort. The complexity of the information content is the defining factor.

Much of the added information value in modern products comes from semiconductors. The semiconductor industry itself is one of the most impressive examples of the energy-conservative nature of information-intensive industries—which is one reason why it is so important to a resource-poor nation such as Japan. A typical semiconductor manufacturing plant that produces $1 billion of output consumes just a fraction of the power wattage of a steel plant or an aluminum plant of the same level of output.

In an information-intensive world, supplying information and providing the capability to process it can add billions of dollars to the value of products without requiring much, if any, additional energy use. For example, the business of supplying electronic information is a $12 billion industry; the value of software annually sold in the U.S. with computer systems currently is $52 billion;[19] and information publishing in the United States is an industry of more than $14 billion. Yet all three consume relatively little energy other than that required to cool, warm, or light the offices of their employees. In just this way, the virtual corporation will depend upon the power of information, not electricity, to create value.[20]

One can make a good case that the virtual corporation will be significantly less capital intensive than today's business enterprise. "Lean production is lean because it uses less of everything than does mass production"[21] (see [a later chapter]).

When companies successfully implement such systems they make more efficient use of capital equipment, reduce the need for very much working capital, and increase the output per square foot of their factories. The quick response experiment of the textile industry demonstrates how more efficient production, distribution, and retailing can boost inventory turns and thus reduce the need for working capital.

Taiichi Ohno, inventor of the Toyota production system, has been quoted as saying that his current project is "looking at the time line from the moment the customer gives us an order to the point where we collect the cash. And we are reducing that time line by removing the non-value added wastes."[22] By squeezing wasted time out of the system, sizable amounts of working capital will be saved as goods speed their way more quickly through production and into the customers' hands.

That is the impact on manufacturing. One can add that the generation of information-intensive products is less capital intensive as well. One of the purest examples of this is software, the quintessential case of which is Microsoft. The dominant supplier of software for personal computers—$1.8 billion in sales—Microsoft has reached its present size with one of the fastest growth rates in American business history, while still generating the capital it needs internally. The company's public stock offering was primarily a way just to create liquidity for its owners.

Businesses that add value to their products by using information generally enjoy very high gross margins. Take a database company, such as Lexus/Nexus, a supplier of information to the legal profession. Once it has incurred the cost of installing the computers and collecting the core data, that information can be sold repeatedly with little additional expense. By the same token, the variable costs associated with handling more reservations on an airline reservation system such as SABRE are practically zero.

One of the best examples of an information-intensive product is the Intel microprocessor. These microprocessors power most of the world's personal computers, and Intel enjoys an estimated 80 percent gross margin on each one it sells. Obviously, the value of these products rests not in the cost of their production but in the information processing power they bring to customers.

BUSINESS AS INFORMATION

So pervasive and fundamental is the role of information—from the words in this book to the strands of DNA in each of the ten trillion cells of your body—that we often look right past it. Most of this information is clustered into databases, collections of information that range from addresses in a Rolodex to memories in a human brain to the banks of billions of bytes of data supporting a Cray supercomputer. The creation of the virtual corporation will result from linking relevant databases into ever more extensive and integrated networks.

The database we most often use during a typical day is stored in our own memory. In it we carry patterns of behavior, records about our friends and business associates, and rules about how to deal with the vagaries of daily life. We augment this body of information with a growing number of other databases. For example, there are notes we write to ourselves, to-do lists, address books, calendars, and computer databases. We also transmit this information to others via written and spoken word, delivery systems such as the postal service and Federal Express, and electronic means such as fax and the telephone.

Not only are we receptacles of information, we are also generators. And the information that we generate often induces and controls the actions of others. Take an average workday. An engineer generates designs that encode information in the form of specifications that are transported to others to define the nature and form of a manufacturing process. An architect does the same thing in the blueprint for a building. A stockbroker transmits information and its analysis to clients about market behavior to induce buy and sell orders. In fact, a significant portion of the population that works in service industries does little else but process and manipulate information. Consider the work of lawyers, accountants, advertising account managers, newspaper reporters, and thousands of other service persons.

Here at the end of the twentieth century, four decades into the computer age, it is increasingly obvious that the very nature of business itself is information. Many of the employees in any corporation are involved in the process of gathering, generating, or transforming information. In a typical modern automated industrial firm only a small fraction of the workers—perhaps less than 5 percent—is actually involved in physical work. But even among that tiny population, information has revised the workplace.

In the age of numerically controlled machines and robotics, manufacturing has become yet another information process where machine instructions stored in computer memory describe how a piece of metal should be rolled, lathed, stamped, welded, bolted, or painted. Fewer and fewer human beings are actually involved in the production process. Instead, most workers in manufacturing companies are now involved in producing services. They deal mostly with information. They sell products to customers and service their needs; they are involved in manufacturing overhead processes to ensure that the right products are produced and that the proper materials are readily available; they administer and control the operation; they develop plans and strategies; and they design the products and services they have determined the customer desires. This is as true in the most traditional of industries—steel, automobiles, railroads, tool and die, and construction—as it is in the most modern, such as computer workstations and bioengineering.

In service industries as well, major portions of the work force engage in processing information. In a typical airline, a sizable percentage of employees are involved in generating and using the information required to run the business. Similarly, the vast majority of employees in a typical financial services firm is involved in information gathering, information processing, and generating of customer services based on information. The same is true in newspaper, television, and advertising companies.

THE PRODUCTIVITY DILEMMA

What we have discussed so far suggests that the rate of progress in modern corporations depends on the ability of business to generate and process information. Not everyone agrees, however. As Nobel laureate Robert Solow has said, "We see computers everywhere but in the productivity statistics."[23] Harvard economist Gary Loveman stunned computer industry executives at the 1991 Stewart Alsop computer conference with a similar conclusion about this "productivity paradox":

> *I'm here to tell you that after several years, my results have been poor and the results of many of my colleagues who have tried similar things also remains poor. Poor in the sense that we simply can't find evidence that there*

has been a substantial productivity increase—and in some cases any produc-tivity increase—from the substantial growth in information technology.[24]

With tens of billions of dollars spent—enough to put an average of $10,000 worth of computer equipment on the desk of each U.S. white-collar worker—how can Loveman be correct? One answer comes from Michael Borrus, of BRIE: "It simply isn't good enough to spend money on new technology and then use it in old ways. I suspect that for every company using computers right, there is one us-ing it wrong—and the two negate each other."[25]

This suggests that perhaps the real impact of computers is still ahead of us, to be found in the virtual corporation. Historical support for this comes from the research of Paul David of the Center for Economic Policy Research at Stanford. David studied an analogous technological breakthrough of the last century—that of the arrival of electricity—and found a similar lag between technology and a jump in productivity: "In 1900 contemporaries might well have said that the elec-tric dynamos were to be seen 'everywhere but in the economic statistics.'"[26]

What David concluded was that the social, organizational, and industrial changes required to pass from one technological regime to the next are so com-plex and profound as to require a half-century to complete. Thus, just as the early steam engines in England were used to pour water into old water wheels rather than to drive the factory shafts themselves,

> *the same phenomenon has been remarked upon recently in the case of the computer's application in numerous data processing and recording func-tions, where old paper-based procedures are being retained alongside the new, microelectronics-based methods—sometimes to the detriment of each system's performance.*[27]

The computer era is now approaching its own half-century mark. We would suggest that just as the dynamo finally moved from being a mere replacement source of power to a central role in daily life, defining its era, so too, with the ad-vent of the virtual corporation, will information processing soon take its proper place as the heart of the new industrial paradigm.

LEVELS OF UNDERSTANDING

In a discussion about the power of information, it is important to ask about what kind of information we are talking of. Accuracy aside, all information is not equal. In fact, the information that is of use to a corporation falls into four dis-tinct categories: content, form, behavior, and action. Until recently, only the most elementary category has been available to industry in any systematic and manage-able way. Obtaining or generating the other three has become economically feasi-ble only in recent years. Learning how to acquire and work with these other information forms not only will be important but will be the basis of the virtual corporation.

Content Information

Content information formed the basis for the modern corporation, as described by Chandler.[28] It is information about quantity, location, and types of items. For example, a simple inventory system includes information about the number of parts of a particular type and where they are located. Other related files may describe the specifications of these parts. Databases on personnel can contain addresses, employment and salary histories, and even personal data on employees. And customer files will contain data on such items as credit history, past activity, and current orders.

Content information is historical in nature. It records what an employee has done; when an individual was born; where inventory has been stored; what a customer has ordered. Content information is what typically used to reside in a file cabinet and then was transferred to punched cards and now fills the memory of a personal computer, for instance, in a personnel department or on a loading dock.

Until the 1980s, the computer industry was built on the ability to process content information for business. IBM's dominance of the commercial computer business was a direct result of its doing a better job of processing and integrating content information for business than any of its competitors.

Form Information

Form information describes the shape and composition of an object. In comparison with content information, this type of information can be quite voluminous. For example, the content information about a Ford Taurus might describe its color, the type of options installed in the car, the price, and where the vehicle is located in the distribution system. The form information on the same car would describe the shape of every component in the system. It would contain data on the precise shape of a piston, fender, and engine block. Millions of bytes of data are required to store the form data for the same automobile that would be described by a few hundred bytes of content data.

Another illustration of the differences between content and form information can be found in the data associated with a typical American home. The content information on such a house—lot size, square footage, tax burden, mortgage payable—constitutes a few hundred bytes on a tax roll or in the computer at a title office. But to describe the form of that house on a computer system using, say, Autodesk software, would require millions of bytes of storage and millions of computer operations.

Billions of computer operations are often needed to generate the huge data bases that describe form. Twenty years ago this data might have taken weeks, even months, to generate. As computers have become faster it has become possible to generate comparable form data in a matter of hours, even minutes. That compression of time, and its commensurate reduction in processing cost, has made the use of form information feasible for a growing number of businesses.

Content information is a record of the past, and form information describes shape—neither offer much of a glimpse into the future. Yet successful forecasting is a hallmark of business competitiveness, requiring the ability to simulate, often in real time, how a system is going to perform. Such forecasting enables us to understand each system's potential behavior.

Behavior Information

Behavior information often begins with form information and usually requires massive amounts of computer power. To predict the behavior of a physical object a computer must be able to simulate its motion in three-dimensional space through numerous discrete steps in time.

For instance, to simulate the performance of a microprocessor circuit containing one million devices and operating at 100 megahertz (100 million cycles per second) for a single second means the computer must determine the states of one million devices for every one hundred millionths of a second of simulated time. The computers and information processing techniques required to perform these kinds of computations are only now coming within reach. Powerful workstations supplied by companies such as Sun and Silicon Graphics make it possible for engineers to do this type of analysis at their desks.

Computer simulations have also proved to be an extremely effective tool for molecular design. The simulation of a complex organic molecule on a Molecular Simulations system may require anywhere from eighteen billion to two trillion computer operations.[29] In an example closer to the lives of most readers, Boeing uses sophisticated simulation information to study the behavior of aircraft wing designs under stress.

The usefulness of behavior information as an alternative to expensive, destructive, or even dangerous real-life testing has even been recognized in more mainstream industries. "We're at a turning point because of the drastically reduced prices of these [new computers]," George Dodd, head of computer science at the research labs of General Motors, told the *Wall Street Journal*. According to Dodd, engineers will soon be doing tasks that they once only dreamed of, such as crash-testing cars on desktop computers, instead of smashing into concrete walls, and, possibly, designing car parts entirely by computer.

With accurate simulations it is often possible to build a flawless or fail-safe device the first time. Of course this is only practical if the cost of simulating the result and the time to perform the simulations are much less than the cost of building the prototype. The extensive use of behavior information in the last few years has become possible as computer processing power has strengthened and memory storage prices have fallen.

The paradigm of this for our time is Boeing's design of its new 777 airliner, the largest project ever undertaken by computer alone. Costing an estimated $5 billion, it requires seven thousand specialists in two hundred "design-build teams" linked together by seven mainframe computers and twenty-eight hundred workstations. The plane will even be electronically preassembled long before it reaches the manufacturing floor. Despite this mammoth production, Boeing believes computer design will cut the total project cost by 20 percent.[30]

With behavior information, many design disasters of the past might have been averted, reduced to mere laboratory curiosities. Using such information, a potential and unforeseen future tragedy can be replaced with a successful and predictable conclusion.[31]

Further opportunities to use behavior information are waiting in the wings—the so-called grand challenges. These include predicting weather, analyzing atomic structure to create new materials, understanding how drugs affect the body, locating and extracting oil, and understanding the interplay of substances in combustion systems. According to Kathleen Bernard of Cray Research, "Problems such as these can require a trillion [operations] per second and billions of words of memory"—power only a thousand times greater than is available today.[32]

Action Information

The final triumph of the information revolution will be the use of a fourth type of information—information that instantly converts to sophisticated action. As computing power grows inexorably cheaper, compact, and more powerful, it is possible to build machines that not only gather and process information but act upon the results.

Of course simple feedback machines capable of basic action have been around for years. The standard home thermostat is a good example: it senses temperature and then turns the heat on or off to maintain the house at a constant temperature. Today's action information machines are vastly more sophisticated. As industrial robots, they can accept information and use it to shape mechanical parts, inspect and pick and place parts, or, in a scenario right out of science fiction, build the next generation of industrial robots.[33] In other incarnations, they can evaluate requests for money at an ATM, laser cut a metal shape to order, understand and execute human voice instructions, or build dishwashers at General Electric's celebrated $300 million Louisville plant.[34]

These are but early applications of action-based information. Just as form information and behavior information need both cheap storage and inexpensive processing power, managing action information requires all that came before it, plus inexpensive interfaces to the natural world. This means analog-to-digital converter chips, man-machine interfaces, inexpensive sensors, and sophisticated machine vision systems.

Most of these technologies are already in development. For example, Synaptics is experimenting with techniques to provide machines with humanlike vision—a process that will require not only massive amounts of computing power but organization of that power into brain-like neural networks.

These advances suggest that our lives will increasingly be dominated by machines that perform tasks for us. In many cases this will be a less personal world; the first clues can be experienced now whenever we deal with an ATM rather than a human teller, or when our phone calls are answered by a voice mail machine. Not all of the changes will be so obvious, of course: when we step on the antilock brakes in our car, it is a computer that tells the system how rapidly to apply and release the pressure.

Work environments will also change. More and more factories will operate with "lights out," devoid of humanity except for the occasional passing guard or visiting repair person. One likely effect of this will be a kind of corporate future shock. For hundreds of years, businesses operated primarily using only one type of information. Each generation found new and more effective ways of gathering, processing, and using this information. Now, in just a single generation, three new kinds of business information will be available. Learning to use these new forms will require cognitive changes in both management and the work force.

As resistant to this change as they might be, many companies will find no alternative but to use form, behavior, and action information—if only for the decisive edge they might also give a competitor. With form information, that competitor might be able to eschew the cost and time of prototyping; with behavior information it might better predict the future; and with action information it would be able to run automated factories and provide customers with adaptable products. That is simply too much of an advantage in a competitor for even the largest firm to withstand for long.

While any precise vision of the future may be clouded, it is obvious that the virtual corporation will increasingly rely on devices that harness, integrate, and effectively use these new types of information. Information will be the core of the virtual corporation. A company's ability to operate and create products and services will be dependent on its information-gathering, -processing, and -integration skills. Content information will continue to determine the state of the business. Form information will make it possible to define the products to be produced. Behavior information will test those models in use. And action information will pull it all together into the actual manufacture, testing, and distribution of the finished goods and services. A virtual corporation will be defined by its ability to master these new information tools.

REFERENCES

1. Womack, Jones, and Roos, *Machine that Changed the World* (Old Tappan, NJ: MacMillan Publishing Company, Inc., 1990), pp. 67, 182.
2. Ibid.
3. Taichi Ohno, *Toyota Production System* (Cambridge, Mass.: Productivity Press, 1988).

4. Maryann Keller, *Rude Awakening* (New York: Harper Perennial, 1989), p. 127.
5. Womack, Jones, and Roos, *Machine that Changed the World* (Old Tappan, NJ: MacMillan Publishing Company, Inc., 1990), p. 173.
6. Ibid.
7. Joseph D. Blackburn, "The Quick Response Movement in the Apparel Industry: A Case Study in Time Compressing Supply Chains," Chapter 11 in *Time-Based Competition* (Homewood, Ill.: Business One/Irwin, 1991), p. 36.
8. "Best Practice Companies," *FW,* 17 September 1991, p. 36.
9. Ibid.
10. Blackburn, "The Quick Response Movement," pp. 254–255.
11. Ibid.
12. Ibid., p. 258.
13. Chandler, *The Visible Hand,* p. 280.
14. Ibid., p. 94.
15. "GM Will Run Big Car Group Like Japanese," *Wall Street Journal,* 10 June 1991, p. A3.
16. Rosabeth Moss Kanter, "Attack on Pay," *Harvard Business Review,*" Mar–Apr. 1987, p. 60.
17. Brian Dumaine, "The Bureaucracy Busters," *Fortune,* 17 June 1991, p. 46.
18. John S. McLenahen, "Factory Automation," *Industry Week,* 20 June 1998, p. 44.
19. Gary H. Anthos, "U.S. Sees Industry Growth in '92," *Computerworld,* 6 January 1992, p. 88.
20. Standard & Poor's, *Industry Surveys,* 17 October 1991, p. C96.
21. Womack, Jones, and Roos, *Machine that Changed the World* (Old Tappan, NJ: MacMillan Publishing Company, Inc., 1990), p. 13.
22. Ohno, *Toyota Production System,* from the Publisher Foreword by Norman Bodek, p. ix.
23. Quoted by Gary Loveman, "Why Personal Computers Have Not Improved Productivity," minutes of Stewart Alsop 1991 Computer Conference, p. 39.
24. Ibid.
25. Author interview with Michael Borris.
26. Paul A. David, "Computer and Dynamo: The Modern Productivity Paradox in a Not-Too-Distant Mirror," CEPR pub. no. 172, July 1989, from abstract.
27. Ibid., pp. 16, 20.
28. Chandler, *The Visible Hand,* section 2.
29. Per Barry D. Olafson, Molecular Simulations.
30. George Tibbits, "Change Is in the Air as Boeing Builds New 777," *San Francisco Examiner,* 6 October 1991, p. E3; and "Picture Perfect," photo essay, *Business Week/Quality 1991,* p. 96.
31. See the Tacoma Narrows Bridge Story.
32. Kathleen Bernard, "Ordering Chaos," in *Technology 2001* (Cambridge, Mass.: MIT Press, 1991), p. 82.
33. This appears to be what is going on at the very secretive Japanese robotics firm Fanuc.
34. Thomas M. Rohan, "Factories of the Future," special section, *Industry Week,* 21 March 1998, p. 44.

4

The Importance of Information Services for Productivity "Under-recognized" and Under-invested

Michael Koenig

The relationship between the provision of information services and the productivity of the organization is a topic of great importance. The reason organizations build and maintain information services is to enhance the effectiveness and productivity of people and units supported by those services. That relationship is a topic that has been relatively little researched, largely because of the difficulty of assessing the productivity of the information-intensive people, processes, and units supported by information services, much less the interrelationship itself. What research has been done, however, is remarkably uniform and consistent in pointing to the conclusion that information services are cost-effective investments, and that information-dependent organizations consistently under-invest in information services. This article analyzes and reports on the literature driving that conclusion, and is meant to enhance the ability of librarians and information officers in promoting their operations.

BACKGROUND

There is a significant amount of work addressing the relationship of library and information services to the productivity of the organizations they support.

Reprinted from *Special Libraries* 83, no. 4 (1992), pp.192–210 by Special Libraries Association. Web address (www.sla.org). Michael Koenig is the dean of the Graduate School of Library and Information Science, Rosary College in River Forest, IL.

The impact of that work has been very modest, however. One reason for the lack of impact is that the work is very scattered, and has appeared, as a glance at the list of referenced to this article will indicate, in relatively obscure places. Much of the work has appeared in technical reports little noticed by the business and professional community, and a good chunk of it—some of the best—has appeared in proprietary consulting reports which are not in the public domain at all. The most thorough review of this literature is a recent chapter in *Annual Review of Information Science and Technology* by Koenig,[1] a previous chapter in 1982 by Griffiths[2] on the "Value of Information and Related Systems, Products, and Services," though now slightly dated, is also very relevant.

There are also three other reviews of interest. Two, by Bearman et al.,[3,4] and by Cronin and Gudim, discuss the importance of the problem, but do not discuss specific results; one by Bawden[5] looks specifically at the topic of information systems and creativity, and pulls together a very disparate literature.

STUDIES ATTEMPTING TO CALCULATE THE VALUE OF INFORMATION SERVICES

One way of looking at the relationship of information services and productivity is to attempt to derive a value for the information services.

What is perhaps the seminal work on attempting to value and evaluate the effect of providing information services was conducted by Margaret Graham and her colleagues at the Exxon Research Center in the mid-1970s. Not atypical for work in this field, it appeared first in an internal technical report, but was fortunately picked up by the Eugene Jackson for his *Special Librarianship, A New Reader*.[6] However, the fact that it never appeared in the sort of venue, the journal literature, where one would expect to see important new findings, was a major missed opportunity.

The findings were new and dramatic. The study built on previous research in user studies but was novel in its attempt to extrapolate and quantify the effect the services provided. The study participants (Exxon researchers) logged information-impacted events on 20 randomly selected days. The participants reported that 62% of those events were beneficial, and in 2% of the cases they were able to estimate the value of the benefit quantitatively. By extrapolating from only that 2%, and assigning no value to the remaining 60% of the impacts that were beneficial but not quantifiable, and subtracting the cost of the researcher's time spent in gathering information from the benefits, the authors concluded that the observable benefits were 11 times greater than the cost of providing external literature information services to the Exxon research community. One can conclude this is a lower bound for the benefits, based as it is on only a small percentage of the beneficial outcomes.

A much larger study, using similar techniques, was conducted in the late 1970s on NASA's information services.[7] This study was conducted on a much broader scale than the one at Exxon. A stratified sampling procedure was used to elucidate data about the use and impact of seven different NASA information products and services. Respondents were asked three basic questions: 1) what was the nature of the consequent utility (termed "application mode") of the use of the information source? (Responses to answer 1 were classified as: 0—not relevant or no application; 1—information use only; 2—improved products or processes; 3—new products or processes.); 2) (if the response was application mode 2 or 3) what were the estimated benefits likely to be achieved or costs to be saved?; and 3) what was the probability of accomplishing those benefits or cost savings? For each of the seven services the study reports the probability for "application modes" 2 and 3, the unit cost (to NASA) for the information transaction, the cost to the user, and the expected net benefit (likely benefit X probability) per transaction.

Unfortunately, the study did not aggregate the data and failed to draw the salient conclusions that could and should have been drawn. Working from the published data, the aggregate data can be extrapolated as follows: The cost to NASA of providing the information service over the five-year period 1971-1976 was $14.3 million ($2.9 million per year) and the expected benefit was $191 million ($28 million per year). The ratio between expected benefits and NASA costs is 13:1. The author, Mogavero,[7] recommends that the user cost be subtracted from the expected benefit in calculating a cost-benefit ratio (the same technique as used in the Exxon study). Thus,

$$\text{Cost–benefit ratio} = \frac{\text{Gross Estimated Benefit} - \text{Gross User Cost}}{\text{NASA Production Cost}}$$

Calculated this way, the cost benefit ratio is 7.6 to 1.

While not quite so dramatic as the Exxon results, this result is still compelling. Note that the methodology, which asks for both the anticipated benefit and the likelihood of achieving that benefit (in effect a deflator index), is a cautious and conservative tone.

One can argue that the formula used is not the appropriate one, that from the organization's perspective, the salient ratio is that between benefit and cost (benefit foregone). (See the article by Bickner[8] for further discussion of this point.) That is, from the organization's perspective, the formula should be:

$$\text{Cost–Benefit Ratio} = \frac{\text{Gross Estimated Benefit}}{\text{NASA Production Cost} + \text{Gross User Cost}}$$

which yields:

$$\frac{\$191 \text{ million}}{\$14.3 \text{ million} + \$82 \text{ million}} \text{ or } 1.98$$

as the ratio (effectively two to one) of benefit to cost. Note the very dramatic internal ratio of user expended cost of accessing information to the cost of providing information services, a ratio of almost 6 to 1. This implies that there is substantial opportunity for systems or service enhancements that diminish user costs and thereby enhance the cost-benefit ratio. It also points out that the nominal cost of providing information services is only the tip of the iceberg. In this case, for every dollar expended in providing information services, another six dollars are spent by the user in using those services.

Using a related methodology Mason & Sassone,[9] also in the late 1970s, analyzed the operations of an information analysis center (IAC). In this technique the investigators, working with the users, tried to estimate only the employee's time saved and then assigned value by calculating the burdened salary cost of the employee's time. This technique was applied to an unidentified IAC, and the net present value of the time saved exceeded the net present value of the invested resources and operating cost by 4%.

The costing techniques are more rigorous and sophisticated than most because the present value if invested resources is included as well as operating costs. Mason and Sassone call this technique a "lower bound cost benefit" because the calculations are based solely on the user's time and costs, and no attempt is made to estimate either any larger benefits to the organization or any societal benefits. If the transaction saved $500 of the researcher's time compared with getting the information in some other fashion, but also results in $50,000 worth of benefits or savings, then the utility of the transaction is calculated as merely $500, not $50,000. Even with such stringent limitations, looking only at the cost of alternative processes for gathering information, not at the benefit provided by the information, the center shows a positive net present value.

Valuation methodologies of this general type have been most fully developed and most widely applied by King Research, Inc.[10-18] Some of the studies involve government agencies and the reports are to some degree in the public domain and thus accessible though generally obscure; the bulk have been done for private corporations, are proprietary, and are accessible if at all only via personal contacts. Thus, their work, though very important, is generally little known, particularly to the general business community outside of professional information circles.

First, the methodology[10,12,18] analyzes the value of the information services to the organization in terms of the value of the time (as measured by salary and overhead) that the users are willing to expend on those services. This is taken as an indication of the organization's willingness to pay for the services. With this methodology the cost to the user, as indicated by time the user spends in accessing information, is treated as an indicator of implicit value rather than as a debit to savings to value achieved as in the three studies above. To be sure, such a measure is an indicator of the motivation to seek information, but as King points out,[17] it seems to be fairly constant across organizations and therefore not likely to be very sensitive to the quality of service provided. In five different organizations studied, the ratios are reported in Table 4-1.

The spread of ratios is very wide, an order of magnitude in fact, but in all cases the value of the service as measured by the time users were willing to spend using it was very substantial. If, as King points out, the time information workers spend seeking information is relatively constant across different organizations, then the numbers [in Table 4-1] may also serve as an indicator of the intensity of

TABLE 4-1 Ratios of Willingness to Pay (measured in terms of user professionals' time) to Nominal Cost of Providing Information Services

Institution	Ratio
Major Diversified Chemicals Company A[19]	2.5 to 1
Major Diversified Chemicals Company B[10]	4.3 to 1
Major Electronics and Communications Company[20]	4.4 to 1
Major Public Utility[11]	19 to 1
U.S. Department of Energy[16]	26 to 1

the information services provided, the lower the ratio the more intense the information services provided. Note that Poppel[21] in his study of managers in business organizations reports a very similar (21% as opposed to 25%) proportion of time spent in information seeking.

Second, value is attached to the information services by calculating the additional cost that would be incurred if there were no in-house information service and the documents had to be obtained elsewhere. The values calculated for this approach are shown in Table 4-2.

TABLE 4-2 Ratio of Cost to Use Alternative Services to the Nominal Cost of Providing Information Services

Institution	Ratio
Major Diversified Chemicals Company A[19]	2.6 to 1
Major Diversifies Chemicals Company B[10]	2.7 to 1
Major Electronics and Communications Company[20]	3.6 to 1
Major Public Utility[11]	8 to 1

Again all the ratios are highly favorable.

Thirdly, based on the observations that professionals tend to spend a relatively fixed proportion of their time seeking information and reading (a homeostatic function?), the methodology calculates the number of readings that would have to be foregone by the requirement to spend more time seeking information if no in-house information service were available. From this figure one can derive a value of the savings (or research cost avoidance) that would be lost or incurred if the library or information center did not exist. Knowledge workers surveyed at each institution estimate the savings (or benefit) achieved by reading. However, these estimates are applied only to the transactions foregone, not to all transactions.

The intermediary results from a number of studies are summarized by Griffiths & King[10] in Table 4-3.

TABLE 4-3 Proportion of Readings of Which Various Levels of Savings (Benefit) Are Reported to Be Achieved

Savings ($)	Proportion
0	73.9
1–11	12.5
11–100	3.9
101–1,000	4.2
1,001–10,000	3.4
>10,000	2.1

Calculated over the various studies, Griffiths & King[11] report the data for the value of reading an item in Table 4-4.

TABLE 4-4

$385	for reading a journal article
$1,160	for reading a book
$706	for reading an internal technical document

The value calculated at specific institutions for this approach are reported in Table 4-5.

King Research also examined the value of the Energy Data Base (EDB) of the U.S. Department of Energy (DOE).[14,16] The apparent value—the burdened salary cost of the time spent using the database—was approximately $500 million, out of a total research budget of $5.8 billion (including principal users of the database such as contractors, not just DOE). Estimated total savings attributed to those readings were approximately $13 billion. Thus, Table 4-6 can be interpreted as an investment of $5.8 billion, yielding a return on investment of approximately 2.2 to 1.

TABLE 4-5 Ratios of Research Cost Avoidance to the Nominal Cost of Providing Information Services

Institution	Ratio
Major Diversified Chemicals Company A[11]	4.8 to 1
Major Diversified Chemicals Company B[20]	14 to 1
Major Electronics and Communications Company[10]	16 to 1
Major Public Utility[11]	17 to 1
US Department of Energy[16]	25 to 1

TABLE 4-6

Generation of Information	+	Information Processing and Use	=	Future Savings to DOE Scientists
$5.3 billion	+	$500 million	=	$13 billion

Using the research-cost avoidance approach discussed above, assuming that there were to be no energy databases, there would be a loss of over 300,000 searches and almost 2.5 million readings (a value equivalent to $3 billion). If the current R&D budget is $5.8 billion, then without the EDB, an R&D budget of $8.8 billion would theoretically be required to maintain the same level of output. That is equivalent to saying that the EDB increases organizational productivity by 52%.

Griffiths & King estimate that, if one extrapolated these techniques broadly, the readings by all scientists and engineers in the United States resulted in savings of about $300 billion for the year 1984 alone.[13] They admit this figure sounds enormous, but ask what would scientists and engineers accomplish without access to information? They calculate that the actual time value that scientists and engineers spend in reading exceeds $20 billion per year, based on an average burdened salary, which is in effect a ratio of 15 to 1 for benefit to cost invested in reading.

The calculation of cost-benefit figures is a complex and disputatious exercise, of rather more subtlety than is often realized. The article by Bickner on "Concepts of Economic Cost"[8] is an excellent analysis of the issues and of some of the fallacies to avoid. The calculation of cost-benefit figures where a principal commodity is information, a commodity particularly ill-addressed by conventional economies, is even more fraught with peril.

The caveat above not withstanding, the magnitude of the effects reported in these studies is quite striking, as is the very high degree of their consistency, both across different techniques and across different cases. This creates a high degree of confidence that the findings are not mere artifacts, but that they reflect a genuine phenomenon.

ECONOMETRIC CALCULATIONS

A few attempts have been made to calculate the overall effect of information as a factor in industrial productivity. Perhaps the first of these was the use by Hayes & Erickson[22] of the Cobb-Douglas production function to estimate the value added by information services. In the basic Cobb-Douglas formula, the value of goals and services sold is calculated to be the product of a constant times the values of different inputs, labor, capitol, etc., each raised to a different power (exponent). The exponents are solved for by seeing which exponents best fit a number of separate cases. In the Hayes and Erickson formulation, the value added

(V) in manufacturing industries is a function of labor (L), capital (K), purchase of information services (l), and purchase of other intermediate goods and services (X), and takes the form:

$$V + AL^a K^b I^c X^d, \text{ or}$$
$$\text{Log } V = \text{Log } A + a \log L + b \log K + c \log l + d \log X$$

(where A, a, b, c, d are constants). Braunstein[23] developed this approach further, arguing that the standard Cobb-Douglas production function is too specific, that it inappropriately requires that the substitutability between each pair of factors be constant and equal to 1. Braunstein substitutes the "constant elasticity of substitution" (CES) and the "translog" production functions, both of which permits elasticities other than 1. The marginal product of information estimated by the Cobb-Douglas function was 2.54, with Hayes and Erickson's 1972 data, and a 2.50 as calculated by Braunstein with 1980 data. The CES function yielded a marginal product of information between 2.43 and 2.92, and the translog function yielded values between 2.34 to 3.67. There is striking consistency in these results, Braunstein argues, and they indicate substantial underinvestment in the purchase of information.

Also striking is the similarity of these numbers to the 2.2 to 1 value for the return on information investment calculated by King Research, Inc., in their analysis of the value of the Energy Data Base,[16] and the 1.98 to 1 reported by Mogavero in his analysis of NASA's information services,[7] values which were derived in an entirely independent fashion.

CHARACTERISTICS OF THE INFORMATION ENVIRONMENT IN PRODUCTIVE ORGANIZATIONS

While they do not directly address the question of value and degree of underinvestment, there have been a number of studies of characteristics of productive companies. These studies shed a great deal of light on the relationship between information services and organizational productivity; a very consistent thread is the importance of information access and information services.

Orpen[24] examined productivity in R&D intensive electronics/instrumentation organizations and analyzed the behavior of research managers as perceived by the research staff. He found that in the more productive organizations (as defined by rates of growth and return on assets) the managers were perceived to be significantly more characterized by the following three behaviors: 1) they routed literature and references to scientific and technical staff; 2) they directed their staff to use scientific and technical information (STI) and to purchase STI services; and 3) they encouraged publication of results and supported professional visits and continuing education.

Equally striking was the finding that managerial behavior not directly concerned with information, such as planning future work changes, initiating personnel changes, hiring exemplars, or altering hiring and promotion policies, did not differentiate between the "high-performance" and the "low performance" companies. In short, information-related behavior strongly tended to discriminate between "high-performance" and "low performance" companies, while non-information-related behavior did not—a distinction that, interestingly enough, Orpen did not make.

In reviewing the corpus of work on R&D innovation, Goldhar, et al.[25] conclude that there are six characteristics of environments that are conducive to technological innovations. Of the six, four are clearly related to the information environment—specifically: 1) easy access to information by individuals; 2) free flow of information both into and out of the organizations; 3) rewards for sharing, seeking, and using "new" externally developed information sources; and 4) encouragement of mobility and interpersonal contacts. The other two characteristics are rewards for taking risks and for accepting and adapting to change. These findings and their implicit prioritization (in Goldhar's ordering, 1, 2, 3, & 6, that is the top three of Goldhar's six factors are all information related factors) are striking in that except for the work of Allen,[26-28] who found that more productive teams and individuals had more diverse information contacts outside the project team, none of the work reviewed by Goldhar comes from the traditional areas of information science, or communications; it comes almost entirely from the literature of economics and management. And like Orpen, Goldhar fails to make much of the predominance of information related factors.

A consistent macrotheme in this literature is that of the link between productivity and diversity of information contacts. Koenig[33-37] has studied the relationship between research productivity and the information environment, using the pharmaceutical industry as the setting. A gross measure of productivity can be calculated simply as the number of approved new drugs per research dollar expended. That output measure is refined further by weighting it in regards to: 1) whether the FDA regards the drug as an important therapeutic advance, 2) the drug's chemical novelty, and 3) the filing company's patent position with regard to the drug, and indication of where the bulk of the research was done. Research productivity, thus measured, differs greatly among large pharmaceutical companies.[35] In comparing the information environment of the more-productive companies with the less-productive, the former are characterized by:[37]

- Greater openness to outside information;
- Somewhat less concern with protecting proprietary information;
- Greater information systems development effort;
- Greater end-user use of information systems and more encouragement of browsing and serendipity;
- Greater technical and subject sophistication of the information services staff; and
- Relative unobtrusiveness of managerial structure and status indicators in the R&D environment.

To the degree that data were available, there did not seem to be any significant distinction between the more versus the less productive companies in terms of the extent of resources expended on information services (as measured by the number of information center staff).

These findings (above) are a part of a larger body of literature that finds contact with external information sources and diversity of information sources are key factors in successful innovation. Project Sappho (Scientific Activity Predictor from Patterns with Heuristic Origins) conducted by the University of Sussex[38] deliberately studied failures as well as successes. Twenty-nine "pairs" (one successful and one failure) of innovation attempts in a similar industry segment were analyzed to determine what led to success. One of the five major conclusions was that "successful innovators make more effective use of outside technology and scientific advice, even though they perform more of the work in-house. They have better contacts with the scientific community, not necessarily in general, but in the specific areas concerned."

After reviewing a number of studies on innovation, principally from the management literature, Utterback[39,40] concluded, "In general, it appears that the greater the degree of communications between the firm and its environment at each stage of the process of innovation, other factors being equal, the more effective the firm will be in generating, developing, and implementing new technology,"[40] Wolek & Griffith[41] reviewed the sociologically-oriented literature on this topic and came to substantially the same conclusion. McConnell, writing on how to improve productivity from an operational standpoint, and reviewing the literature in a less formal fashion, remarks: "Information flow, through both formal and informal networks, should be full and free—up, down, and across the organization. This required continuous effort and attention. . . . The more open and free communication is in the organization, the greater will be the productivity."[42]

Kanter[43,44] conducted an extension survey of innovations initiated by middle managers. From her findings, she made six major recommendations for structuring organizations to support creativity. The second recommendation was "a free and somewhat random flow of information."[44] She further reports that to accomplish productive changes, a manager needs "information, resources, and support,"[44] in that order.

When examining the literature about what characterizes productive organizations it is clear that not only does a consistent theme emerge of greater openness toward and greater access to information, both internal and external, but that information access related factors emerge in positions of very high priority in comparison to other factors under management control. Also striking, and very corroboratory in its implications is the fact that these findings are consistent whether the investigator or the literature received is from the areas of library and information science, management science and economics, or sociology.

CHARACTERISTICS OF PRODUCTIVE INFORMATION WORKERS

There is also a large body of literature on the characteristics of productive information workers, and the findings are quite consistent with and complementary to those above. King Research,[10] in evaluating information use at Oak Ridge National Laboratories has documented a significant and positive relationship between the productivity of professionals and the amount of time spent in reading. Several indicators were used to measure productivity: number of formal records (i.e., of research, of project management), number of formal publications, number of proposals or research plans, number of formal oral presentations, and number of times the professionals were consulted for advice. All of these indicators were found to be positively correlated with the amount of reading done.

Mondschein[45] studied the productivity of researchers in several major corporations, as measured by publishing activity, vis-à-vis their use of automated current awareness services (SDI or selective dissemination of information). He found that scientists who use SDI frequently appear to be more productive than their colleagues who either do not use such services or use them only infrequently. Further, the productive researchers were characterized by their use of a wider variety of information sources, particularly by the extent of their efforts to stay current and by their use of patent information sources.

Ginman,[46] in studying the information use of CEOs, observes a very different information style for CEOs in companies in the revival phase as compared with those in the stagnation phase. The former are more extroverted in their information use style, and have an information culture that is characterized by greater width and depth, with greater use of external information sources and greater ability to pinpoint and recall specific items of information input, such as specific authors, articles, etc.

Chakrabarti & Rubenstein,[47] in studying NASA innovations adopted by industry, conclude that quality of information as perceived by the recipient is a major factor in the adoption of innovations. That is, of course, an extension to the high-tech environment of the classic work by Rogers[48] on innovation and change agency (use of agents who deliberately introduce beneficial change), most of which was done in relatively low-tech situations, and is consistent with Rogers findings.

Johnston & Gibbons[49] examined the characteristics of information that contributed to the resolution of technical problems with some 30 ongoing innovations in British industry. They found that 1) information obtained from the literature contributed as much as information obtained from personal contact; 2) different sources were selectively used to acquire different types of information; and 3) a wide range of information sources is important.

The studies reported above are typical of the larger body of research finding. The consistent theme is that more productive individuals make greater access to and greater use of information services.

CONCLUSION

There is an extensive literature that indicates very strongly that access to information is a very critical component of the productivity of information workers and consequently the productivity of the information dependent organization employing those persons. This phenomenon is generally recognized, but its comparative importance is still "under-recognized," even ill-recognized in the very literature that reports the findings (see particularly the discussion above of the work by Orpen[24] and Goldhar[25]). More importantly, there is an emerging body of research findings, emerging in very scattered locations, but perhaps now approaching some critical mass in size that quite consistently indicates that information-dependent organizations under-invest in information services and that to maximize their productivity, those organizations should substantially increase their investment in information services.

The agenda before the information profession is obvious:

We need more research on the relationship between the information environment and organizational productivity.

We need to integrate and disseminate the increasing body of knowledge we do have on the subject.

The importance of organizational productivity and productivity enhancement is well understood and almost totally accepted; the importance of the information environment and of information services to productivity is only beginning to be understood and is very much "under-recognized." Recent work by Matarazzo[50] documents the general lack of awareness of managers about the real contributions made by libraries and information centers. We need to change that state of affairs.

REFERENCES

1. Koenig, Michael, E.D. "Information Services and Downstream Productivity," in Williams, Martha E., ed. *Annual Review of Information Science and Technology: Volume 25.* New York: Elsevier Science Publishers for the American Society for Information Science, 1990. 55–86.

2. Griffiths, José-Marie. "The Value of Information and Related Systems, Products and Services," in Williams, Martha E., ed. *Annual Review of Information Science and Technology: Volume 17.* White Plains, NY: Knowledge Industry Publications, Inc. for the American Society for Information Science, 1982. 269–284.

3. Bearman, Toni Carbo, Polly Guynup, and Sandra N. Milevski. "Information and Productivity," *Journal of the American Society for Information Science* 36(6): 369–375 (November 1986).

4. Cronin, Blaise and Mairi Gudim. "Information and Productivity: A Review of Research," *International Journal of Information Management* 6(2): 85–101 (June 1986).

5. Bawden, David. "Information Systems and the Stimulation of Creativity," *Journal of Information Science* 12(5): 203–216 (1986).

6. Weil, Ben H. "Benefits from the Research Use of the Published Literature at the Exxon Research Center," in Jackson, Eugene B., ed. *Special Librarianship: A New Reader.* Metuchen, NJ: Scarecrow Press, 1980. 586–594.

7. Mogavero, Louis N. "Transferring Technology to Industry through Information," in *Information and Industry; Proceedings of the North Atlantic Treaty Organization, Advisory Group for Aerospace Research and Development (AGARD), Technical Information Panel's Specialists' Meeting;* October 18–19 1978; Paris, France. Neuilly-sur-Seine, France: AGARD. January 1979. 14:1–14:6 (AGARD CP-246).

8. Bickner, Robert E. "Concepts of Economic Cost," in King, Donald E., Nancy K. Roderer, and Harold A. Olsen, eds. *Key Papers in the Economics of Information Systems* White Plains, NY: Knowledge Industry Publications, Inc. for the American Society for Information Science, 1983. 107–146.

9. Mason, Robert M. and Peter G. Sassone. "A Lower Bound Cost Benefit Model for Information Services," *Information Processing & Management* 14(2): 71–83 (1978).

10. Griffiths, José-Marie and Donald W. King. *A Manual on the Evaluation of Information Centers and Services.* Oak Ridge. TN: King Research, 1990. 370 pp. Submitted to the North Atlantic Treaty Organization, Advisory Group for Aerospace Research and Development. Available by permission from King Research, Inc., PO Box 572, Oak Ridge, TN 37831.

11. Griffiths, José-Marie and Donald W. King. *An Information Audit of Public Service Electric and Gas Company Libraries and Information Resources; Executive Summary and Conclusions.* Rockville, MD: King Research, Inc., Spring 1988, 15 pp.

12. King, Donald W. and José-Marie Griffiths. "Evaluating the Effectiveness of Information Use," in: *Evaluating the Effectiveness of Information Centers and Services.* Material to Support a Lecture Series Presented Under the Sponsorship of the North Atlantic Treaty Organization, Advisory Group for Aerospace Research and Development (AGARD), Technical Information Panel and the Consultant and Exchange Programme; September 5–6, 8–9, 12–13 1998; Luxembourg; Athens, Greece; Lisbon, Portugal; Neuilly-sur-Seine, France; AGARD. 1998. 1:1–1:5.

13. Griffiths, José-Marie and Donald W. King. *The Contribution Libraries Make to Organizational Productivity.* Rockville, MD: King Research, Inc., 1985. 12 pp. OCLC: 16389522. Available by permission from King Research, Inc., PO Box 572, Oak Ridge, TN 37831.

14. King, Donald W., and José-Marie Griffiths, Ellen A. Sweet, and Robert R.V. Wiederkehr. *A Study of the Value of Information and the Effect on Value of Intermediary Organizations, Timeliness of Services and Products, and Comprehensiveness of the EDB.* Rockville, MD: King Research, Inc., 1984, 3 volumes in 1. (Submitted to the U.S. Department of Energy, Office of Scientific and Technical Information). NTIS: DE85003670; OCLC:11712088; DOE: NBM-1078. Available by permission from King Research, Inc., PO Box 572, Oak Ridge, TN 37831.

15. Roderer, Nancy K., Donald W. King, and Sandra E. Brouard. *The Use and Value of Defense Technical Information Center Products and Services.* Rockville, MD: King Research, Inc., June 1983. 115 pp. (Submitted to the Defense Technical Information Center). OCLC: 12987688, 11599947. Available by permission from King Research, Inc., PO Box 572, Oak Ridge, TN 37831.

16. King, Donald W., and José-Marie Griffiths, Nancy K. Roderer, and Robert R.V. Widerkehr. *Value of the Energy Data Base.* Rockville, MD; King Research, Inc., October 1982, 81p. Submitted to the U.S. Department of Energy, Technical Information Center. NTIS: DE82014250; OCLC: 9004666; DOE: OR11232-1. Available by permission from King Research, Inc., PO Box 572, Oak Ridge, TN 37831.

17. King, Donald W., Dennis O. McDonald, and Nancy K. Roderer, *Scientific Journals in the United States: Their Production, Use, and Economics*. Stroudsburg, PA: Hutchinson Ross Publishing Co., 1981. 319 pp.

18. King, Donald W. and Nancy K. Roderer. "Information Transfer Cost/Benefit Analysis," in: *Information and Industry: Proceedings of the North Atlantic Treaty Organization, Advisory Group for Aerospace Research and Development (AGARD), Technical Information Panel's Specialists' Meeting;* October 18–19, 1978; Paris, France. Neuilly-sur-Seine, France; AGARD; January 1979, 8:1–8:10 (AGARD CP-246).

19. Griffiths, José-Marie. Proprietary Report, presented at a research seminar, June 1987.

20. King, Donald W., José-Marie Griffiths, Lawrence W. Lannow, and Helen M. Kurtz. "Study of the Use and Value of Library Network Services." Proprietary Report prepared by King Research.

21. Poppel, Harvey L. "Who Needs the Office of the Future?" *Harvard Business Review* 60(6):146–155 (November/December 1982).

22. Hayes, Robert M. and T. Erickson. "Added Value as a Function of Purchases of Information Services," *Information Society* 1(4): 307–338 (1982).

23. Braunstein, Yale M. "Information as a Factor of Production: Substitutability and Productivity," *Information Society* 3(3): 261–273 (1985).

24. Orpen, Christopher. "The Effect of Managerial Distribution of Scientific and Technical Information on Company Performance," *R&D Management* 15(4): 305–308 (October 1985).

25. Goldhar, Joel D., Louis K. Bragaw, and Jules J. Schwartz. "Information Flows, Management Styles, and Technological Innovation," *IEEE Transactions on Engineering Management* EM-23(1): 51–61 (February).

26. Allen, Thomas J. *Managing the Flow of Technology: Technology Transfer and the Dissemination of Technological Information within the R&D Organization* Cambridge, MA: MIT Press, 1977. 320 pp.

27. Allen, Thomas J. "Roles in Technical Communications Networks," in Nelson, Carnot E. and Donald K. Pollack, eds. *Communication Among Scientists and Engineers.* Lexington, MA: Heath Lexington Books, 1970. 191–208.

28. Allen. Thomas J. "The Utilization of Information Sources during R&D Proposal Preparation." Cambridge, MA: MIT Press, 1964, 31p (MIT Alfred P. Sloan School of Management working paper no. 97-34).

29. Albrecht, Terrance L. and Vickie A. Ropp. "Communicating about Innovation in Networks of Three U.S. Organizations," *Journal of Communication* 34(3):78–91 (Summer 1984).

30. Pelz, Donald C. and Frank M. Andrews. "Diversity in Research" in Allison, David, ed. *The R&D Game: Technical Men, Technical Managers, and Research Productivity.* Cambridge, MA: MIT Press, 1969. 73–89

31. Pelz, Donald C. and Frank M. Andrews. *Scientists in Organizations: Productive Climates for Research and Development.* New York: Wiley, 1966. 318 pp.

32. Shilling, Charles W. and Jessie S. Bernard. *Informal Communications among Bioscientists, Part II.* Washington, DC: George Washington University, 1964. 1 volume (discontinuous paging). (Biological Science Communications Project Report no. 16A.)

33. Koenig, Michael, E.D. "The Information and Library Environment and the Productivity of Research," *Inspel* 24(4): 157–167 (1990).

34. Koenig, Michael, E.D. "Bibliometric Indicators versus Expert Opinion in Assessing Research Performance," *Journal of the American Society for Information Science* 34 (2): 136–145 (March 1983).

35. Koenig, Michael, E.D. "A Bibliometric Analysis of Pharmaceutical Research," *Research Policy* 12(1):15–36 (February 1983).

36. Koenig, Michael, E.D. "Determinants of Expert Judgement of Research Performance," *Scientometrics* 4(5): 361–378 (1982).

37. Koenig, Michael E.D. and Daniel J. Gans "The Productivity of Research Effort in the U.S. Pharmaceutical Industry." *Research Policy* 4(4): 331–349 (October 1975).

38. University of Sussex, Science Policy Research Unit. "Success and Failure in Industrial Innovation," report on Project Sappho, London, England: Center for the Study of Industrial Innovation. February 1972. 37 pp.

39. Utterback, James Milo, "Innovation in Industry and the Diffusion of Technology." *Science* 15; 183(415): 620–626 (February 1974).

40. Utterback, James Milo. "The Process of Technological Innovation within the Firm," *Academy of Management Journal* 14: 75–88 (March 1971).

41. Wolek, Francis W. and Belver C. Griffith. "Policy and Informal Communications in Applied Science and Technology," *Science Studies* 4(4): 411–420 (July 1974).

42. McConnell, J. Douglas. "Productivity Improvements in Research and Development and Engineering in the United States," *Society of Research Administrators Journal* 12(2): 5–14 (Fall 1980).

43. Kanter, Rosabeth Moss. *The Change Masters: Innovations for Productivity in the American Corporation.* New York: Simon and Schuster, 1983. 432 pp.

44. Kanter, Rosabeth Moss. "The Middle Manager as Innovator," *Harvard Business Review* 60(4): 95–105 (July/August 1982).

45. Mondschein, Lawrence G. "SDI Use and Productivity in the Corporate Research Environment," *Special Libraries* 81(4): 265–279 (Fall 1990).

46. Ginman, Mariam. "Information Culture and Business Performance," *IATUL Quarterly* 2(2): 93–106 (1988).

47. Chakrabarti, Alok K. and Albert H. Rubenstein. "Interorganization Transfer of Technology: A Study of Adoption of NASA Innovations," *IEEE Transactions on Engineering Management* EM-23(1): 20–34 (February 1976).

48. Rogers, Everett M. *Diffusion of Innovations.* 3rd edition. New York: Free Press, 1983. 453 pp.

49. Johnston, Ron and Michael Gibbons, "Characteristics of Information Usage in Technical Innovation," *IEEE Transactions on Engineering Management* EM-22(1): 27–34 (February 1975).

50. Matarazzo, James M., Laurence Prusak, and Michael R. Gauthier. *Valuing Corporate Libraries: A Survey of Senior Managers.* Washington, DC: Special Libraries Association in cooperation with Temple, Barker & Sloane, Inc., 1990, 11 pp.

5

How Information Gives You Competitive Advantage: The Information Revolution Is Transforming the Nature of Competition

Michael E. Porter and Victor E. Millar

It is hard to underestimate the strategic significance of the new information technology. This technology is transforming the nature of products, processes, companies, industries, and even competition itself. Until recently, most managers treated information technology as a support service and delegated it to EDP departments. Now, however, every company must understand the broad effects and implications of the new technology and how it can create substantial and sustainable competitive advantages.

The authors of this article provide a useful framework for analyzing the strategic significance of the new information technology. They show how and why the technology is changing the way companies operate internally as well as altering the relationships among companies and their suppliers, cus-

Reprinted by permission of Harvard Business Review, from "How Information Gives You Competitive Advantage" by Michael E. Porter and Victor E. Millar, 4, 1985 Copyright © 1985 by President and Fellows of Harvard College; all rights reserved.

Authors' note: We wish to thank Monitor Company and Arthur Andersen for their assistance in preparing this article. F. Warren McFarlan also provided valuable comments Editor's note: All notes appear at the end of the article.

Mr. Porter is professor of business administration at the Harvard Business School. He is the author of the best-seller *Competitive Advantage* (Free Press, 1985) and *Competitive Strategy* (Free Press, 1980), and he recently served on the Presidential Commission on Industrial Competitiveness.

Mr. Millar is the managing partner for practice of Arthur Andersen & Co. and is responsible for the professional practices of the firm worldwide. He has worked extensively with executives to increase their understanding of information in the management function.

tomers, and rivals. They go on to identify three specific ways that the technology affects competition: it alters industry structures, it supports cost and differentiation strategies, and it spawns entirely new businesses. They outline five steps to help managers assess the impact of the information revolution on their own companies.

The information revolution is sweeping through our economy. No company can escape its effects. Dramatic reductions in the cost of obtaining, processing, and transmitting information are changing the way we do business.

Most general managers know that the revolution is under way, and few dispute its importance. As more and more of their time and investment capital are absorbed in information technology and its effects, executives have a growing awareness that the technology can no longer be the exclusive territory of EDP or IS departments. As they see their rivals use information for competitive advantage, these executives recognize the need to become directly involved in the management of the new technology. In the face of rapid change, however, they don't know how.

This article aims to help general managers respond to the challenges of the information revolution. How will advances in information technology affect competition and the sources of competitive advantage? What strategies should a company pursue to exploit the technology? What are the implications of actions that competitors may already have taken? Of the many opportunities for investment in information technology, which are the most urgent?

To answer these questions, managers must first understand that information technology is more than just computers. Today, information technology must be conceived of broadly to encompass the information that businesses create and use as well as a wide spectrum of increasingly convergent and linked technologies that process the information. In addition to computers, then, data recognition equipment, communications technologies, factory automation, and other hardware and services are involved.

The information revolution is affecting competition in three vital ways:

It changes industry structure and, in so doing, alters the rules of competition.

It creates competitive advantage by giving companies new ways to outperform their rivals.

It spawns whole new businesses, often from within a company's existing operations.

We discuss the reasons why information technology has acquired strategic significance and how it is affecting all businesses. We then describe how the new technology changes the nature of competition and how astute companies have exploited this. Finally, we outline a procedure managers can use to assess the role of information technology in their business and to help define investment priorities to turn the technology to their competitive advantage.

STRATEGIC SIGNIFICANCE

Information technology is changing the way companies operate. It is affecting the entire process by which companies create their products. Furthermore, it is reshaping the product itself: the entire package of physical goods, services, and information companies provide to create value for their buyers.

An important concept that highlights the role of information technology in competition is the "value chain."[1] This concept divides a company's activities into the technologically and economically distinct activities it performs to do business. We call these "value activities." The value a company creates is measured by the amount that buyers are willing to pay for a product or service. A business is profitable if the value it creates exceeds the cost of performing the value activities. To gain competitive advantage over its rivals, a company must either perform these activities at a lower cost or perform them in a way that leads to differentiation and a premium price (more value).[2]

A company's value activities fall into nine generic categories (see Figure 5-1). Primary activities are those involved in the physical creation of the product, its marketing and delivery to buyers, and its support and servicing after sale. Support activities provide the inputs and infrastructure that allow the primary activities to take place. Every activity employs purchased inputs, human resources, and a combination of technologies. Firm infrastructure, including such functions as general management, legal work, and accounting, supports the entire chain. Within each of these generic categories, a company will perform a number of discrete activities, depending on the particular business. Service, for example, frequently includes activities such as installation, repair, adjustment, upgrading, and parts inventory management.

A company's value chain is a system of interdependent activities, which are connected by linkages. Linkages exist when the way in which one activity is per-

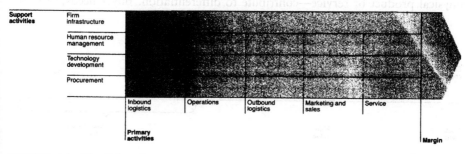

FIGURE 5-1 The Value Chain

formed affects the cost or effectiveness of other activities. Linkages often create trade-offs in performing different activities that should be optimized. This optimization may require trade-offs. For example, a more costly product design and more expensive raw materials can reduce after-sale service costs. A company must resolve such trade-offs, in accordance with its strategy, to achieve competitive advantage.

Linkages also require activities to be coordinated. On-time delivery requires that operations, outbound logistics, and service activities (installation, for example) should function smoothly together. Good coordination allows on-time delivery without the need for costly inventory. Careful management of linkages is often a powerful source of competitive advantage because of the difficulty rivals have in perceiving them and in resolving trade-offs across organizational lines.

The value chain for a company in a particular industry is embedded in a larger stream of activities that we term the "value system" (see Figure 5-2). The value system includes the value chains of suppliers, who provide inputs (such as raw materials, components, and purchased services) to the company's value chain. The company's product often passes through its channels' value chains on its way to the ultimate buyer. Finally, the product becomes a purchased input to the value chains of its buyers, who use it to perform one or more buyer activities.

Linkages not only connect value activities inside a company but also create interdependencies between its value chain and those of its suppliers and channels. A company can create competitive advantage by optimizing or coordinating these links to the outside. For example, a candy manufacturer may save processing steps by persuading its suppliers to deliver chocolate in liquid form rather than in molded bars. Just-in-time deliveries by the supplier may have the same effect. But the opportunities for savings through coordinating with suppliers and channels go far beyond logistics and order processing. The company, suppliers, and channels can all benefit through better recognition and exploitation of such linkages.

Competitive advantage in either cost or differentiation is a function of a company's value chain. A company's cost position reflects the collective cost of performing all its value activities relative to rivals. Each value activity has cost drivers that determine the potential sources of a cost advantage. Similarly, a company's ability to differentiate itself reflects the contribution of each value activity toward fulfillment of buyer needs. Many of a company's activities—not just its physical product or service—contribute to differentiation. Buyer needs, in turn,

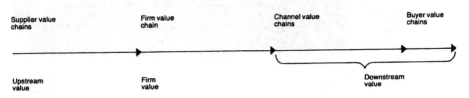

FIGURE 5-2 The Value System

depend not only on the impact of the company's product on the buyer but also on the company's other activities (for example, logistics or after-sale services).

In the search for competitive advantage, companies often differ in competitive scope—or the breadth of their activities. Competitive scope has four key dimensions: segment scope, vertical scope (degree of vertical integration), geographic scope, and industry scope (or the range of related industries in which the company competes).

Competitive scope is a powerful tool for creating competitive advantage. Broad scope can allow the company to exploit interrelationships between the value chains serving different industry segments, geographic areas, or related industries. For example, two business units may share one sales force to sell their products, or the units may coordinate the procurement of common components. Competing nationally or globally with a coordinated strategy can yield a competitive advantage over local or domestic rivals. By employing a broad vertical scope, a company can exploit the potential benefits of performing more activities internally rather than use outside suppliers.

By selecting a narrow scope, on the other hand, a company may be able to tailor the value chain to a particular target segment to achieve lower cost or differentiation. The competitive advantage of a narrow scope comes from customizing the value chain to best serve particular product varieties, buyers, or geographic regions. If the target segment has unusual needs, broad-scope competitors will not serve it well.

TRANSFORMING THE VALUE CHAIN

Information technology is permeating the value chain at every point, transforming the way value activities are performed and the nature of the linkages among them. It also is affecting competitive scope and reshaping the way products meet buyer needs. These basic effects explain why information technology has acquired strategic significance and is different from the many other technologies businesses use.

Every value activity has both a physical and an information-processing component. The physical component includes all the physical tasks required to perform the activity. The information-processing component encompasses the steps required to capture, manipulate, and channel the data necessary to perform the activity.

Every value activity creates and uses information of some kind. A logistics activity, for example, uses information like scheduling promises, transportation rates, and production plans to ensure timely and cost-effective delivery. A service activity uses information about service requests to schedule calls and order parts, and generates information on product failures that a company can use to revise product designs and manufacturing methods.

An activity's physical and information-processing components may be simple or quite complex. Different activities require a different mix of the two components. For instance, metal stamping uses more physical processing than information processing; processing of insurance claims requires just the opposite balance.

For most of industrial history, technological progress principally affected the physical component of what businesses do. During the Industrial Revolution, companies achieved competitive advantage by substituting machines for human labor. Information processing at that time was mostly the result of human effort.

Now the pace of technological change is reversed. Information technology is advancing faster than technologies for physical processing. The costs of information storage, manipulation, and transmittal are falling rapidly and the boundaries of what is feasible in information processing are at the same time expanding. During the Industrial Revolution, the railroad cut the travel time from Boston, Massachusetts to Concord, New Hampshire from five days to four hours, a factor of 30.[3] But the advances in information technology are even greater. The cost of computer power relative to the cost of manual information processing is at least 8,000 times less expensive than the cost 30 years ago. Between 1958 and 1980 the time for one electronic operation fell by a factor of 80 million. Department of Defense studies show that the error rate in recording data through bar coding is 1 in 3,000,000, compared to 1 error in 300 manual data entries.[4]

This technological transformation is expanding the limits of what companies can do faster than managers can explore the opportunities. The information revolution affects all nine categories of value activity, from allowing computer-aided design in technology development to incorporating automation in warehouses (see Figure 5-3). The new technology substitutes machines for human effort in information processing. Paper ledgers and rules of thumb have given way to computers.

Support activities	Firm infrastructure	Planning models				
	Human resource management	Automated personnel scheduling				
	Technology development	Computer-aided design	Electronic market research			
	Procurement	On-line procurement of parts				
		Automated warehouse	Flexible manufacturing	Automated order processing	Telemarketing Remote terminals for salespersons	Remote servicing of equipment Computer scheduling and routing of repair trucks
		Inbound logistics	Operations	Outbound logistics	Marketing and sales	Service
		Primary activities				Margin

FIGURE 5-3 Information Technology Permeates the Value Chain

Initially, companies used information technology mainly for accounting and record-keeping functions. In these applications, the computers automated repetitive clerical functions such as order processing. Today information technology is spreading throughout the value chain and is performing optimization and control functions as well as more judgmental executive functions. General Electric, for instance, uses a database that includes the accumulated experience and (often intuitive) knowledge of its appliance service engineers to provide support to customers by phone.

Information technology is generating more data as a company performs its activities and is permitting it to collect or capture information that was not available before. Such technology also makes room for a more comprehensive analysis and use of the expanded data. The number of variables that a company can analyze or control has grown dramatically. Hunt-Wesson, for example, developed a computer model to aid it in studying distribution-center expansion and relocation issues. The model enabled the company to evaluate many more different variables, scenarios, and alternative strategies than had been possible before. Similarly, information technology helped Sulzer Brothers' engineers improve the design of diesel engines in ways that manual calculations could not.

Information technology is also transforming the physical processing component of activities. Computer-controlled machine tools are faster, more accurate, and more flexible in manufacturing than the older, manually operated machines. Schlumberger has developed an electronic device permitting engineers to measure the angle of a drill bit, the temperature of a rock, and other variables while drilling oil wells. The result: drilling time is reduced and some well-logging steps are eliminated. On the West Coast, some fishermen now use weather satellite data on ocean temperatures to identify promising fishing grounds. This practice greatly reduces the fishermen's steaming time and fuel costs.

Information technology not only affects how individual activities are performed but, through new information flows, it is also greatly enhancing a company's ability to exploit linkages between activities, both within and outside the company. The technology is creating new linkages between activities, and companies can now coordinate their actions more closely with those of their buyers and suppliers. For example, McKesson, the nation's largest drug distributor, provides its drugstore customers with terminals. The company makes it so easy for clients to order, receive, and prepare invoices that the customers, in return, are willing to place larger orders. At the same time, McKesson has streamlined its order processing.

Finally, the new technology has a powerful effect on competitive scope. Information systems allow companies to coordinate value activities in far-flung geographic locations. (For example, Boeing engineers work on designs on-line with foreign suppliers.) Information technology is also creating many new interrelationships among businesses, expanding the scope of industries in which a company must compete to achieve competitive advantage.

So pervasive is the impact of information technology that it confronts executives with a tough problem: too much information. This problem creates new uses of information technology to store and analyze the flood of information available to executives.

TRANSFORMING THE PRODUCT

Most products have always had both a physical and an information component. The latter, broadly defined, is everything that the buyer needs to know to obtain the product and use it to achieve the desired result. That is, a product includes information about its characteristics and how it should be used and supported. For example, convenient, accessible information on maintenance and service procedures is an important buyer criterion in consumer appliances.

Historically, a product's physical component has been more important than its information component. The new technology, however, makes it feasible to supply far more information along with the physical product. For example, General Electric's appliance service data base supports a consumer hotline that helps differentiate GE's service support from its rivals'. Similarly, some railroad and trucking companies offer up-to-the-minute information on the whereabouts of shippers' freight, which improves coordination between shippers and the railroad. The new technology is also making it increasingly possible to offer products with no physical component at all. Compustat's customers have access to corporate financial data filed with the Securities and Exchange Commission, and many companies have sprung up to perform energy use analyses of buildings.

Many products also process information in their normal functioning. A dishwasher, for example, requires a control system that directs the various components of the unit through the washing cycle and displays the process to the user. The new information technology is enhancing product performance and is making it easier to boost a product's information content. Electronic control of the automobile, for example, is becoming more visible in dashboard displays, talking dashboards, diagnostic messages, and the like.

There is an unmistakable trend toward expanding the information content in products. This component, combined with changes in companies' value chains, underscores the increasingly strategic role of information technology. There are no longer mature industries; rather, there are mature ways of doing business.

DIRECTION AND PACE OF CHANGE

Although a trend toward information intensity in companies and products is evident, the role and importance of the technology differs in each industry. Banking and insurance, for example, have always been information intensive. Such industries were naturally among the first and most enthusiastic users of data processing. On the other hand, physical processing will continue to dominate in industries that produce, say, cement, despite increased information processing in such businesses.

Figure 5-4, which relates information intensity in the value chain to information content in the product, illuminates the differences in the role and intensity of information among various industries. The banking and newspaper industries have a high information-technology content in both product and process. The oil-refining industry has a high use of information in the refining process but a relatively low information content in the product dimension.

Because of the falling cost and growing capacity of the new technology, many industries seem to be moving toward a higher information content in both product and process. It should be emphasized that technology will continue to improve rapidly. The cost of hardware will continue to drop, and managers will continue to distribute the technology among even the lower levels of the company. The cost of developing software, now a key constraint, will fall as more packages become available that are easily tailored to customers' circumstances. The applications of information technology that companies are using today are only a beginning.

Information technology is not only transforming products and processes but also the nature of competition itself. Despite the growing use of information technology, industries will always differ in their position in Figure 5-4 and their pace of change.

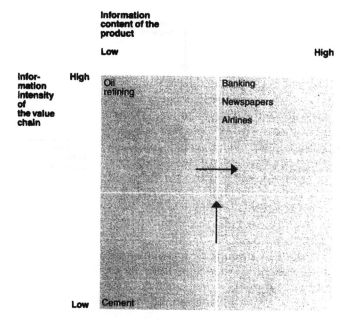

FIGURE 5-4   Information Intensity Matrix

CHANGING THE NATURE OF COMPETITION

After surveying a wide range of industries, we find that information technology is changing the rules of competition in three ways. First, advances in information technology are changing the industry structure. Second, information technology is an increasingly important lever that companies can use to create competitive advantage. A company's search for competitive advantage through information technology often also spreads to affect industry structure as competitors imitate the leader's strategic innovations. Finally, the information revolution is spawning completely new businesses. These three effects are critical for understanding the impact of information technology on a particular industry and for formulating effective strategic responses.

CHANGING INDUSTRY STRUCTURE

The structure of an industry is embodied in five competitive forces that collectively determine industry profitability: the power of buyers, the power of suppliers, the threat of new entrants, the threat of substitute products, and the rivalry among existing competitors (see Figure 5-5). The collective strength of the five forces varies from industry to industry, as does average profitability. The strength of each of the five forces can also change, either improving or eroding the attractiveness of an industry.[5]

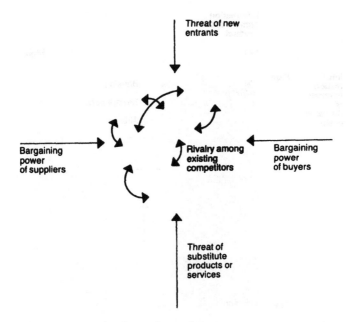

FIGURE 5-5   Determinants of Industry Attractiveness

Information technology can alter each of the five competitive forces and, hence, industry attractiveness as well. The technology is unfreezing the structure of many industries, creating the need and opportunity for change. For example:

- Information technology increases the power of buyers in industries assembling purchased components. Automated bills for materials and vendor quotation files make it easier for buyers to evaluate sources of materials and make-or-buy decisions.
- Information technologies requiring large investments in complex software have raised the barriers to entry. For example, banks competing in cash management services for corporate clients now need advanced software to give customers on-line account information. These banks may also need to invest in improved computer hardware and other facilities.
- Flexible computer-aided design and manufacturing systems have influenced the threat of substitution in many industries by making it quicker, easier, and cheaper to incorporate enhanced features into products.
- The automation of order processing and customer billing has increased rivalry in many distribution industries. The new technology raises fixed costs at the same time as it displaces people. As a result, distributors must often fight harder for incremental volume.

Industries such as airlines, financial services, distribution, and information suppliers (see the upper right-hand corner of Figure 5-4) have felt these effects so far.[6] (See Table 5-1, "Information Technology and Industry Structure," for more examples.)

Information technology has had a particularly strong impact on bargaining relationships between suppliers and buyers since it affects the linkages between companies and their suppliers, channels, and buyers. Information systems that cross company lines are becoming common. In some cases, the boundaries of industries themselves have changed.[7]

Systems that connect buyers and suppliers are spreading. Xerox gives manufacturing data to suppliers electronically to help them deliver materials. To speed up order entry, Westinghouse Electric Supply Company and American Hospital Supply have furnished their customers with terminals. Among other things, many systems raise the costs of switching to a new partner because of the disruption and retraining required. These systems tend to tie companies more closely to their buyers and suppliers.

Information technology is altering the relationship among scale, automation, and flexibility with potentially profound consequences. Large-scale production is no longer essential to achieve automation. As a result, entry barriers in a number of industries are falling.

At the same time, automation no longer necessarily leads to inflexibility. For example, General Electric rebuilt its Erie locomotive facility as a large-scale yet flexible factory using computers to store all design and manufacturing data. Ten types of motor frames can be accommodated without manual adjustments to the

TABLE 5-1   Information Technology and Industry Structure

Buyer power	Videotex home shopping services, such as Comp-U-Card, increase buyers' information. Buyers use their personal computers to browse through electronic catalogs and compare prices and product specifications. Customers can make purchases at any hour at prices typically 25% to 30% below suggested retail levels. Comp-U-Card is growing quickly: revenues have quintupled in two years to $9.5 million and membership is now 15,000. According to some projections, by the mid-1990s, 75% of U.S. households will have access to such services.
Buyer power	Shelternet, an electronic information exchange offered by First Boston Corporation, allows real estate brokers to determine quickly and easily what mortgage packages are available and whether the buyer will qualify for financing. This improves the position of both brokers and homebuyers in shopping for mortgages. The parties can make preliminary commitments within 30 minutes.
Substitution	Electronic databases, such as NEXIS, are substituting for library research and consulting firms. NEXIS subscribers can quickly search the full text of any article in 225 periodicals. Users drastically reduce the time spent in literature searches. In addition, the buyer avoids the cost of journal subscriptions and pays only for the information required.

machines. After installation of a "smart" manufacturing system, BMW can build customized cars (each with its own tailored gearbox, transmission system, interior, and other features) on the normal assembly line. Automation and flexibility are achieved simultaneously, a pairing that changes the pattern of rivalry among competitors.

The increasing flexibility in performing many value activities combined with the falling costs of designing products has triggered an avalanche of opportunities to customize and to serve small market niches. Computer-aided design capability not only reduces the cost of designing new products but also dramatically reduces the cost of modifying or adding features to existing products. The cost of tailoring products to market segments is falling, again affecting the pattern of industry rivalry.

While managers can use information technology to improve their industry structure, the technology also has the potential to destroy that structure. For example, information systems now permit the airline industry to alter fares frequently and to charge many different fares between any two points. At the same time, however, the technology makes the flight and fare schedules more readily available and allows travel agents and individuals to shop around quickly for the lowest fare. The result is a lower fare structure than might otherwise exist. Information technology has made a number of professional service industries less attractive by reducing personal interaction and making service more of a commodity. Managers must look carefully at the structural implications of the new technology to realize its advantages or to be prepared for its consequences.

CREATING COMPETITIVE ADVANTAGE

In any company, information technology has a powerful effect on competitive advantage in either cost or differentiation. The technology affects value activities themselves or allows companies to gain competitive advantage by exploiting changes in competitive scope.

Lowering Cost

As we have seen, information technology can alter a company's costs in any part of the value chain.[8] The technology's historical impact on cost was confined to activities in which repetitive information processing played a large part. These limits no longer exist, however. Even activities like assembly that mainly involve physical processing now have a large information-processing component.

Canon, for example, built a low-cost copier assembly process around an automated parts-selection and materials-handling system. Assembly workers have bins containing all the parts needed for the particular copier. Canon's success with this system derives from the software that controls parts inventory and selection. In insurance brokerage, a number of insurance companies usually participate in underwriting a contract. The costs of documenting each company's participation are high. Now a computer model can optimize (and often reduce) the number of insurers per contract, lowering the broker's total cost. In garment production, equipment such as automated pattern drawers, fabric cutters, and systems for delivering cloth to the final sewing station have reduced the labor time for manufacturing by up to 50%. (See Table 5-2, "Aim: A Competitive Edge," for further examples.)

In addition to playing a direct role in cost, information technology alters the cost drivers of activities in ways that can improve (or erode) a company's relative cost position. For example, Louisiana Oil & Tire has taken all ten of its salespeople off the road and made them into telemarketers. As a result, sales expenses have fallen by 10% and sales volume has doubled. However, the move has made the national scale of operations the key determinant of the cost of selling, rather than regional scale.

Enhancing Differentiation

The impact of information technology on differentiation strategies is equally dramatic. As noted earlier, the role of a company and its product in the buyer's

TABLE 5-2   Aim: A Competitive Edge

Lowering Cost	Casinos spend up to 20% of revenues on complimentary services for high rollers. One assignment for pit bosses has always been to keep an eye out for the big spenders. Now, however, many casinos have developed computer systems to analyze data on customers. Caesar's Palace lowered its complimentary budget more than 20% by developing a player-rating system for more accurate identification of big spenders.
Enhancing Differentiation	American Express has developed differentiated travel services for corporate customers through the use of information technology. The services include arranging travel and close monitoring of individual expenses. Computers search for the lowest airplane fares, track travel expenses for each cardholder, and issue monthly statements.

value chain is the key determinant of differentiation. The new information technology makes it possible to customize products. Using automation, for instance, Sulzer Brothers has increased from five to eight the number of cylinder bore sizes of new low-speed marine diesel engines. Shipowners now choose an engine that is more precisely suited to their needs and thereby recoup significant fuel savings. Similarly, Digital Equipment's artificial intelligence system, XCON, uses decision rules to develop custom computer configurations. This dramatically reduces the time required to fill orders and increases accuracy—which enhances Digital's image as a quality provider.

By bundling more information with the physical product package sold to the buyer, the new technology affects a company's ability to differentiate itself. For example, a magazine distributor offers retailers processing credits for unsold items more efficiently than its competitors. Similarly, the embedding of information systems in the physical product itself is an increasingly powerful way to distinguish it from competing goods.

Changing Competitive Scope

Information technology can alter the relationship between competitive scope and competitive advantage. The technology increases a company's ability to coordinate its activities regionally, nationally, and globally. It can unlock the power of broader geographic scope to create competitive advantage. Consider the newspaper industry. Dow Jones, publisher of the *Wall Street Journal,* pioneered the page transmission technology that links its 17 U.S. printing plants to produce a truly national newspaper. Such advances in communication plants have also made it possible to move toward a global strategy. Dow Jones has started the *Asian Wall Street Journal* and the *Wall Street Journal—European Edition* and shares much of the editorial content while printing the papers in plants all over the world.

The information revolution is creating interrelationships among industries that were previously separate. The merging of computer and telecommunications technologies is an important example. This convergence has profound effects on the structure of both industries. For example, AT&T is using its position in telecommunications as a staging point for entry into the computer industry. IBM, which recently acquired Rolm, the telecommunications equipment manufacturer, is now joining the competition from the other direction. Information technology is also at the core of growing interrelationships in financial services, where the banking, insurance, and brokerage industries are merging, and in office equipment, where once distinct functions such as typing, photocopying, and data and voice communications can now be combined.

Broad-line companies are increasingly able to segment their offerings in ways that were previously feasible only for focused companies. In the trucking industry, Intermodal Transportation Services, Inc. of Cincinnati has completely changed its system for quoting prices. In the past, each local office set prices using manual procedures. Intermodal now uses microcomputers to link its offices to a center that calculates all prices. The new system gives the company the capacity to introduce a new pricing policy to offer discounts to national accounts, which place their orders from all over the country. Intermodal is tailoring its value chain to large national customers in a way that was previously impossible.

As information technology becomes more widespread, the opportunities to take advantage of a new competitive scope will only increase. The benefits of scope (and the achievement of linkages), however, can accrue only when the information technology spread throughout the organization can communicate. Completely decentralized organizational design and application of information technology will thwart these possibilities, because the information technology introduced in various parts of a company will not be compatible.

SPAWNING NEW BUSINESSES

The information revolution is giving birth to completely new industries in three distinct ways. First, it makes new businesses technologically feasible. For example, modern imaging and telecommunications technology blend to support new facsimile services such as Federal Express's Zapmail. Similarly, advances in microelectronics made personal computing possible. Services such as Merrill Lynch's Cash Management Account required new information technology to combine several financial products into one.

Second, information technology can also spawn new businesses by creating derived demand for new products. One example is Western Union's EasyLink service, a sophisticated, high-speed, data-communications network that allows personal computers, word processors, and other electronic devices to send messages to each other and to telex machines throughout the world. This service was not needed before the spread of information technology caused a demand for it.

Third, information technology creates new businesses within old ones. A company with information processing embedded in its value chain may have excess capacity or skills that can be sold outside. Sears took advantage of its skills in processing credit card accounts and of its massive scale to provide similar services to others. It sells credit-authorization and transaction-processing services to Phillips Petroleum and retail remittance-processing services to Mellon Bank. Similarly, a manufacturer of automotive parts, A.O. Smith, developed data-communications expertise to meet the needs of its traditional businesses. When a bank consortium went looking for a contractor to run a network of automated teller machines, A.O. Smith got the job. Eastman Kodak recently began offering long-distance telephone and data-transmission services through its internal telecommunications system. Where the information technology used in a company's value chain is sensitive to scale, a company may improve its overall competitive advantage by increasing the scale of information processing and lowering costs. By selling extra capacity outside, it is at the same time generating new revenue.

Companies also are increasingly able to create and sell to others information that is a by-product of their operations. National Benefit Life reportedly merged with American Can in part to gain access to data on the nine million customers of American Can's direct-mail retailing subsidiary. The use of bar-code scanners in supermarket retailing has turned grocery stores into market research labs. Retailers can run an ad in the morning newspaper and find out its effect by early afternoon. They can also sell this data to market research companies and to food processors.

COMPETING IN THE AGE OF INFORMATION

Senior executives can follow five steps to take advantage of opportunities that the information revolution has created.

1. *Assess information intensity.* A company's first task is to evaluate the existing and potential information intensity of the products and processes of its business units. To help managers accomplish this, we have developed some measures of the potential importance of information technology.

    It is very likely that information technology will play a strategic role in an industry that is characterized by one or more of the following features:

    - Potentially high information intensity in the value chain—a large number of suppliers or customers with whom the company deals directly, a product requiring a large quantity of information in selling, a product line with many distinct product varieties, a product composed of many parts, a large number of steps in a company's manufacturing process, a long cycle time from the initial order to the delivered product.

- Potentially high information intensity in the product—a product that mainly provides information, a product whose operation involves substantial information processing, a product whose use requires the buyer to process a lot of information, a product requiring especially high costs for buyer training, a product that has many alternative uses or is sold to a buyer with high information intensity in his or her own business.

These may help identify priority business units for investment in information technology. When selecting priority areas, remember the breadth of information technology—it involves more than simple computing.

2. *Determine the role of information technology in industry structure.* Managers should predict the likely impact of information technology on their industry's structure. They must examine how information technology might affect each of the five competitive forces. Not only is each force likely to change but industry boundaries may change as well. Chances are that a new definition of the industry may be necessary.

   Many companies are partly in control of the nature and pace of change in the industry structure. Companies have permanently altered the bases of competition in their favor in many industries through aggressive investments in information technology and have forced other companies to follow. Citibank, with its automated teller machines and transaction processing; American Airlines, with its computerized reservations system; and *USA Today,* with its newspaper page transmission to decentralized printing plants, are pioneers that have used information technology to alter industry structure. A company should understand how structural change is forcing it to respond and look for ways to lead change in the industry.

3. *Identify and rank the ways in which information technology might create competitive advantage.* The starting assumption must be that the technology is likely to affect every activity in the value chain. Equally important is the possibility that new linkages among activities are being made possible. By taking a careful look, managers can identify the value activities that are likely to be most affected in terms of cost and differentiation. Obviously, activities that represent a large proportion of cost or that are critical to differentiation bear closest scrutiny, particularly if they have a significant information-processing component. Activities with important links to other activities inside and outside the company are also critical. Executives must examine such activities for ways in which information technology can create sustainable competitive advantage.

In addition to taking a hard look at its value chain, a company should consider how information technology might allow a change in competitive scope. Can information technology help the company serve new segments? Will the flexibility of information technology allow broad-line competitors to invade areas that were once the province of niche competitors? Will information technology provide the leverage to expand the business globally? Can managers harness information technology to exploit interrelationships with other industries? Or, can the technology help a company create competitive advantage by narrowing its scope?

A fresh look at the company's product may also be in order:

Can the company bundle more information with the product?
Can the company embed information technology in it?

4. *Investigate how information technology might spawn new businesses.* Managers should consider opportunities to create new businesses from existing ones. Information technology is an increasingly important avenue for corporate diversification. Lockheed, for example, entered the database business by perceiving an opportunity to use its spare computer capacity.

Identifying opportunities to spawn new businesses requires answering questions such as:

What information generated (or potentially generated) in the business could the company sell?
What information-processing capacity exists internally to start a new business?
Does information technology make it feasible to produce new items related to the company's product?

5. *Develop a plan for taking advantage of information technology.* The first four steps should lead to an action plan to capitalize on the information revolution. This action plan should rank the strategic investments necessary in hardware and software, and in new product development activities that reflect the increasing information content in products. Organizational changes that reflect the role that the technology plays in linking activities inside and outside the company are likely to be necessary.

The management of information technology can no longer be the sole province of the EDP department. Increasingly, companies must employ information technology with a sophisticated understanding of the requirements for competitive advantage. Organizations need to distribute the responsibility for systems development more widely in the organization. At the same time, general managers must be involved to ensure that cross-functional linkages, more possible to achieve with information technology, are exploited.

These changes do not mean that a central information-technology function should play an insignificant role. Rather than control information technology, however, an IS manager should coordinate the architecture and standards of the many applications throughout the organization, as well as provide assistance and coaching in systems development. Unless the numerous applications of information technology inside a company are compatible with each other, many benefits may be lost.

Information technology can help in the strategy implementation process. Reporting systems can track progress toward milestones and success factors. By using information systems, companies can measure their activities more precisely and help motivate managers to implement strategies successfully.[9]

The importance of the information revolution is not in dispute. The question is not whether information technology will have a significant impact on a company's competitive position; rather the question is when and how this impact will strike. Companies that anticipate the power of information technology will be in control of events. Companies that do not respond will be forced to accept changes that others initiate and will find themselves at a competitive disadvantage.

NOTES

1. For more on the value chain concept, see Michael E. Porter, *Competitive Advantage* (New York: Free Press, 1985).
2. For a discussion of the two basic types of competitive advantage, see Michael E. Porter, *Competitive Strategy* (New York: Free Press, 1980), Chapter 2.
3. Alfred D. Chandler, Jr., *The Visible Hand* (Cambridge: Belknap Press of Harvard University Press, 1977), p. 86.
4. James L. McKenney and F. Warren McFarlan, "The Information Archipelago—Maps and Bridges," HBR September–October 1982, p. 109.
5. See Michael E. Porter, "How Competitive Forces Shape Strategy," HBR March–April 1979, p. 137.
6. See F. Warren McFarlan, "Information Technology Changes the Way You Compete," HBR May–June 1984, p. 98.
7. James J. Cash, Jr. and Benn R. Konsynski, "IS Redraws Competitive Boundaries," HBR March–April 1985, p. 134.
8. See Gregory L. Parsons, "Information Technology: A New Competitive Weapon," *Sloan Management Review.* Fall 1983, p. 3.
9. Victor E. Millar, "Decision-Oriented Information," *Datamation,* January 1984, p. 159.

Part Two

The Special Library as a Business Asset

Part Two

The Special Library as a Business Asset

6

Toward a Better Understanding of New Special Libraries

Elin Christianson and Janet L. Ahrensfeld

Research undertaken to explore and better define the phenomenon of the new special library is described. Growth rate, types of organizations that establish new special libraries, where they are located, and the specific pressures or events that spark establishment are documented. Factors relating to goals, management relations, management attitudes, users, economics, and politics are assessed in terms of their importance to the new special library in its first years of life. Conclusions are drawn regarding the role of SLA and its public relations, consultation, employment and education programs in fostering the establishment of successful new special libraries.

The continuing growth in the existing number of special libraries has been a significant characteristic of the modern special library movement over the entire 60 years of its history. Even the influence of another, less pleasant, characteristic—the frequency with which special libraries go out of existence—does not diminish the vigor of the formation of new special libraries.

Despite our awareness of the new special library phenomenon and the important part it plays in the growth potential for special libraries as a whole, we actually *know* little about it. This is not to say we do not understand anything about how and why special libraries begin. Common sense, intuition, and years of experience have provided some implicit assumptions on which we draw when called upon to describe this phenomenon of growth. Intuition and common sense

Reprinted from *Special Libraries* 71, no. 2 (March 1980), pp. 146-153 by Special Libraries Association. Web Address (www.sla.org). Elin Christianson chairs the Committee on New Special Libraries, Illinois Chapter, SLA, Chicago, Illinois. Janet L. Ahrensfeld is library director, Blue Cross/Blue Shield Associations Library, Chicago, Illinois.

also tell us that this phenomenon is likely to continue, and that there is still a potential for growth in the number of special libraries.

Edward Strable raised the question of SLA's involvement in fostering the growth of new special libraries as one of the larger issues of the profession during his Special Libraries Association presidency in 1972-73.[1] His discussion centered on these questions: Are we doing nearly enough to stimulate the establishment of new special libraries to serve the large segment of the population that does not have any special professional information services in their work-related lives? How do we attack the problem more effectively than we now are doing? Strable's questions drew a spectrum of response which ranged from examples of specific activities underway in certain Chapters to arguments against the continued proliferation of small, ineffectual company libraries.[2]

About two-and-a-half years ago [1977] Strable again raised these questions, addressed this time to the Illinois Chapter. He proposed that the Chapter initiate a special project to study the origins of new special libraries and the means by which they might be more effectively encouraged. The Committee on New Special Libraries (CONSL) was formed to undertake the project (see the Appendix [in this chapter] for a listing of Committee members).

CONSL first examined the "lore" or empirical knowledge of new special libraries, surveying not only the professional literature for prior research and articles, but also the messages on the value of special libraries which SLA has directed to management through its publications and articles. CONSL then undertook a series of research projects designed to test this knowledge and to provide further insights on such questions as:

- How many new special libraries are there?
- What is the growth rate of new special libraries?
- What kinds of organizations do these new special libraries serve?
- What are the influences which operate to bring them into existence?
- What are the influences or factors at work during the early years of life that help the new special library become successfully established or that lead to its failure?
- Are there patterns of factors or common factors which can be identified and used to stimulate the establishment of new special libraries and ensure their success?

The Illinois Chapter area was used for the research. This decision was based both on convenience and on the wide spectrum of organizations found throughout the Chapter area.

Three studies, employing various research techniques, were conducted:

1. A census of new special libraries in the Illinois Chapter area, conducted by mail questionnaire.
2. In-depth interviews with librarians and managers from organizations that had successful new special libraries, and similar in-depth interviews

with librarians who had been involved with new special libraries that had failed.

3. A study of selected critical factors in new special libraries, again studied by mail questionnaire.

This report synthesizes the results of CONSL's investigations, committee discussions, and conclusions.*

THE DEMOGRAPHY OF NEW SPECIAL LIBRARIES

While the primary purpose of the census of new special libraries was to identify such libraries for further research, the results of the census are of interest in themselves since they provide the basic dimensions of the universe of new special libraries in the area.

Fifty-six new special libraries were reported to have been established in the Illinois Chapter area in a period of just over five years, that is, between Jan 1, 1973 and Mar 1978. Measuring the rate of new library establishment over this period produces a 5-year growth rate of 27%, which is in the range suggested for somewhat earlier periods by Kruzas (25% in the five-year period 1963-68) and Woods (16.7% between 1964 and 1970).[3]

The majority of new special libraries—48 or 86%—are located within the Chicago metropolitan area. Of these, two thirds are in the city; the one third in the suburbs correspond to the trend of organizations to locate outside the central city.

Not-for-profit organizations accounted for 40% of the new special libraries. This was influenced by the large number of health science libraries, although not-for-profit organizations in other subject areas also contributed to the total. In terms of broad subject area, business accounted for 19 new special libraries; science-technology, 16; the health sciences, 10; and law, 5 new special libraries. Six other subjects in the social sciences and humanities accounted for the remaining 6 new special libraries.

THE PRE-ESTABLISHMENT PERIOD

What situations and attitudes occur in organizations and lead to the establishment of a library? Part of CONSL's research was directed toward obtaining information about these influences.

What kind of information resources existed in the organization before the librarian was hired? The need for information was well recognized. Over 80% of the librarians indicated that in the pre-establishment period their managements

---

*The full report of this study, entitled *New Special Libraries: A Summary of Research*, is available from Special Libraries Association, ISBN 0-87111-271-X.

were aware that they needed information and that their information resources were poor. Just over two thirds of the librarians indicated that employees were already using published materials.

In about one third of the organizations, there already was or had once been a library—either a former library now being revived, a library staffed by a clerk, or, in a few cases, division or departmental libraries which were being consolidated. In two thirds of the organizations, the librarians actually started the library, either from unorganized materials or from a collection in some stage of development (47.8% of the organizations), or from "scratch" (17.4%).

What primary reason did management have for establishing a special library? While 80.4% realized their information resources were poor or disorganized, the primary reasons for establishing a library were equally divided between a desire for organization of materials and a desire for information service. Although this response indicates that management was aware of its need for information and had perceived that it needed a library, only 13% of the librarians indicated that their management had a realistic picture of what a library could or should do for them.

Were there any specific pressures which transformed the library idea into action? Over 90% of the librarians were able to identify one or more specific pressures which led to the organization's decision. The two most frequently mentioned were pressure from an increased need for information resources (37.4%), and the pressure from professional standards which required a library (31.4%). Other specific pressures mentioned were the desire for economy or coordination (in the cases of the libraries which were consolidations or expansions of departmental libraries), and the availability of grant funds that could be applied to the establishment of a library.

One question of particular interest to CONSL was the possibility of a "trigger" to establishment. Given the presence of a quasi-library (a collection of materials more or less organized), and the impetus from the various pressures, what actually set the library planning process in motion? Eighty percent of the librarians were able to identify a specific trigger event or person. For half of the libraries, the trigger was a person or persons who took an active interest in the idea. Thirty percent of the librarians identified an event as the trigger. While in these cases there undoubtedly was a person who took an active part, nevertheless, the identification of an event pinpoints an additional influence which, in combination with the other influences, may tip the balance toward establishment.

Most of the events arose from major organizational changes—physical moves, consolidations of several departments, or a reorganization of the company. In a few cases the library was planned as a component of the new organization and was established along with the opening of the organization's offices.

Where do these organizations turn for help in planning the library? In hiring the librarian? Actual contact with Illinois Chapter consultation or employment services was minimal. Only 17.3% of the organizations were familiar with or had used SLA publications or consultation, although the Illinois Chapter has an active consultation service. The first step for the majority of the organizations was to hire a librarian. Two thirds of the librarians obtained their jobs in these new special libraries through non-library-connected channels of communication. Word of mouth or personal contact accounted for 26.1% of the hirings. The other major sources were newspaper advertisements and employment agencies. Only one third of the librarians were hired through library channels, with library school contacts accounting for most of the hirings. The Illinois Chapter employment service accounted for 8.7% of the hirings. Half of the librarians hired to establish the special libraries had previous professional experience in special library work; half did not.

CRITICAL FACTORS IN NEW SPECIAL LIBRARIES

CONSL realized early in its work that the formation of a new special library is a continuing process and that the hiring of a librarian, which CONSL defined as the establishment of the library, is part of this process. The hiring of the librarian may make the new special library visible, but it does not necessarily make it viable. Since the purpose of encouraging the establishment of new special libraries is to encourage the spread of *successful* new special libraries, it is important to identify the influences at work in the first few critical years of life, as well as those at work before the library is established.

The axiom that each special library is unique is as true of new special libraries as it is of long-established ones. CONSL developed an extensive list of factors that are potential influences on special library development, reflecting the many different situations in which new special libraries are found. Nevertheless, as research and discussions continued, certain of these factors became dominant and coalesced into areas of common concern: goals, management, the librarian, users, and economics. These considerations are important to all special libraries but they are particularly important to the new special library whose newness makes it particularly vulnerable.

The interpretation which follows is synthesized from the in-depth group interviews with successful and failed libraries and from the critical factors study of new special libraries.

Goals and/or the goal-setting process are important to the new special library. However, the specific goal statement, policy, statement of purpose, job description, and so on, is not so important as the opportunity for continuing communication between management and the librarian as they engage in the process. Librarians should develop their own goals for the new special library. Most do and such individual goals reflect the personal commitment and initiative of the librarians. Only 40 to 65% of the new special libraries were engaged in some sort of goals process with management. Libraries less than three years old and libraries which were in shaky condition were even less likely to be involved in goal setting with management.

While goals, statements of purpose, policies, or job descriptions are not a critical factor—that is, their absence does not automatically doom the library—

they are an important indicator of the communication and understanding between management and the librarian that are necessary for the new special library's success.

Management attitudes toward and expectations of the library are critical factors. Two aspects of management attitudes and expectations have already been described: i.e., management's involvement in library goals, and the organization's familiarity with information service and expectations of the library's function.

Such factors as a stable organizational location, management-level position for the librarian, and job description are important indicators of management attitudes. Although just over 75% of the librarians indicated they held a management-level position, 13% indicated that theirs was a clerical-level position. Almost 11% *did not know* how they were classified. Only half of the librarians had job descriptions. Less than half indicated that management recognized that a special library required undivided attention and did not expect the librarian or library staff to take on non-information service functions. About 75% of the librarians indicated there was a clear-cut chain of command from the library to a top executive. Almost as many, about 70%, indicated the library's organizational location was stable, that is, it had not been transferred to a succession of managers. In some cases, unclear chains of command or organizational reshuffling are symptoms of problems in the organization. Whether it is the organization or the library that is the problem, such dislocation and relocation can be a warning signal.

Another aspect of management's attitude toward the new special library is the question of the individuals or groups of individuals who are active supporters of the library. A very high percentage of the librarians, 95.5%, indicated they have at least one important executive who is a friend of the library. They considered having a "friend at the top" to be highly important. However, about three fourths of the librarians also recognized that the library must have a sizable group of users to survive. The older libraries were more likely to have acquired such a group than were the newer libraries, who had had less time to build a clientele.

Although a friend at the top is important, and such a person may be the trigger for the establishment of a new special library, the interviews with new special libraries that failed underlined the importance of having wider support. If the continued presence of the friend at the top is *the* critical factor in the life of the new special library, then the library is going to fail when that support is withdrawn.

A librarian who is assertive and can promote the library effectively is an important factor. The librarians in the new special libraries recognized that the factors which depended on their initiative—such as learning about the organization and its information needs, developing information services, and communicating with management and users—were highly important, and almost all the librarians indicated they were attempting to do these things. In part this highly positive response is due to respondent bias. But CONSL also observed that most of the librarians had a definite commitment to the success of their special library. Their effectiveness varied, however, according to the responsiveness of their management and the librarian's own expertise in knowing what message needed to get across.

Almost all of the librarians interviewed were able to identify their users and potential users by department or interest and were attracting users from all levels of management. Middle management had the slight edge in providing users, but the most important management level varied from organization to organization. In some, lower management or general staff levels were the most important users; in others, top management was.

Two aspects of economics were considered: the economic environment of the organization as a whole, and the specific support of the library. Financial problems can be an early-warning signal of cutbacks that may affect the new special library or sometimes the critical factor in promulgating the demise of the new special library. Many librarians lacked a sensitivity to the economic climate in which their organization operated. Although the more experienced special librarians recognize the importance of the organization's financial status, the relatively inexperienced librarians in new special libraries are not yet attuned to this strong influence upon the library.

The librarians were able to respond more clearly to the library's own economic condition in terms of adequate space, budget, and staff. Seventy percent of the new special libraries had adequate funds, although many did not have formal budgets. Sixty percent had adequate space. Only 41.3% of the new special libraries had adequate professional and clerical staff.

CONCLUSION

The formation of new special libraries is a phenomenon which occurs with little direct influence or assistance from the special library profession. Thus, while organizations may be aware of their need for better information resources and conclude that they need a library, they are not likely to have a realistic understanding of how such a library should function or of the resources that must be committed to it. The action the organization takes to establish its library is most likely to be the hiring of a librarian. Since the librarian of the new special library is likely to lack experience in special librarianship, the establishment of a new special library becomes a process of trial and error, for both the organization and the librarian.

While there seem to be no cookbook formulas for encouraging the establishment of new special libraries, certain needs and influences recur and are identifiable. CONSL proposes that a goal of Special Libraries Association should be the establishment of successful new special libraries. This can best be accomplished by acknowledging the needs of librarians *and* management. To achieve this goal, SLA should reach out more actively to management decision-makers with a message on special libraries more pertinent to these times. The need for information, for better information resources, and for organization and coordination of materials—all traditional selling points—are generally accepted within organizations. The message that needs to be conveyed centers on improving management's perceptions of the role and status of the library in the organization and on the librarian as a professional information specialist.

Similarly, SLA should reach out more actively to assist inexperienced librarians in new special libraries. Many new librarians do seek help by joining SLA, by using the Chapters' consultation services, and by contacting other special librarians, but these contacts are usually for specific purposes and are limited in terms of the time spent and the amount of information exchanged.

CONSL made a number of specific recommendations to the Illinois Chapter, including continued promotion of the special library idea via exhibits and articles but with a "new, improved" message. In addition, a more viable Consultation Service is needed with a larger pool of consultants and more visibility. Visibility could be enhanced by publicizing the Service, not only directly to management but also to public libraries, trade associations, library schools, and other intermediary contact points where organizations seek assistance in establishing their libraries.

The Illinois Chapter's increasing size has made informal exchange of information a formidable task. It has been recommended that the Chapter look into more formal means of providing interaction among its members. Finally, the Chapter Education Committee might design future programs geared to the needs of librarians in new special libraries. CONSL's research indicates that such programs could draw a small but fairly steady supply of participants.

The Illinois Chapter project was envisioned as a model or pilot study. It is hoped that disseminating the results will not only foster discussion of its findings and the philosophies underlying its conclusions but also encourage similar studies to confirm or extend its work. At a time when information and information management is becoming increasingly important and the competition among methods of information management is rising, the development of new special libraries requires greater attention; their success reflects advantageously on all special libraries and their failure reflects negatively. Successful new special libraries contribute to total information resources once they become established and able to engage in cooperative programs. It is in all our interests to develop effective programs for sharing expertise in order to enhance their chances for success.

APPENDIX: ILLINOIS CHAPTER COMMITTEE ON NEW SPECIAL LIBRARIES

The members of the Illinois Chapter Committee on New Special Libraries (CONSL) were Janet L. Ahrensfeld, library director, Blue Cross and Blue Shield Associations; Eva Brown, interlibrary cooperation coordinator, Chicago Library System; William S. Budington, executive director and librarian, The John Crerar Library; Lorraine Ciboch, head, Information Services, ITR Biomedical Research; Richard A. Davis, associate professor, Graduate School of Library Science, Rosary College; Jane Kelsey, assistant librarian, Northern Trust Company; and Peggy A. Sullivan, assistant commissioner, Extension Services, Chicago Public Library. Edward G. Strable, manager, Information Services, J. Walter Thompson Company, was CONSL chairman, (1977/78). Elin B. Christianson, library consultant, was chairman (1978/79).

LITERATURE CITED

1. Strable, Edward G./Lets Talk Together. *Special Libraries* 63 (no. 9): 13A. (Sep 1972).
2. Strable, Edward G./We Talked Together. *Special Libraries* 64 (no. 10): 464-466 (Oct 1973).
3. Woods, Bill M./The Special Library Concept of Service. *American Libraries* 3 (no. 7): 759-768 (Jul-Aug 1972).

7

The Library as a Business Asset—When and How

D. N. Handy

An asset, in business, is a debt-satisfying possession. In determining business solvency Assets are set over against Liabilities, and if the former exceed the latter, the business is said to be solvent. The term Assets is applied technically to *material* possessions. But there are possessions other and even more essential than material: these are the *moral*, out of which material assets grow. At the foundation of every Business lie courage, competency, integrity, perseverance. These cannot be computed or averaged, but their commercial value is everywhere recognized.

Wherefore, let us at the outset agree that when we speak of the Library as a business-asset, we speak not of its value as so many books and pamphlets, but of its value as a contributing agency to those more fundamental possessions to which material assets owe their existence.

What then, has the Library contributed and what may it in the future hope to contribute that will add to business courage, integrity, competency, perseverance? In a word, to Business efficiency?

The answer is found in a measure in our conception of a Library and its function. Shall we then describe what we have in mind when we speak of the Library that may become a business asset?

It certainly is not *any* collection of books and pamphlets under *any* custodian and handled probably more often by the Janitor than the Manager. That is not the kind of Library that we have in mind. Our Library is a collection organized and planned for a definite end. Nothing in it is purposeless. Accession and discardure proceed hand in hand. Correlation and division of material advance together. Every process and method is subject to closest scrutiny and all are called upon to answer to the final test of efficiency. The real value of such a Library is its use; it is a tool. As a collection of books its value in the open market may not be

Reprinted from *Special Libraries* 3, no. 8 (October 1912), pp. 162–166 by Special Libraries Association. Web address (www.sla.org). D. N. Handy was the librarian of The Insurance Library Association of Boston, Massachusetts.

great. If sold at a forced sale it might not bring a fortune. But in its power to help and inspire those who make the business what it is, its value is incalculable.

The measure of this value is to be sought in increasing efficiency of personnel; wider outlook, clearer vision, firmer grasp, greater fortitude.

It would be pleasant to think of the precise manner in which a Library might entrench itself in business favor, until it became admittedly indispensable. Such an experience is not uncommon. Libraries there are today—adjuncts of successful business houses—which stand on a plane of equality with every other department; whose directors are in every sense advisers; whose position in importance and dignity yields precedence to none. They add efficiency to the entire staff, and by breadth and merit bring distinction to the business they serve.

But it is not my purpose to describe in detail the ways in which the Library may justify itself as an Asset of Business. Purposely I have confined myself to broad, general lines along which the argument may safely proceed.

The asset value of a Library is dependent upon a variety of conditions some of which are, but more of which are not within the control of the Library itself. Let us see what some of these conditions are:

Foremost among them, I should say, must be a condition of receptivity on the part of Business itself. If Business does not see fit to recognize the aid that the Library can bring to it, it will be useless for the Library to try to force itself upon Business.

Again, and only second in importance is the attitude of the Library towards Business. If the Library shall cling to traditional aims; shall overestimate the importance of conventional methods; shall hold disdainfully aloof from those adaptations and changes which alone can make it useful to business, then its asset value will never be large or general.

Finally, assuming Business and the Library agree as to their mutual helpfulness, the lines along which they are to co-operate, if the results are to be satisfying to both, must be susceptible of being easily seen and followed. We shall try in the time that remains, to consider briefly the problems which these introductory paragraphs suggest.

At no time in the history of the modern business world, has the opportunity been so favorable for a lasting alliance between the Library and Business. Business was never more complex, nor more moral. Greater wisdom is required to develop it. It is more sensitive. Results come quicker: failure follows more promptly on the heels of error—success almost anticipates the footsteps of sound judgment. Consequences are more far reaching. Disaster to one involves many—while bankruptcy carries overthrow and panic to hundreds of others.

The greater demands of Business are seen not only in the enormous growth of industrial enterprises, and the larger responsibilities of management, but in the increasing numbers of college and university men who are seeking business careers. Our leading universities, recognizing this field are organizing their own activities to cultivate it, so that in Harvard, Dartmouth, Ann Arbor and other great colleges and universities in the States, we have courses in business administration leading in some cases to business degrees.

Business itself is awakening to a sense of its need and is not only aiding colleges and universities in their work, but in many cases is blazing new trails on its own account.

In England for some years the Insurance Institute of Great Britain and Ireland has provided courses of instruction in insurance. In the United States of America four years ago was organized The Insurance Institute of America, a conference body representing insurance men all over the country, which has for its main purpose the planning of courses in insurance, and the holding periodically of examinations. All with a view to the better training of young men in this field. It is done in recognition of the larger demands of present day business.

Again, an almost revolutionary change has taken place in the public attitude towards Business of every kind. It matters not what it is. The idea now is that men live for service; that men organize socially, commercially, and industrially for service. And if any organization is unable to undergo this test it must reform, or stand aside and let a better take its place. This I take it, is the interpretation of the great unrest which has possessed England and America in the last decade.

This means Business organized on a bigger and better scale—organized more efficiently and more morally. Organized not on caprice but on law—conducted not in the spirit of careless opportunism, but of social righteousness. Corporate business is coming back to the same sense of social responsibility that characterized private business when every employer treated his employe and his patron as a friend and neighbor.

All these—this increasing complexity, growing sense of social responsibility, demand for and increasing inflow of college men into business—spell opportunity for the Library as an indispensable adjunct of business enterprise. Answering for our first condition, then, it may be said that Business *is* in a *receptive* mood, and that it stands ready today, to welcome among its productive forces the Library organization.

But if the Library is to be truly an asset to Business enterprise, the Library itself must recognize not only its opportunity but its responsibility. The failure of the general library to lead in this work of aiding business in the solution of its problems has been inevitable. The general library aims at popular service. It is the popular subscription which maintains it. And the satisfaction of a popular constituency in any city of from 25,000 to a million of inhabitants, will take the most liberal budget. Business wants its own technology; it wants pamphlets, clippings, reports—all sorts of special things which no public library with all its other obligations could ever hope to get and to classify.

Hence, the need of specialized libraries and special methods. It is evident that the Special Library has a whole field of methods yet to amplify, systematize, and unify.

If the Library is to help Business, it must be organized as Business is organized. It must be alert, systematic, sacrificing many times scholarship and thoroughness to speed, clearly seeing the fact that adequacy of information is the thing and organizing its means to that end. To get everything on a subject may be necessary for some purposes, and is always interesting to the bibliographer; but to get the *adequate* thing is the Business-librarian's ideal of service, and if he misses it he may wake up surprised to find his labor unappreciated. Superficial? It may be so. But it should be remembered that we Business Librarians labor to get results and not for the sake of laboring. We apply methods to accomplish ends, not to enjoy the precision of the methods.

Here the general Librarian is likely to slip into pitfalls. He cannot always understand why, if the system says go through A, B, C, and D to E, he should be asked a dozen times a day to skip B, C, and D, a jump from A to E direct. But if the library is to serve Business it must do so, or it will not receive much consideration. Business is multiplying short-cuts, motion-savers, "efficiency" getters in every department: it will tolerate nothing less from the Library. It is for the Library to prove its value—to demonstrate its practical worth by adjusting itself to the business environment. It must not follow too closely the traditions of general library work. It ought to be familiar with general library methods; but it should never lose sight of the fact that general library methods were devised with an eye single to general library problems. The problems of a business library are different.

This, then, is the duty of the business library if the title to Asset-value is to go unchallenged. And the library may be certain that Business will not take it at its own appraisal but will demand to see for itself whether its claims are justified.

It is pleasing to feel that under conditions of handicap and often of inadequate support, Business Libraries in many cities are justifying their existence and are gradually making for themselves a secure place among the assets of the enterprises which they represent. So much for the second condition of our thesis.

Finally, how are the Library and Business to co-operate for their mutual advantage.

It is evident that in this respect Business has to perform a duty even greater than we have laid upon the Library itself. If the Library is under obligation to adapt itself to the needs of business, Business is under special obligation to place its resources more completely at the disposal of the Library. It must take the Library seriously and plan for it accordingly.

The library as a tool needs to be made more effective. Because many business men who have caught the vision of an efficient management of business have failed to see the part the printed page is to play in its realization, libraries still lag far behind business offices in adequacy of organization.

Business organizes for results. To get them it concentrates responsibility: coordinates supervisory functions; supplies the material and moral means of achievement. It has superintendents, and foremen: chief clerks and assistants; stenographers and filing clerks; messengers and office boys. As methods develop, more attention is given to details. Specialization increases. No man's time is allowed to be wasted. Time is the great factor. The office boy may dawdle; but the man at the head of the machine may not—he must be isolated and apart. Everything comes to him. His vital forces are conserved for the main work in hand.

So all along the line, each man according to his importance is surrounded by system—the orderly unfolding of the day's routine—intended to shield him from confusion and distractions that his mind may be concentrated on his work.

Except here and there, no business Library has anything approaching such organization as this. Library work is one of unceasing detail. It is one, too, requiring constant supervision. It should be given the means for its development.

Business fails to appreciate the ally that it might have in the well conducted library. It appreciates and at times is mildly grateful for the Library's service; but it has shown no great discernment when it came to an understanding of the means by which the service was rendered. It asks for and expects results; but has little appreciation of the price at which results must be bought.

The manager, pressed for time, impatiently demands information which only an expert can place before him, and wonders why it is not more readily given. He seldom faces the facts. If he did the answer would be forthcoming. He has spent money on a few books, periodicals, pamphlets, and newspaper clippings and scampingly on a librarian, thinking that somehow under pressure, this combination will tell him the things he wants to know.

Of course it will do nothing of the kind. A Library so organized will never become an asset of any business. And so long as it is organized in this way, it will be a *liability*—the target each year for criticism and the first to suffer cuts in the budget.

An indispensable requisite of a Business library is a librarian thoroughly conversant with the main facts of the business. He must know its theory and history. He must be freed from routine at least to the extent necessary to enable him to become an expert in the materials which he handles. He must be treated as a literary adviser and given the opportunity to develop literary discrimination and judgment in the field which he covers. Then he becomes more than a custodian of books: he is a counselor, impressing his personality upon a unique source of business inspiration, namely, the business literature of his collecting, and bringing direct to his superiors the information which they will know how to use for the good of the business as a whole.

Subordinates, working under him, will assemble, classify, card index, bulletin, and distribute, while the Library itself will stand on a level with manufacturing, accounting, and selling. It will be a department of the business, organized like other departments for efficiency.

This principle is being recognized more and more. Many of the larger business libraries have developed around the office desk of an executive whose business it was to handle the theories connected with the business. In some of the large life insurance companies vast collections have grown up about the actuarial office, usually the result of one man's enthusiasm. In other lines of business it has been in the publicity department that the Library has had its beginning, where the demand for the literature of the business and for publicity literature was most pressing.

In each case the necessity for an expert in the literature in question, to supervise its collection, has been naturally recognized. But in any case, these all resolve themselves into questions of organization and financing, questions which in the final analysis Business alone can answer.

The Library may adapt itself to Business, but it is for Business to say whether the adaptation shall be thorough going and effective.

Is the Library then, *a business asset?* My answer is that it is such, just in proportion as Business is willing to let it be. When Business shall treat it as it treats other factors of business success, discerning its possibilities of usefulness, encouraging and planning for its development, adapting it to the requirements of business activity, then it will justify itself unquestionably.

But it is for Business to make of it what it will. It can be a tool with which work may be done, or a burden requiring the loss of energy carrying it. The Library cannot answer the question alone.

When Business shall frankly admit that result-getting from the printed page is as much a practical possibility as result-getting from forces which business has always accustomed itself to use, then the machinery by which the printed page shall be assembled and made available for business uses will be set in motion and the Special or Business Library will come into its own.

I would not have you suppose that I regard this as wholly a problem of the future. Business has already awakened to the possibilities of Library help, and wherever it has done so with insight and courage it has answered for itself the question which we have here proposed. In banking, in finance, in engineering, in applied chemistry, in insurance, and in numerous other fields, Business has set itself to the task of adapting Library methods to business needs. Special collections administered for special requirements are springing up in every large city, and the liberality with which these are beginning to be supported is in some respects an indication of Business's own estimate of their value.

DISCUSSION

F. N. Morton

Mr. Handy, in his paper says, "Business fails to appreciate the ally that it might have in the well conducted library. It appreciates and at times is mildly grateful for the library's service."

There is, unfortunately, a reason for this lukewarmness, and one for which the library, no matter how efficient, is not responsible. Take for example, an engineering concern such as that with which I am connected. The contracting and construction department shows by the cash profit at the end of the year its value to the company. Similarly, the operating department shows by the lessened cost of production per unit of output, its value as an asset. The library, on the other hand, by producing a few lines in a periodical or reference book may save the company from a costly error; but this does not show upon the balance sheet and is forgotten accordingly—until the next time. This is a handicap under which reference libraries have labored in the past and under which they will work for some time to come.

The foregoing may seem to indicate a pessimistic view on my part, but this is not the case. The fact that firms and corporations are extending more and more their libraries, and are spending more and more their money upon them, both directly and indirectly, shows that an awakening is taking place and that the asset value of libraries is becoming appreciated. Hard headed corporations do not spend money on liabilities except, possibly, to turn them into assets. The library is coming into its own and will, in the not very distant future, be appreciated according to its merits. It will never be able to show a balance on the year's profit and loss statement any more than does the legal department in which, like the library, all is disbursement and nothing is receipt, but it will assume a standing comparable therewith; and there is no question as to the recognition of the standing of the legal department.

In our own case the consultation part of our work is continually on the increase, and the department is becoming, not only a bureau of information on the past history of the branches covered, but a general source of information on all subjects. In fact, much of the information needed does not exist in written or printed form at all, but has to be supplied by the knowledge and training of the librarian and his staff. I do not mean that the library is often called upon to decide in matters entirely of judgment: this would be resented, and very properly, by those whose positions keep them in immediate and direct contact with the work under consideration, although in these cases the library is consulted as to what has been done in the past under similar conditions. The particular function of which I speak is to produce incontrovertible facts. For example, information C is needed. This does not exist as far as the available literature is concerned. Reliable experiment has, however, determined A, and the laws B of chemistry or physics, are known. By combining these and making the proper calculations, C may be deduced. The library has A and B, determines C and gives the exact information desired without trouble to the one asking the question. The latter, left to his own resources might know A or B; the fact that he does not know C shows that he does not know both A and B.

An instance may be cited as an illustration. The department was asked the horsepower that would be required to compress a million cubic feet of natural gas an hour to 300 lbs. per square inch. First, the ratio of the specific heats at constant volume and at constant temperature respectively, had to be looked up. This might be called A. Then from the formula for the power required to compress gas with an allowance for the efficiency of the compressor (B) the required power, or C, was calculated. In this case, the inquirer did not know either A or B.

Among the subjects upon which the library has proved itself an asset, were information affecting the validity of franchise of patents both of our own and of others, processes of manufacture, past experiences in the art, recent progress applicable to our conditions, information regarding legal and commission decisions, and many others which can hardly be classified in a general list of this sort.

To give in brief an idea of the asset value of the special library. I should say that, by records of the past, its saves the expense of errors in the present, and points the way to economic developments in the future.

R. H. Pack, Toronto Electric Light Co. (Discussion by letter)

I am a great believer in special libraries being maintained by large corporations, and I do not know of any better way to make additions to this library, in order to keep thoroughly up to date, than by keeping in close touch with an Association such as yours. Through the medium of your magazine, "Special Libraries," we have more than once been enabled to obtain copies of some book or of or some report or pamphlet which we have found of the greatest value.

Even in this day of great mergers and combinations, competition in business is very keen, if not to keep business from a rival concern, at least to produce a better article in a more efficient and economical way than has been done before. For this reason it is highly important that the members of an organization of a modern Company should be kept thoroughly posted in regard to the very latest developments in their business.

I suppose this applies even more particularly to the business of public service corporations in which the political factor entered to such a great extent, and speaking from my own point of view, I am satisfied that if public service corporations had sooner grasped the political and economic questions involved in their business and had properly applied the knowledge thus gained, there would not today exist to the same extent, public dissatisfaction with large corporations.

The cost of keeping up a special library is not great, and I feel that the work of your Association in providing references so helpful to the maintenance and upbuilding of these special libraries is excellent in every way.

8

Valuing Corporate Libraries: A Survey of Senior Managers

James M. Matarazzo, Laurence Prusak, and
Michael R. Gauthier

PREFACE

This study summarizes the opinions expressed by senior-level managers at 164 corporations about their libraries and information centers and the information specialists who run them. By presenting this information in a concise report, the investigators have provided data useful for planning and strategy development by members of the Special Libraries Association.

The report emphasizes the importance of *disseminating information* from company libraries and information centers. Also highlighted is the need to develop and deliver effective services, especially those services that both respond to user needs and meet the overall goals of the organization. These key results bring to mind a thought Peter Drucker expressed in the *Wall Street Journal*:

> *The information-based organization does not require advanced "information technology." All it requires is a willingness to ask who requires what information, when and where.*

Like all good research, the investigation raises questions that call for additional research, suggests new explorations, and proposes possible solutions to some of the problems identified. For example, the study notes that only three of the librarians at these 164 library/information centers report to an individual who has some background in library and information science. The finding thus raises questions about the career paths of information managers. Similarly, the senior-

Reprinted from James Matarazzo, Laurence Prusak, and Michael R. Gauthier. *Valuing Special Libraries: A Survey of Senior Managers* © 1990 Special Libraries Association, Washington, DC. James M. Matarazzo is a professor in the Graduate School of Library and Information, Simmons College, Boston, Massachusetts. Laurence Prusak and Michael R. Gauthier are principals at Temple, Barker & Sloane, Inc., Lexington, Massachusetts.

level managers interviewed heap praise on librarians and the roles libraries play, yet we know that salaries paid to librarians lag those paid to other types of information specialists in corporations. Why this occurs should be the focus for future research, as should other topics raised by the findings reported.

The results of the study thus should stimulate the reader to ask additional questions as well as present him or her with the realities and possibilities evident for libraries and information centers in a dynamic and ever-changing corporate sector.

The Special Libraries Association is deeply indebted to James Matarazzo and Laurence Prusak for the investigative research they undertook. Their contribution to the literature of our profession is most significant.

—David R. Bender, Ph.D., Executive Director, Special Libraries Association

ACKNOWLEDGMENTS

The authors acknowledge with gratitude the assistance of the following individuals: Carolyn D. Schroeder, Technical Librarian, Storage and Information Management Group, Digital Equipment Corporation; Debra Maher, Associate, Temple, Barker & Sloane, Inc.; Deborah Smith-Cohen, Assistant Librarian, U.S. Army Cold Regions Research & Engineering Laboratory; Mark Gabriel, Design Manager, Temple, Barker & Sloane, Inc.; Katherine C. Teele, Designer, Temple, Barker & Sloane, Inc.; and Donna B. Doucette, Analytical Editor, Temple, Barker & Sloane, Inc. Additional assistance on this project was received from Linda Willey, Robert P. Rich, and Sherry Roess.

We also thank Dr. David R. Bender, Executive Director of the Special Libraries Association, for his support and assistance with this project from its inception.

The survey was made possible by a grant from the Special Programs Fund (1987) of the Special Libraries Association and a matching grant from Temple, Barker & Sloane, Inc., a management consulting firm based in Lexington, Massachusetts. Additional funds were received from the Emily Hollowell Research Fund at the Simmons College Graduate School of Library and Information Science, Mr. Richard Goldberg, and CLSI.

We would like to thank the following firms for participating in the survey:

Abbott Laboratories
Aetna Life & Casualty
Agway, Inc.
Air Products & Chemicals, Inc.
Alberto-Culver Co.
Alexander & Alexander Services, Inc.
Allied-Signal, Inc.
Alumax, Inc.
Aluminum Company of America
Amax, Inc.

Amerada Hess Corp.
American Express Co.
American International Group, Inc.
American Management Systems, Inc.
American Telephone & Telegraph Co.
Ametek, Inc.
AMP, Inc.
Anheuser-Busch, Inc.
Apple Computer, Inc.
Archer-Daniels-Midland Co.
Armstrong Rubber Co.
Armstrong World Industries, Inc.
Avon Products, Inc.
The B. F. Goodrich Co.
Bain & Company
Ball Corp.
Bell Atlantic Corp.
Bethlehem Steel Corp.
The Boeing Company
Boise Cascade Corp.
Borg-Warner
Braxton Associates
Campbell Soup Co.
CBS, Inc.
Chesebrough-Pond's, Inc.
Chi Systems
Cincinnati Milacron, Inc.
The Coca-Cola Co.
Columbia Gas Systems Service Corp.
Combustion Engineering, Inc.
Commonwealth Edison Co.
Compaq Computer Corp.
Computer Sciences Corp.
Consolidated Edison Co. of New York
Consumers Power Co.
Contel Corp.
Continental Illinois National Bank & Trust Co.
Control Data Corp.
Coopers & Lybrand
Cray Research, Inc.
Cubic Corp.
Data General Corp.
Dayton Hudson Corp.
Deere & Co.
Deluxe Check Printers, Inc.

Digital Equipment Corporation
Dow Chemical Co.
Dow Corning Corp.
Dow Jones & Co., Inc.
E-Systems, Inc.
Eastman Kodak Co.
Eaton Corp.
Ecolab, Inc.
Eli Lilly & Co.
Englehard Corp.
Equifax, Inc.
Ernst & Whinney
Ethyl Corp.
Farmland Industries, Inc.
Federated Department Stores
Fluor Daniel, Inc.
General Dynamics Corp.
General Mills, Inc.
General Motors Corp.
General Public Utilities Corp.
Georgia-Pacific Corp.
Gillette Co.
Goldman, Sachs & Co.
GTE Corp.
Gulf States Utilities Co.
Harvest States Cooperatives
Helene Curtis Industries, Inc.
Henkel Process Chemicals, Inc.
Hercules, Inc.
Hewitt Associates
Hospital Corporation of America
Ingersoll-Rand Co.
Inland Steel Co.
Intel Corp.
International Paper Co.
Irving Trust Co.
ITT Corp.
James River Corporation
John Hancock Mutual Life Insurance Co.
Johnson & Johnson
Johnson Controls, Inc.
Kemper Corporation
Kerr-McGee Corp.
Ketchum Communications, Inc.
Kline & Co., Inc.

Land O'Lakes, Inc.
Laventhal & Horwath
Lockheed Corp.
Loral Electro-Optical Systems, Inc.
Manville Sales Corp.
Marmon Corp.
Marriott Corp.
Massachusetts Mutual Life Insurance Co.
May Department Stores
McDonnell Douglas Corp.
McGraw-Hill, Inc.
MCI Communications Corp.
Mead Corp.
Mead Data Central, Inc.
Media General, Inc.
Medtronic, Inc.
Mercer-Meidinger-Hansen
Metropolitan Life Insurance Co.
Minnesota Mining & Manufacturing Co.
Monsanto Co.
Moore Business Forms, Inc.
Morrison-Knudsen Co., Inc.
Motorola, Inc.
Mutual Benefit Life Insurance Co.
National Semiconductor Corp.
Nationwide Advertising Services, Inc.
Navistar International Corp.
NBD Bancorp, Inc.
NCR Corp.
New York Times Co.
NL Industries, Inc.
Northeast Utilities
Noxell Corp.
NYNEX Corp.
Occidental Chemical Corp.
Ogden Food Products Corp.
Ogilvy & Mather
Ohio Edison Co.
PACCAR, Inc.
Pacific Resources, Inc.
Pennwalt Corp.
Philip Morris, Inc.
PPG Industries, Inc.
Prudential Insurance & Financial Services
Rockwell International Corp.

Rohm & Haas Co.
Rorer Group, Inc.
Safeway Stores, Inc.
Scott Paper Co.
Sears, Roebuck & Co.
Security Pacific National Bank
Sherwin-Williams Co.
A. E. Staley Manufacturing Co.
Stanley Consultants, Inc.
Sunkist Growers, Inc.
Texas Eastern Corp.
Thom McAn
TRW, Inc.
Union Carbide Corp.
Unisys Corp.
Varian Associates
Wal-Mart Stores, Inc.
Warner-Lambert Co.
Wells Fargo & Co.

INTRODUCTION

The Special Libraries Association, in a report from its Task Force on the Value of the Information Professional, highlighted a need for additional research on how the corporate world values information. Specifically, the task force recommended a study of the value placed by senior executives on both the information professional and the corporate library/information center. We conducted this survey in response to that recommendation. The survey focused on two issues: emerging trends for special libraries, and how the work traditionally associated with those libraries is valued. We hope our findings will help corporate librarians in formulating plans and strategies.

The Survey Sample

In conducting the survey, we followed an approach different from that commonly found in today's self-referential professional literature. Rather than interview the librarians, we interviewed those individuals to whom the heads of libraries report. In this way, we sought to obtain objective evidence that corporations value libraries and information centers.

The corporate officials interviewed represented different functions and had different titles. The most common functions reported were finance and administration, marketing, and information services. Titles ranged from manager to senior vice president.

The survey sample of 164 companies was developed from an in-house analysis based on contributions of for-profit sectors to the Gross National Product (GNP). In this way, we obtained a sample approximating the contributions of each major sector of the GNP and representing the spectrum of American business and industry. We also avoided undue concentration on "information intensive" industries or, conversely, on struggling industries or those with libraries under obvious survival pressures. The interview list has a range and balance that reflects the scope of business in the United States.

The largest firms in each GNP sector were selected for interviews. We chose the larger companies because they were deemed more likely to have a fully functioning library and to have used those services for some reasonable period of time. This methodology seemed best, since we sought thoughtful and seasoned commentary from those interviewed. Our expectations were borne out by the respondents. Because the executives selected for interviews frequently have the task of justifying the library to upper management, many already had given some thought to our questions and were well prepared to answer them.

EXECUTIVE SUMMARY AND CONCLUSIONS

The survey findings characterized the current position of corporate libraries as follows:

The typical corporate library is a centralized unit staffed with fewer than five full-time employees. It is designed to identify, acquire, and disseminate information. Users of these libraries place the highest value of service on database searching as a means of information delivery. The most frequent user groups are in marketing/sales and technical departments. While the development of effective services is rated highly, there is little consensus on which of the library services brings the most value to the firm or on how to evaluate the library's impact.

On the basis of the comments we received during the course of the interviews, as well as an analysis of the data, we have concluded that:

- Librarians evaluate their performance based on standardized library methodologies. Their managers use far different, and often subjective, evaluation criteria.
- There is little managerial consensus on how the library adds specific value to the firm's performance or how value should be measured.
- Librarians have little say on the firm's information policies and mission. Few respondents could state what exact function the library performs within the firm's information structure.
- Growing end-user usage of database systems and other information technologies will have a serious impact on business operations as well as on

the role of the library within the firm. Will the librarian perform as purchasing agent, gatekeeper, network manager, internal trainer, information specialist, or chief information officer? Librarians and their managers have done very little planning on this critical issue.

• There is still a strong reservoir of goodwill and affection for the library and librarians—often based on an intuitive "feel" that the service is valuable and worthy of continued support. However, in the increasingly volatile business climate, it is questionable whether libraries can grow based on these forms of approval. Considerable work must be done to ensure future growth!

REASON FOR INITIAL ESTABLISHMENT

The need for quantitative and qualitative information and its subsequent identification and dissemination led companies to establish information centers. These reasons were cited more often than any others by the respondents in the survey [see Figure 8-1].

The responses also reveal a contradiction between the value sought from the centers and the methods of measuring the value received. For example, although no respondent cited cost control or employee productivity as a reason for establishment, libraries often are asked to justify themselves using such categories. The contradiction can perhaps be explained by the difficulties inherent in measuring qualitative factors.

Relatively few respondents cited analysis of data as a reason for establishment, indicating a need for improving library capabilities in this area. Librarians are rarely viewed as analysts; the acquisition, organization, and dissemination of information do not imply that librarians possess the knowledge or skills needed

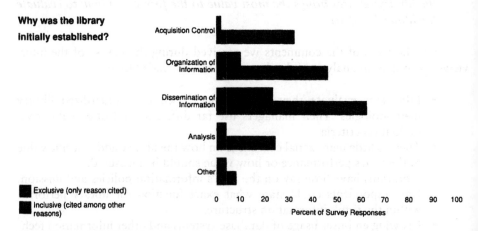

FIGURE 8-1 Why Was the Library Initially Established?

for data analysis. Adding these skills, where appropriate, would enhance the value of the libraries/information centers. Further research on this issue should be conducted to help librarians develop services and products in this area.

LIBRARY SERVICE ORGANIZATION

No common organizational mode emerged among the libraries at the 164 companies surveyed, although use of a central library—with or without satellites or archives—proved to be relatively typical [see Figure 8-2]. Thirty-one percent of the companies have a central library with satellites, 24 percent maintain only a central library, and 20 percent support a central library with an archive. In addition to those with central libraries, 20 percent of the companies reported using only satellite libraries, and 5 percent have libraries serving a small unit or individual, or collecting only a specific form of literature.

SIZE OF STAFF

Staff size among the special libraries is weighted clearly toward the small. The majority (55 percent) of the libraries and information centers in the survey have staffs of five full-time equivalents or fewer [see Figure 8-3]. Another 21 percent have staffs of 6 to 10 full-time equivalents. Libraries/information centers

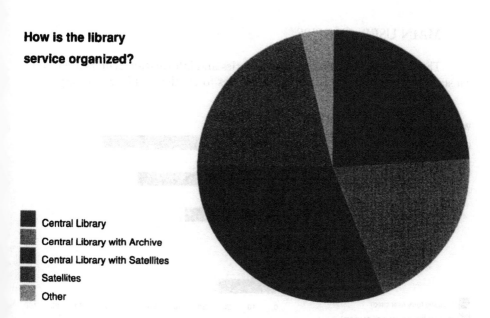

How is the library service organized?

- Central Library
- Central Library with Archive
- Central Library with Satellites
- Satellites
- Other

FIGURE 8-2   How Is the Library Service Organized?

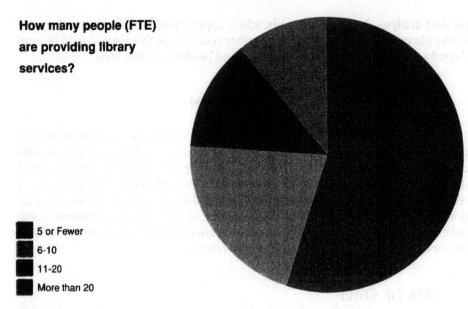

How many people (FTE) are providing library services?

Legend:
- 5 or Fewer
- 6-10
- 11-20
- More than 20

FIGURE 8-3   How Many People (FTE) Are Providing Library Services?

with staff sizes of 11 to 20 accounted for 13 percent of those surveyed, and 11 percent reported staffs of more than 20 full-time equivalents.

MAIN USER GROUPS

The primary users of corporate libraries and information centers are technical staffs [see Figure 8-4]. Marketing and sales forms the next largest group of us-

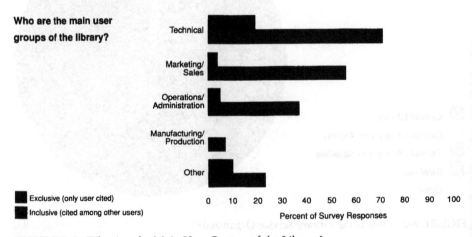

Who are the main user groups of the library?

User groups:
- Technical
- Marketing/Sales
- Operations/Administration
- Manufacturing/Production
- Other

Legend:
- Exclusive (only user cited)
- Inclusive (cited among other users)

X-axis: 0 10 20 30 40 50 60 70 80 90 100
Percent of Survey Responses

FIGURE 8-4   Who Are the Main User Groups of the Library?

ers, followed by operations/administration (which includes use of law and tax libraries). Such results should surprise no one.

Among the user types cited in the "other" category were systems/MIS personnel, investor relations staffs, and a separate "CEO library."

CRITERIA FOR EVALUATING LIBRARIES

No criterion used to evaluate libraries received even a 40 percent plurality in the survey responses, but "quality of information" seems to be the single most important component [see Figure 8-5]. In addition to citing quality as an important criterion, the respondents frequently mentioned other issues related to service quality, such as accuracy and timeliness (summarized as "other").

Interestingly, a substantial proportion of the respondents declared that they had no procedures for measuring the value of the library. This issue should be studied further, given that the library is often perceived as a "discretionary" business need rather than as an essential operation such as accounting.

Libraries face an additional problem because they lack formal measurements for evaluation. In other operations, the labor/management ratios, productivity measures, and even sales volumes can be used to determine "value." But libraries often exist simply because a firm is so information-intensive that it could not survive without a library, or because a CEO or other highly placed individual argued for its establishment and insists on its maintenance. Without formal value measurements, the library may face difficulties in justifying its continued existence, especially if the individual who argued for and defended the library leaves the firm or transfers to another operational area.

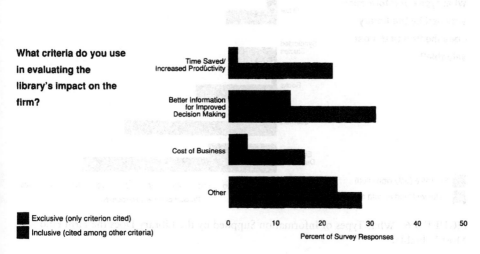

What criteria do you use in evaluating the library's impact on the firm?

- Time Saved/ Increased Productivity
- Better Information for Improved Decision Making
- Cost of Business
- Other

■ Exclusive (only criterion cited)
■ Inclusive (cited among other criteria)

0   10   20   30   40   50
Percent of Survey Responses

FIGURE 8-5 What Criteria Do You Use in Evaluating the Library's Impact on the Firm?

MOST VALUABLE TYPES OF INFORMATION

Print materials still show good value, but databases are valued more highly [see Figure 8-6]. Almost 80 percent of the survey respondents cited database searching as a key service.

The increased importance of databases presents some potential problems for librarians because it leads to increased pressure for end-user searching. Vendors promote the end-user-initiated search for commercial reasons; end users, especially those with computer knowledge, often see no need for an intermediary to do the searches. In some fast-paced environments, the use of a librarian can be viewed as a hindrance—a gatekeeper who adds little value in the database search.

The practice of letting end-user searching occur has proven on occasion to be quite expensive to firms, due to seriously inexperienced and ill-trained searchers. In several cases, the firms eliminated the practice and went back to giving the library the monopoly on database searching. However, more frequent and better training by vendors, consultants, and librarians may make this practice more viable.

Cutting costs and boosting efficiency should be an integral part of librarians' efforts to demonstrate the value of using an intermediary in database searches. In validating the intermediary's role, librarians should stress the following:

- The increased proliferation of databases and the problems in choosing the right one
- The need to apply specialized skills to the search process, which is more than simply following procedures
- The need for in-depth knowledge of database pricing to control costs

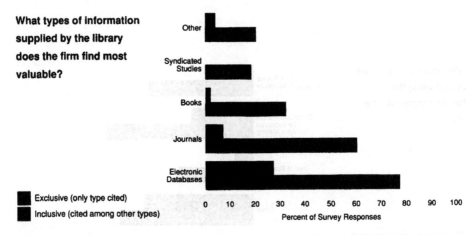

FIGURE 8-6 What Types of Information Supplied by the Library Does the Firm Find Most Valuable?

VALUE OF SERVICES

Librarians usually spend considerable amounts of money, and management must have a clear vision as to what the organization receives for that investment. Management does not ask, "How good is the library?" It asks, "How much good does the library do?" On the basis of the responses to this survey, librarians must do much more to demonstrate value.

When asked to say which library services added the most value to the company, nearly two-thirds of the respondents either did not know or chose not to respond [see Figure 8-7]. This lack of knowledge is especially serious because these individuals not only exercise management control over the libraries but also are the chief evaluators of the library manager and services. These same individuals also may be asked to justify library budgets and to defend against any proposals to reduce library expenditures. Some remedial efforts toward demonstrating the value of specific services would seem prudent, given the survey responses. Perhaps the library manager should conduct appropriate studies, then convey those results to upper management.

VALUE OF THE LIBRARIAN

Librarians generally rated high in the five major categories assessed for the survey. More than 70 percent of the respondents rated the librarians high in devel-

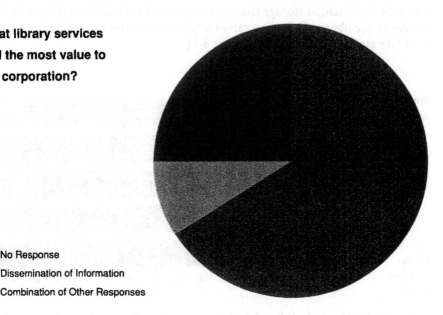

What library services add the most value to the corporation?

- No Response
- Dissemination of Information
- Combination of Other Responses

FIGURE 8-7 What Library Services Add the Most Value to the Corporation?

oping effective services, delivering effective services, and responding to changing needs [see Figure 8-8]. More than 60 percent gave the librarians high ratings in making the company's staff productive.

Ratings on controlling expenditures were lower, although still relatively favorable: More than 40 percent of the respondents rated librarians high in this category, and those who gave them lower ratings acknowledged that librarians cannot control all the related costs. This lack of control may occur because others, such as the controller's office, make the financial decisions. Or it may occur because library expenses run below expenses for other functions, so that cost control is deemed less vital in libraries than elsewhere.

Comments on the survey questions indicated the importance of developing and delivering effective services. Some respondents pointed out that added value comes in the development of customized services, not in the creation of menu-type selections. The services deemed important include those customized and tailored for specific users or specific divisions within the company.

EMERGING TRENDS

The respondents showed a clear appreciation of the growing importance of information technology for corporate libraries. That appreciation, in turn, influenced other responses. For example, an expectation that corporate staff would grow with no concurrent growth in library size can be explained by the increasing use of information technologies rather than the more space-consuming print products. Information storage space can be created without increasing the physical size of the library. That expectation might also explain the anticipated growth in library staffs and budgets [see Figure 8-9].

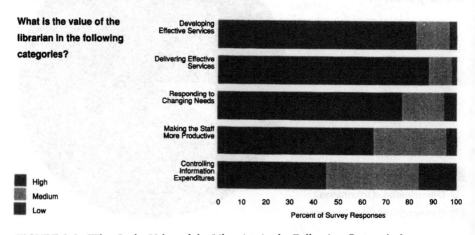

FIGURE 8-8   What Is the Value of the Librarian in the Following Categories?

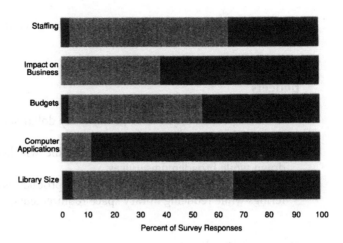

What trends do you see in corporate libraries over the next five years in terms of staffing, budgets, computer applications, library size, and general impact on the operations of the business?

FIGURE 8-9   What Trends Do You See in Corporate Libraries over the Next Five Years in Terms of Staffing, Budgets, Computer Applications, Library Size, and General Impact in the Operations of the Business?

The role of computer applications in libraries and information centers will also grow, leading to a potential recasting of current operations. For example, will the library become a function of and report to an MIS-type organization or directly to a CIO (Chief Information Officer)? Will librarians themselves aspire to CIO status?

RESPONDENTS' COMMENTS ON EMERGING TRENDS

The summary of comments we received on the question about emerging library trends provides a glimpse of other expectations. A sampling of these comments follows:

Staffing

- More end-user involvement will mitigate staff growth.
- Growing centralization and consolidation will reduce the number of separate libraries.

Impact on Business

- A library's impact grows when the library is strategically linked with other functions, such as marketing.

- Libraries will provide more value-added services and broaden their traditional services to increase impact.

Budgets

- Libraries will be required to justify every dollar spent based on real business needs.
- CD-ROM and full texts available on-line will help keep library costs down while broadening services.
- The ease of using CD-ROM technology products will enhance service offerings while reducing library space requirements.

Computer Applications

- More end-user involvement in database searching and retrieval can be expected.
- Awareness and use of new technologies will enhance the library's status.
- Librarians will be required to know more about business-related computer applications.

9

The Value of Corporate Libraries: Findings from a 1995 Survey Of Senior Management

James M. Matarazzo and Laurence Prusak

PARTICIPATING FIRMS

Abbott Laboratories
Aetna Life & Casualty Company
Air Products and Chemicals, Inc.
Alberto-Culver Company
Alexander and Alexander Services, Inc.
AlliedSignal, Inc.
Alumax, Inc.
Aluminum Corporation of America
American International Group
American Management Systems, Inc.
American Telephone & Telegraph
AMP, Inc.
Anheuser-Busch Companies, Inc.
Apple Computer, Inc.
Armstrong World Industries, Inc.
Asea Brown Boveri
Avon Products, Inc.
Bain & Company
Ball Corporation

Reprinted from James Matarazzo and Laurence Prusak. *The Value of Corporate Libraries: Findings from a 1995 Survey of Senior Management* © 1995 Special Libraries Association, Washington, DC. James M. Matarazzo is dean of the Graduate School of Library and Information Science, Simmons College, Boston, Massachusetts. Laurence Prusak is a principal with the Ernst & Young Center for Business Innovation, Boston, Massachusetts.

Bell Atlantic Corporation
Bethlehem Steel Corporation
B. F. Goodrich
Boeing Company
Boise Cascade Corporation
Braxton Associates
Campbell Soup Company
CBS Inc.
Chesebrough-Ponds, Inc.
Chi Systems
Cincinnati Milacron, Inc.
Coca-Cola Company
Commonwealth Edison
Compaq Computer Corporation
Consolidated Edison Co. of New York
Consumers Power Company
Coopers & Lybrand L.L.P.
Cray Research, Inc.
Data General Corporation
Dayton Hudson Corporation
Deere & Company
Deluxe Corporation
Digital Equipment Corporation
Dow Chemical Company
Dow Corning Corporation
Dow Jones & Company, Inc.
Eastman Kodak Company
Eaton Corporation
Eli Lilly and Company
Entergy Corporation
Equifax, Inc.
Ethyl Corporation
Fluor Corporation
General Electric Company
General Mills, Inc.
General Public Utilities Corporation
Gillette Company
Goldman Sachs Group, L.P.
GTE Corporation
Helene Curtis Industries, Inc.
Henkel Corporation
Hercules, Inc.
Hewitt Associates
Ingersoll-Rand Company
Inland Steel Industries, Inc.
Intel Corporation

International Paper Company
James River Corporation of Virginia
John Hancock Mutual Life Insurance Co.
Johnson Controls, Inc.
Kemper Corporation
Kerr-McGee Corporation
Ketchum Communications
Land O'Lakes, Inc.
Lexis-Nexis
Lockheed Corporation
Loral Corporation
Marriott International, Inc.
Massachusetts Mutual Life Insurance Co.
McDonnell Douglas Corporation
McGraw-Hill, Inc.
MCI Communications Corporation
Medtronic, Inc.
Minnesota Mining & Manufacturing
Monsanto Company
Motorola, Inc.
Nationwide Advertising Services, Inc.
Navistar International Corporation
NBD Bancorp, Inc.
New York Times Company
NL Industries, Inc.
NYNEX Corporation
Occidential Petroleum Corporation
Ohio Edison Company
Ogilvy & Mather
PACCAR, Inc.
Philip Morris Companies, Inc.
Rockwell International Company
Rohm & Haas Company
Schuller International
Sears, Roebuck and Co.
Sherwin-Williams Company
Warner Lambert Company
Wells Fargo & Company

ACKNOWLEDGMENTS

The authors acknowledge with gratitude the contributions of Sara Frost Schoman who, through countless hours devoted to phone interviews, was able to gather all the necessary data, and of Suzanne Dusseault, Librarian of the Ernst & Young Center for Business Innovation, for the analysis and summarization of the findings. Julia Kirby, Communications Director of the Ernst & Young Center for Business Innovation, also assisted by overseeing the design and production of this report. The project could not have been completed without their support.

We would also like to thank David R. Bender, Executive Director of the Special Libraries Association, and Tobi Brimsek, Assistant Executive Director of Information Services, who commissioned and encouraged this work. Our thanks to them for their tireless interest—and modest pressure on us to complete the work. Naturally, gratitude is also due to Simmons College and Ernst & Young for allowing us the time to survey and document the changing world of corporate libraries.

Our final and most profound thanks goes to the 103 senior managers who took the time to share their views with us. Their assistance, based on a shared conviction that the questions we asked really matter, has been the great reward of the work.

INTRODUCTION

It has been over five years since our last survey appeared on the perceived value of corporate libraries.[1] During that time, much has happened within business and its environment, which has had and will continue to have a strong influence on information professionals. The three most powerful of these external trends are:

- The growth of computing power and the expansion of network capabilities, including the Internet and the World Wide Web;
- A dramatic increase in target-marketing and sales of on-line products and services directly to end-users; and
- Massive corporate downsizing and reengineering.

These events have been accompanied by a level of hoopla and hand-wringing which makes it all the more difficult to gauge their impact. However, it is clear to us that the first two developments are of, at best, questionable advantage to librarians. The drastic decrease in price and rise in speed of computers allows IT expertise and experience to be widely dispersed within firms. Now, every manager with a budget is a target of innumerable vendors spreading an appealing (if deceiving) gospel: that every man and woman is a knowledge worker, and that all one needs to access the knowledge of the world is a computer and modem.

No profession knows as well as the librarian's the shallowness of this position; it leaves the whole issue of information expertise and quality out of the equation. However, only a little over twenty percent of the senior managers we surveyed listed reference services (which includes answering questions) as the most valued service the library performs. For librarians hoping to preserve their function's *distinctive* value in the new, wired-up world, much internal marketing and business case development will need to be done.

The great waves of downsizing and reengineering undergone by many of our surveyed firms has also put great pressure on librarians continuously to justify their activities and budgets in terms of *business value*. Unfortunately, there is no universally acknowledged way to make this case, as this survey shows. But the need to prove the library's worth will only continue to grow as a generation raised from childhood with computers assumes leadership of tomorrow's "lean and mean" enterprises.

Unfortunately, within the profession, life goes on as usual. In spite of exhortations to change, and some new ideas for doing so,[2] most librarians continue to operate in much the same way as when they started their careers. Responding to increased pressure, they fall into a predictable trap; working ever harder to do more of what they are doing, they fail to do the new and different things that would provide them with differentiation.

Reorienting the library to today's business realities begins with a simple shift in perspective. Top executives in service and manufacturing industries are realizing that their most important competitive asset is their organizational knowledge—that what they own is less important than what they know. Yet how many librarians focus on internal expertise and knowledge (as opposed to internal documents)? A new position, the Chief Knowledge Officer, is already appearing in many firms and will soon be commonplace. A potentially huge area of value exists here for libraries, untouched by the MIS department and other competing functions.

Meanwhile, those librarians who continue to focus primarily on acquisition and distribution of information, in paper or on-line form, will likely be absorbed into other functions (perhaps MIS), or be increasingly relegated to the sidelines of an exciting business environment. Either fate is too severe for such a smart and dedicated group, and one with such potential value.

A NOTE ON METHODOLOGY

In this study, we have attempted to better understand how US corporate libraries are valued by the senior management of the firms they serve. To achieve this goal, we sought the opinion of the individual, usually a director or vice president-level person, to whom the library manager reports. By focusing on those managers charged with providing corporate "cover" for the library, we expected to report an informed yet objective assessment.

We have for our survey chosen a large, diverse sample of corporate America, with the main bias being toward larger rather than smaller firms, given these firms' tradition of having a library. An effort was made to solicit input from firms that had responded to the last survey, several years ago: nearly three-quarters of the firms surveyed here also participated in that earlier survey. A list of participating firms is included [at the beginning] of this report. In all, 103 senior managers chose to respond.

Three points about the survey population are worth noting here:

- Only three interviewees had ever been librarians or had any library training.
- Of the approximately seventy-five percent of firms surveyed here that were also surveyed in the last survey, less than ten percent were repre-

sented by the same individual (*i.e.*, responsibility for oversight of the library had changed).

• Most target respondents were identified with the assistance of the librarians who, in facilitating access to their corporate management, expressed great interest in learning the results of the study.

The survey instrument was developed by the authors with input from sponsors at the Special Libraries Association. Given the overlap with the earlier survey population, some trend analysis was performed, as noted in the text accompanying each chart. In several cases, however, new questions were developed to reflect a changed business and library environment.

The majority of firms surveyed have small library staffs as compared with past years. Seventy-one percent now have staffs of five full-time employees or fewer [see Figure 9-1]. Another fourteen percent have staffs of six to fifteen full-

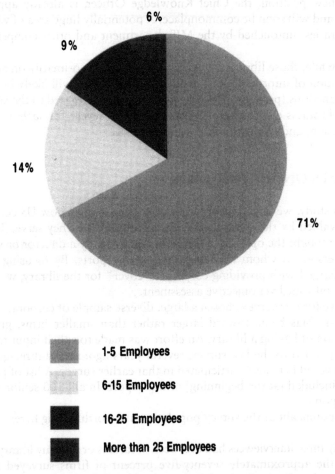

FIGURE 9-1   Number of Full-Time Employees in Libraries Surveyed

time employees; and nine percent have between sixteen and twenty-five employees. Libraries with staff sizes of more than twenty-five employees accounted for only six percent of those surveyed. These large staffs tend to be in firms marked by a tremendous amount of document acquisition and distribution, often in businesses that are information-intensive and subject to government regulation.

The average size of staffs shows a dramatic change from our last survey, when libraries with only one to five employees made up just fifty-five percent of the population. One possible explanation is a proliferation of libraries within firms. We know of many departments (especially in marketing functions) that now have dedicated library staffs, obviously smaller than the library tasked with supporting the whole business. Still, it would appear that, at least in terms of people, many libraries are being asked to do more with less. If so, the numbers point to the most critical question facing librarians today: if only five people are to be dedicated to improving the information environment of a large and diverse firm, how can they apply their time and effort to achieve maximum impact?

Even though corporate libraries tend to be small in terms of people, their budgets are growing by leaps and bounds. Fully two-thirds are now budgeting over $100,000 per year for library-related expenditures, and a good number of those (thirty percent of the total population) budget over $500,000 [see Figure 9-2]. An information-intensive eighteen percent reported spending over a million dollars! Interestingly, there was no correlation among the relative sizes of firms, library staffs, and library budgets. Largest spenders are not necessarily the biggest or most profitable of businesses. And neither does the number of librarians, beyond their salaries, seem to have a direct impact on expenditures. Indeed, many firms may incur higher costs for electronic information retrieval as they cut librarian headcounts.

One disappointment was the large number (twenty-six percent) of senior managers who were unable to make even a ballpark approximation of the library budget. Is this lack of awareness a symptom of indifferenceor worse, a failure on the part of library managers to make it a subject of discussion?

Evaluating the performance of the corporate library has never been a straightforward task. In the years since our last survey, no single standard of measurement has emerged as the best way to gauge the value of library activities to the business. In fact, in fifteen percent of the firms surveyed, evaluations appear to depend simply on the good will and intuition of the library's immediate corporate manager [see Figure 9-3].

Asked to identify the primary means used to assess the library's value, the largest number, at thirty-six percent, cited the use of annual surveys and informal feedback from users. Such surveys are primarily designed to rate products and services provided by the library, but also to give users the opportunity to state what they would like to see the library provide in the future.

The measure cited second most often (by twenty-five percent of respondents) was the volume of requests handled by the library. For most senior managers using this measure, the library's response time in dealing with these requests is also considered. Growing numbers of requests are seen as evidence of perceived value by the organization; faster response times indicate greater productivity.

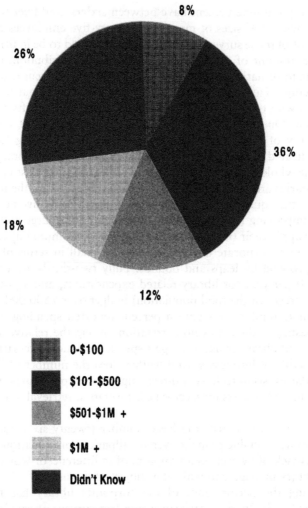

FIGURE 9-2   Annual Budgets of Libraries Surveyed

A few progressive managers prefer to think in terms of the leverage the library provides. Time-saving is the key for ten percent; if using the library allows busy, high-salaried employees more time to do their specialized work, the library's value is high. Seven percent look for even more direct cost savings. As some managers noted, the library is a great resource for identifying the least costly means of purchasing a product or service. Cost savings also accrue from centralizing the use of expensive information retrieval services, and placing them in the hands of skilled users. The same applies, on a lesser scale, to shared use of books and journals that might otherwise be bought separately by many individuals.

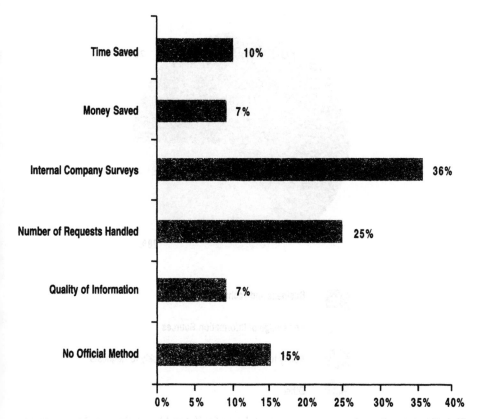

FIGURE 9-3 Methods and Approaches Used to Evaluate the Library's Value

Finally, only seven percent attempt to judge the library on the quality of information provided (including value added to publicly available information). This may have more to do with the difficulty of such assessments than with any preference not to make them.

What becomes a corporate librarian most? In the eyes of senior management, it would appear to be communications skills and speed [see Figure 9-4]. As opposed to their accumulated knowledge of either the business or the tools of their trade, librarians were valued by thirty-six percent of senior managers for their "ability to interpret and respond quickly to requests from users." Certainly, it is true that many, if not most, user requests cannot be simply taken at face value. Interpretation of complex needs must be done before they can be met with available resources. In delivering a response, too, librarians must be able to interpret or reformat information in such a way that it is easy to understand and as concise as possible.

Still, library work is not for the ignorant. Twenty-eight percent of respondents believe that librarians' most important competency is the area that is left to

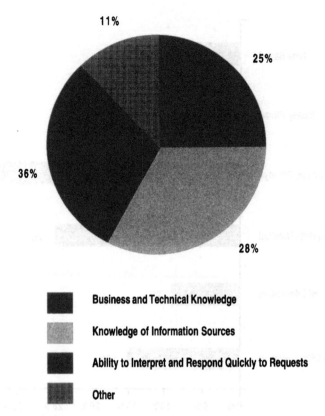

FIGURE 9-4 What Competencies of the Library Staff Are Most Valued by Management

their exclusive domain: the in-depth knowledge of information sources. What was deemed as useful was not simply the librarian's awareness of a broad range of sources, but more importantly, the knowledge of their respective strengths. The ability to identify the best source of information for a given request is critical.

Meanwhile, a good fourth of the population thinks that the business receives greatest value when the librarian has a real understanding of its specific content. Business and technical knowledge covers the firm's own services, products, processes, and performance—and also the broader industries and economies in which it competes. One theory is that librarians who have such understanding are better able to design and develop library services that anticipate the changing needs of the company.

The remaining eleven percent of answers were varied. Some managers chose not to respond or didn't know. Importantly, only a few responded that the most important competencies had to do with acquisition and storage of secondary materials.

Far and away, the most-valuable library service according to senior managers is the retrieval of information from on-line databases [see Figure 9-5]. Almost half (forty-eight percent) of those surveyed singled out this capability for praise—more than twice the number citing the second most popular offering, general reference services (twenty-two percent). Still, it is important to note that the managers placing greatest value on on-line database searches have seen a dramatic reduction in their ranks since the 1990 survey. At that time, seventy-eight percent called it the most valuable service. One force behind the decrease must certainly be the rise of networked databases. As more people gain desktop access to on-line services, and become more proficient in using them, the value of having the library conduct literature searches and retrieve necessary information falls.

This year's survey shows most of the defectors from the on-line camp shifting their support to general reference services, where they believe the library is still able to add unique value. Gains also occurred in other areas. Eleven percent valued "current awareness services," which place the library in a proactive role of providing information to users to keep them aware of what is changing in areas important to them and the business. Another ten percent responded that the circulation of journals and periodicals was the most valuable service (possibly because the cost-savings here are easiest to see). Not surprisingly, in this electronic age,

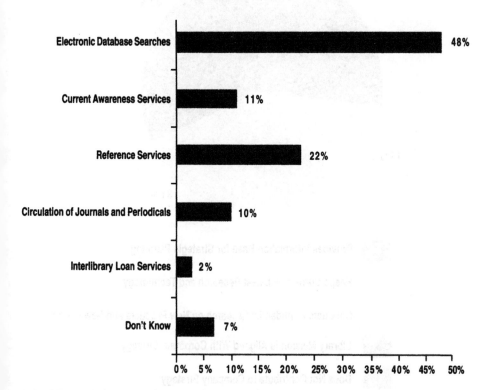

FIGURE 9-5 Library Products and Services Which Provide the Highest Value to Firms

only two percent placed highest value on the very non-virtual information access accomplished through interlibrary book loans.

Asked to characterize the relationship between the library's work and the strategic direction of the firm, most senior managers noted some level of influence. About three-quarters thought the library was contributing to formulation of strategy in some way by providing information valuable to the process [see Figure 9-6]. Only about a third, however, accorded it the highest influence of providing the information base used by management to make strategic decisions. A similar number (thirty-one percent) saw the library contributing to strategy mainly by keeping current on the latest research and technology that might bear on the firm's strategy. In eleven percent of firms, the library helps strategists by conducting confidential research on new products and services.

The relationship between library services and strategy works only in the opposite direction in thirteen percent of firms, where managers report that the li-

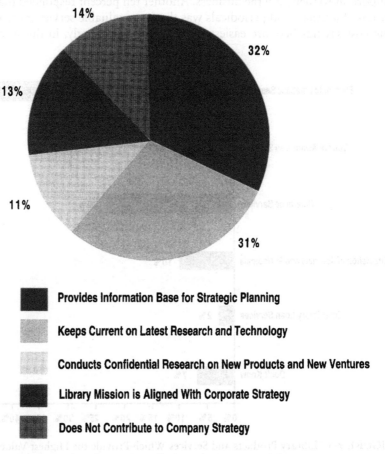

Provides Information Base for Strategic Planning

Keeps Current on Latest Research and Technology

Conducts Confidential Research on New Products and New Ventures

Library Mission is Aligned With Corporate Strategy

Does Not Contribute to Company Strategy

FIGURE 9-6 How Does the Library Contribute to the Strategy of the Firm?

brary simply falls into line with strategy already established, in order to keep its own services and products relevant. Fourteen percent saw no link between library activities and corporate strategy.

On the assumption that all corporate libraries perform basic acquisition, storage, and retrieval of secondary material, we asked senior managers to name an additional type of service provided by the library. Their responses make it clear that libraries are broadening their traditional focus to encompass more value-added services [see Figure 9-7]. Less than one-fifth of senior managers were unable to name any additional services.

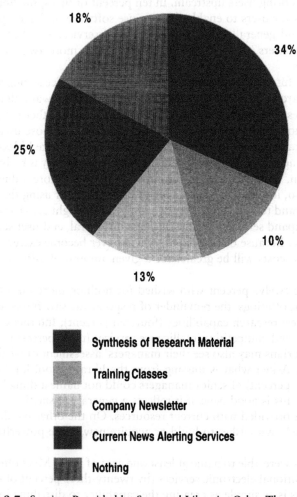

FIGURE 9-7 Services Provided by Surveyed Libraries Other Than Acquisition, Storage, and Retrieval of Secondary Material

In the majority of firms, additional library services are designed to take the library's information gathering and dissemination activities farther downstream. Synthesis of research material collected, for example, means it is presented to users in a more concise and directly relevant form. Rather than merely providing information, the librarian goes a step further to analyze it and make decisions on its value to the user. Thirty-four percent of senior managers observed this kind of synthesis occurring regularly.

Similarly, in a quarter of firms surveyed, libraries are going a step further in disseminating information by becoming proactive in their approach. Such proactivity generally takes the form of current news alerting services. Instead of waiting to respond to inquiries, these librarians recognize that, in many cases, users can't be expected to ask for information they don't know exists.

In some firms, the library has added services that don't so much push their work downstream as bring users upstream. In ten percent of firms, the library offers training sessions for users to enable them to use software packages, perform database searches, and generally engage in library self-service. Another thirteen percent publish newsletters (often electronic) to make users more aware of the library and its services.

Looking to the future, the majority of senior managers voice strong support for increasing the search power of the people: fifty-three percent want all users to have networked access to on-line databases [see Figure 9-8]. Another six percent cast their vote for more end-user training, presumably to make those users more self-sufficient. Naturally, this development would constitute a mixed blessing for librarians. By diverting the many routine requests where the library is truly an unnecessary middleman, it would free up resources to perform more value-added work. But in doing so, it might also get users out of the habit of using the library where it truly does stand to add value. Less demand overall might also hamper the library's ability to expand services. For the business in general, end-user searching also has its downside. Because occasional users will never become extremely efficient in on-line work, costs will be greater for a given amount of information retrieved.

Apart from the twelve percent who wished for nothing more out of the library than its current offerings, the remainder of respondents saw future value in three major categories: research capabilities (fourteen percent); Internet capabilities (twelve percent); and competitive intelligence services (three percent).

Corporate librarians may also see their managers' assessment of weaknesses as a mixed blessing. Asked what is missing from the library "tool kit," a large number (twenty-nine percent) of senior managers could not name a thing [see Figure 9-9]. Of course, this is good news if it reflects a general satisfaction with the level of service being provided with current resources. On the other hand, it may bode ill for librarians' own wishes to build or acquire new, more powerful capabilities.

Most managers were able to name at least one area of need. Most often cited was the need for additional electronic services (by twenty-three percent of respondents). For some, this is as simple as creating the capability to distribute informa-

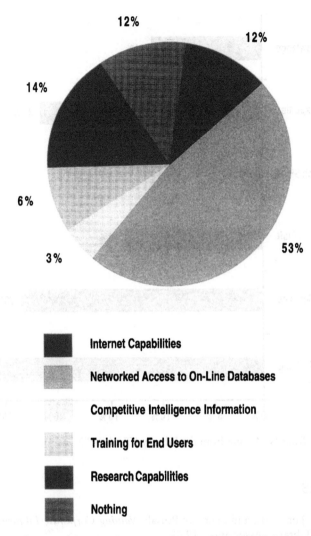

FIGURE 9-8   Products and Services Managers Surveyed Would Like to See in the Future

tion by electronic mail. Other managers have higher hopes, and would like to see all library resources (including books and journals) available on-line. Hand-in-hand with electronic services goes the skill in employing them. Thus, twenty-one percent also cited a weakness in the area of technological expertise.

Few respondents were willing to say that their library's problems came from a lack of warm bodies. Just fourteen percent thought additional staff was needed. Similarly, only eleven percent of these senior managers cited a lack of business knowledge as a problem. Finally, research skills are not perceived to be missing from our nation's corporate libraries, except by two percent of respondents.

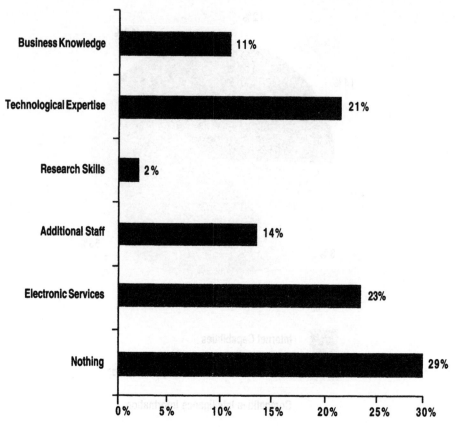

FIGURE 9-9   What Is Missing from the Library "Tool Kit"?

NOTES

1. Matarazzo, James M., and Laurence Prusak, *Valuing Corporate Libraries,* a report of the Special Libraries Association, 1990.
2. See, for example: McGee, James, and Laurence Prusak, *Managing Information Strategically* (New York, NY: John Wiley & Sons, 1993); Cronin, Blaise, and Elisabeth Davenport, *Elements of Information Management* (Metuchen, NJ: Scarecrow Press, 1991); Davenport, T.H., and Laurence Prusak, "Blow up the Corporate Library," *International Journal of Information Management* 13(1993):405–412; and Matarazzo, James, *Corporate Library Excellence* (Washington, DC: Special Libraries Association, 1990).

10

The Librarian as Information Source

Patrick Wilson

So far we have considered only unaided use of library collections. But it is precisely one of the tasks of the librarian to aid people in the use of collections, and we must now consider the sorts and amounts of aid that are and that might be offered.

Enormous amounts of labor and skill go into the preliminary work of organizing collections of documents and providing access instruments. This is work that can conveniently be described as bibliographical work, since it is, insofar as it involves knowledge and judgment rather than clerical routine, work of the same logical character as that involved in the making of a bibliography, an organized list of documents. Creation of a collection is not different in principle from specifying the contents of an imaginary collection by enumeration. Those librarians who have published catalogs of model libraries—public libraries, junior college or college libraries, for example—have done just what the librarian faced with the task of creating a new library would have to do. Procurement of copies of the documents enumerated in a model catalog, their physical preparation and handling, and their circulation, repair, and shelving are jobs the librarian can and often (except in the smallest libraries) does delegate to assistants within the library or agents outside it. Deciding on the contents of a collection, deciding on the ways in which documents are to be made discoverable by potential users, and deciding on devices of physical arrangement and auxiliary access instruments—these are the jobs of the librarian, and they all have their precise analogs in the job of making a bibliography. This is the preparatory work without which a library would be an unusable heap of documents.

The assistance offered to library users, after the preparatory work is done, falls into three categories: bibliographical assistance, question answering, and selection assistance.[17] Let us begin with the first of these. Librarians offer instruction, sometimes formal but usually informal, in the use of bibliographical access tools—catalogs, indexes, bibliographies. In varying degrees, they themselves also use the apparatus on behalf of the library user, preparing bibliographies or, going a step further, assembling for the user copies of the documents corresponding to the bibliography they prepare. This is personalized bibliographical work, and it is done on a significant scale only in special libraries serving restricted and highly professional clienteles. One cannot expect, in a public or academic library, to receive more than a little instruction and advice on the use of the bibliographical apparatus. Bibliographical searching is a time-consuming work, and the amount of time that is devoted to serving any particular library user is generally small. While the amount of assistance in the use of catalogs and other bibliographical works that is offered must vary greatly from library to library and from librarian to librarian, still, in general, it is assumed that library users should be expected, and in fact prefer, to find what they want on their own initiative, with the librarian standing ready to give some assistance if asked to do so. But only some assistance: should the library user pose a general problem and ask what literature there is that might help in solving the problem, he is likely to be referred to an appropriate section of the library shelves, or shown a bibliography, or referred to the card catalog. He is most unlikely to be presented, after a time, with a specially prepared bibliography, and is almost certain not to be presented with a specially prepared report summarizing what is known that would be useful to him. That degree of personal attention is not given except under quite extraordinary circumstances or in highly specialized libraries to a carefully selected clientele. General public libraries and academic libraries are not, as presently organized and staffed, prepared to offer to do their customers' searching for them, to accept descriptions of problems and deliver lists or collections of documents containing information likely to assist in solution of the problems.

But if we are right in supposing that most people are of low degrees of studiousness, then we can suppose that librarians outside of highly specialized institutions serving professional research workers do not offer personalized bibliographical service because it is not wanted. It is not wanted by those of zero studiousness, for they do not want documents at all. It is not wanted by those of studiousness of degree one, for they do not want collections of documents requiring to be used together, compared, analyzed, and evaluated. A bibliography would be of use to them only as a means of selection of a single source, as a vehicle of recommendation. The making of extensive "demand" bibliographies is concentrated in the institutions where are found the very people who, by profession, find search unavoidable but capable of delegation. If, in fact, preparation of personalized bibliographies is not wanted by users of general purpose libraries, this is confirmation of our hypothesis that studiousness of high degrees is rare and found primarily among professional users of documents.[18]

The second sort of assistance to library users is that of question answering—the direct provision of information rather than bibliographical assistance in finding sources from which the information wanted can be derived. The vast bulk of such work is "ready-reference" work, consisting of short answers to specific factual questions, the answers discovered by the use of standard works of reference. This is fact finding, to which Wyer's description of fifty years ago still applies: "It occurs when the objective is specific, clearly stated, and the answer sought nothing more than a name, date, title, statistic, fact, or figure. It is when the question instantly suggests the right book, and the answer when found is usually in one book, often on one page. . . . In nine cases out of ten [it] can be answered from one of the half-dozen most useful reference books."[19] The librarian undertakes to answer questions insofar as direct answers can be discovered in standard sources; the librarian does not undertake to engage in computations, analyses and criticism of sources, evaluation, interpretation, inference, synthesis, application of information to particular problems. The recommended practice, indeed, is to answer by quoting from sources, identifying the source of the quotation. Paraphrasing unidentified sources and answering out of one's own knowledge are not standard professional practices. While standard professional practice does not exclude the use of nonstandard sources, primary reliance is on the use, wherever possible, of the relatively small corpus of standard reference works. Until recently, library question answering has been thought almost invariably successful, both by reference librarians and by patrons.[20] But experiments in which the same factual questions are asked of a number of different libraries have indicated that the information given is often not the best information available.[21] Wyer, in 1930, posed as a "thought question," to which he did not supply an answer, "How can a patron be made to feel that he has had the best and latest information on his subject?"[22] It appears that, in fact, the patron does not regularly get the best and latest information on his subject. Nor should this be surprising, in view of the evidence that most questions asked are answered from a few standard reference works. For a standard reference work is a dated, incomplete, more or less imperfect representation of public knowledge. The librarian could only claim that what was found in a standard reference work did represent the best and latest information on the subject on the basis of documentary research or on the basis of such knowledge as would justify the assertion that no documentary research was necessary in the particular case. But librarians do not in general claim to have, nor do they have, ability at documentary research in all the fields in which they accept and answer questions. It is not even clear that there is a general recognition of an obligation to try to determine that what the standard reference sources say represented the state of public knowledge when the sources were prepared, and that they still faithfully represent public knowledge. A book published by the American Library Association contains this remarkable comment: "One other puzzling problem in *some* questions is ascertaining that the right answer has been found." This author's view is that "the librarian's chief contribution is the discovery rather than the criticism of information," which is an odd way of saying that the librarian's job is to find answers but not to distinguish right from wrong answers, information from misinformation. On conflicting answers found in different sources, the author says, "In the final analysis, the decision as to which is right may have to be made by the expert, but the librarian can help by bringing together for comparison works by various authorities and by turning up more or less hidden sources."[23] This is not, in fact, attempted as a matter of course; reference librarians do not as a matter of routine practice look for variant answers to one question but give a single answer from a favorite standard reference work. Of course, the librarian consults sources that he supposes to be generally reliable, but he does not undertake to vouch for the accuracy of the answer on the basis of his own independent knowledge or on the basis of independent verification of the accuracy of the source in this particular case. He is not in a position to say, and does not undertake to get into the position to say, "This is the answer given in such and such a standard source, and I have every reason to believe, on the basis of my own investigation, that this answer was and still is correct." The librarian, that is, has nothing to add to the bare report that a certain source gives such and such an answer. "It is never the business of the reference librarian," says Wyer, "to determine the truth or falsity of statements found in books."[24] That is, in our terms, it is never the business of the reference librarian to say, on the basis of his own judgment, This is what is known.

The reference service offered by most libraries is thus drastically limited in two important ways: first, it is largely confined to answering specific factual questions, and second, the answering service is confined to reporting without evaluation what is contained in standard reference sources. The user who has an independent basis for trust in a particular reference source may be happy to have someone else use the source on his behalf, and those who are not overly concerned about the accuracy of the answers they receive may be happy to have a general source of answers to specific factual questions. But those who are unfamiliar with the repertory of standard sources and concerned over accuracy can be expected to be skeptical of the value of an information service whose personnel are not in a position to vouch for the accuracy of the information they give and who take no personal responsibility for the correctness of what they report. The limitation to specific factual questions is also a drastic limitation on utility. As the topical organization of catalogs and bibliographies requires that the functional questions the user would like to ask have to be translated into topical terms, so the reference service's limitation to specific factual questions imposes an analogous burden of translation. The user with a decision problem is in effect told: Tell me exactly what facts you want, and I will find them for you. But the person seeking aid in the improvement of an unsatisfactory decision situation either wants no facts at all, or does not know which facts would help. I want, let us say, to know whether there exists some alternative course of action that I have not considered; this will not count as a specific factual question to which an answer can be found in a standard reference source. Perhaps I want information that will help me clarify my own preferences among alternative actions and outcomes; this is not a specific factual question. I want to know what will be the long-range consequences of following a course of action; again, this is not a specific factual question. It is part of the conventional wisdom of librarians that patrons asking questions at a reference desk never ask for what they really want and require delicate interrogation before their true interest becomes clear.[25] But while patrons may often fail to say bluntly what they want, the librarian may add confusion by wrongly supposing that the patron really does have an acceptable specific factual question in mind that he is concealing; the librarian looks for the only sort of question he is prepared to answer.[26] Library reference service is a severely confined and unresponsible variety of information service, offering a thin surface of unevaluated "facts."

This may seem harsh; but a careful look at library reference service suggests that librarians have no basis for self-satisfaction. It is characteristic of professional judgment that it implies an assumption of personal responsibility; it may turn out to be good or bad, but it is his own personal judgment that the professional offers, and that is what we demand. But the reference librarian tries to avoid personal judgment; he avoids saying anything that would imply, "I am giving you my best judgment as to what the answer to your question is; I stand behind my answer, I accept blame if it is not right." Avoiding responsibility means avoiding professionalism; library reference service is not, by and large, a professional service.[27] How could it be? On what basis could the librarian of no more than the usual amount of general and professional education undertake to give his own judgment or expect anyone else to value it? The librarian will give answers to a question without even understanding the question or the answer, if he can find what looks, on linguistic and formal grounds, like an answer in a standard reference work. It is just as well not to claim any personal responsibility when this can happen.

The last main sort of personal assistance librarians offer is assistance in selection of particular works out of a collection, what is, or once was, called "reader's advisory service." As far as the search for information goes, such work is exactly on a par with ready reference or short-answer information service. The short-answer question is responded to with a direct quotation from a source, the long-answer question is responded to with a long text (a book, an article, or references to them). If people ask for a street address, one reads it to them from a directory. If they want to know about the French revolution, one gives them a book or shows them a collection of books. (The latter is undoubtedly much more common than the former.) Librarians are quite ready to recommend a single source of a small piece of information; they do not think of themselves as recommending, but rather as finding the answer. But they are not so ready to recommend long texts, preferring to show the patron a collection and let him make his own selection.[28] Nor is this at all difficult to understand. The librarian is not, and could not be expected to be, able to make personal recommendations on reading in general; he cannot, and is not expected to, say where accurate representations of public knowledge on all possible topics are to be found. What he can do is to produce others' recommendations—reviews, lists of recommended readings, lists of standard writings. He may be able to say, like the assistant in a bookstore, that one title is very popular, another has been well reviewed, and another has apparently a good scholarly reputation. Again, the librarian avoids making an independent judgment on the accuracy and trustworthiness of a text; he reports the views of others, or gives the patron a collection and lets the patron do the deciding. Ordinarily, he has no basis for an independent judgment, so it is understandable that recommendation of particular texts should play a relatively small part in library service.

It is worth dwelling on what we might call the "logical function of the book," in the information, or question-answering, aspect. Whatever may be the purposes for which books are written, their use in information service consists simply in their constituting already prepared answers to questions. Questions that arise repeatedly but unpredictably might conceivably be answered each time on an ad hoc basis; starting from the research literature, a new discourse might be composed once again explaining the theory of relativity or the reading habits of Americans. But such a pattern of behavior would be absurdly wasteful as well as slow. To prepare explanations in advance of inquiry or to prepare a variety of explanations suited to different sorts of sophistication and interest would be the reasonable plan, and if the device of the book did not exist, it would have to be invented. But it is not the physical format of the printed book that is essential; it is the fact that a certain kind of work has been done in advance of particular need and stored in some fashion that allows presentation of the results of the work on demand. For many sorts of exposition, two-dimensional visual displays are superior to the printed book, and three-dimensional displays may be of similar utility. Not the format, but the simple fact of the pre-prepared presentation is the important function of the maintenance of a collection of documents, as of the maintenance of reference collections of presentations in other formats. Collecting books, the library is collecting, among other things, already formulated responses to inquiries not yet received.

Neither in its ready-reference service nor in its recommendations on selection of documents to satisfy informational requests can the library be said to be offering an independent information service. To do so, the librarian would have to be in a position to do more than report what others say; he would have to be in a position to say on his own account what the state of public knowledge on a particular question was. Of course, anyone can do this; anyone at all can lay down the law. But not everyone deserves to be listened to, or consulted. The conditions under which one could legitimately claim to offer an information service, based on a collection of documents, are those described [in a previous chapter]. Ability in documentary research in the area in which an answer lies is necessary, at least through the analytical stage. One who could not himself construct a representation of public knowledge could not hope to certify another's representation as faithful or unfaithful. It is true, as we have said above, that one may be in a position to say that an account cannot be adequate on the basis of research ability or knowledge of a field other than that under view. But to make a positive judgment that a representation is an accurate one, without ability to do what is necessary to construct an analogous representation oneself, is unwarranted.

Librarians refer patrons to documents for information; they can also, and sometimes do, refer patrons to other people for information. As they have directories of sources of printed information, so they have directories of human sources of information. Instead of providing documentary sources from which I can inform myself, they can refer me to agencies or individuals from whom I may be able to get advice and help. This can be a valuable service, particularly for those with an imperfect understanding of the occupational structure and the institutional arrangements for providing advice and help. Perhaps those most in need of such information are the least likely to know of, or take advantage of, a library referral service. Publicity might overcome that difficulty, at least in part, but there is a bigger difficulty. The utility of a directory service depends on its ability to make recommendations that carry some weight of trustworthiness in those cases where there are multiple independent sources to which referral might be made. If I ask to be referred to a personal information source, I do not expect to be referred to an arbitrary source, but to the best, or at least a good, source. I do not want a list, say, of doctors or lawyers; I can find that in the telephone book. I want to be told which is a good one. Even if there is only one agency or personal source for some sort of information, I want to know whether it is any good or whether I would do better to avoid it. But this sort of advice is not, so far as one can tell from published literature, offered by libraries.[29] The referral service offered is neutral and uncritical. Such service is not without value, but it is the value of a telephone directory. When one lacks a directory of one's own, it is good to have one supplied by the librarian, but selection is the problem that remains, and on this one gets no help.

Much of the foregoing is undoubtedly unfair to particular librarians and not true of information services offered in many special libraries. Many librarians are highly qualified scholars and scientists in their own right, fully prepared to accept personal responsibility for the soundness of the information they give. But these are a minority, and the usual qualifications for the position of librarian promise nothing whatever about the capacity of an individual librarian to make independent judgments on the status of the answers provided for questions or the documents recommended to supply a particular need. Particularly in small libraries, the patron may come, in the course of time, to an accurate estimate of the degree to which the librarian can be trusted as a source of accurate information; in a large library, where the same librarian may not be encountered regularly, no basis for such an estimate may be available. It is here as elsewhere in our information-gathering behavior; we prefer personal sources, and while the librarian regularly seen in a small library may become a trusted personal source, the succession of librarians seen in a large library merge into a single institutional source of unknown credibility. This single institutional source offers, in most general libraries, only a superficial and nonprofessional information source, superficial because it is based where possible on quotation from reference works and limited to small matters of "fact," nonprofessional because it is not based on any individual assumption of responsibility for the quality of the information given.

NOTES

17. On types of service, the development of service policy, etc., see Samuel Rothstein, *The Development of Reference Services through Academic Traditions, Public Library Practice and Special Librarianship,* ACRL Monograph no. 14 (Chicago, 1955).

18. Academic libraries pose rather special problems. Students are expected to do their own biographical work since it is part of the educational task. Faculty members either do their own, on the ground that no one else can be trusted, or delegate it to their students. They might be happy to delegate the more tedious and menial chores to librarians, but would they be willing to delegate, and would librarians be prepared to accept, difficult and also extremely time-consuming jobs? See the section entitled "Some Ideals of Library Service" on library provision of research assistance to research workers.

19. James I. Wyer, *Reference Work: A Textbook for Students of Library Work and Librarians* (Chicago: American Library Association, 1930), p. 116.

20. According to Samuel Rothstein, "The Measurement and Evaluation of Reference Service," *Library Trends* 12 (Jan. 64): 456–472, most questions asked are directional (half the total) or factual; of the latter, 90 to 95 percent are "ready reference" questions answerable in less than ten minutes, and about half are answered from a very small core of reference works (dictionaries, encyclopedias, and almanacs). Librarians report over 95 percent success, and most customers report satisfaction. Few patrons seek advisory service for personal reading. See also "Reference Service in American Public Libraries Serving Populations of 10,000 or More," University of Illinois Library School Occasional Paper no. 61 (Urbana, 1961) Prepared by Mary Lee Bundy.

21. Lowell A. Martin, *Library Response to Urban Change: A Study of the Chicago Public Library* (Chicago: American Library Association, 1969); Terence Crowley and Thomas Childers, *Information Service in Public Libraries: Two Studies* (Metuchen, N.J.: Scarecrow, 1971); Peat, Marwick, Mitchell & Co., *California Public Library Systems: A Comprehensive Review with Guidelines for the Next Decade* (Los Angeles, 1975).

22. Wyer, *Reference Work*, p. 127.

23. Margaret Hutchins, *Introduction to Reference Work* (Chicago: American Library Association, 1944), pp. 33, 34. 37 (my emphasis).

24. Wyer, *Reference Work*, p. 130.

25. Robert S. Taylor, "Question Negotiation and Information Seeking in Libraries," *College & Research Libraries* 29 (May 1968): 178–194.

26. The alternative is that people ask reference librarians only questions they expect the librarian will be able to answer. The remarks of Robert B. Cronenberger, "Public Library: Library for the People," *RQ* (Summer 1973): 344–345, on neighborhood information centers, support this view: "Studies have occurred in Wisconsin and California indicating that a high percentage of questions to information and referral agencies are requests for pure information. The use of trained social workers to answer information questions has been shown to be wasteful. Most of the questions aimed at an information referral center are 'Can you give the telephone number of ---?' . . . In Detroit's experience to date, there have been almost no questions involving a counseling situation" (p. 345).

27. Mary Lee Bundy and Paul Wasserman, "Professionalism Reconsidered," *College and Research Libraries* 29 (Jan. 1968): 8: "In general library situations, that which is requested by or offered to the patron is ordinarily just not complex enough to be considered a professional service. The service provided would not over-tax the capacity of any reasonably intelligent college graduate after a minimum period of on-the-job training." It is hard to see how one can possibly argue with this. One does not have to be a professional librarian to read sentences and numbers out of ready reference

books. But I do not quite see what they propose as a remedy. They speak of the "next stage" in librarians' preparation as the enhancement of subject competence, but to what degree? To full professional competence as a scientist or scholar?

28. As Bundy and Wasserman ("Professionalism Reconsidered") pointed out, it is the children's librarians who are the most "professional," at least in the sense of being most assertive in telling their patrons what they should read. This is easier for them than for other librarians, since they are usually so much larger than their patrons.

29. See note 26, and also see Thomas Childers, "The Neighborhood Information Center Project," *Library Quarterly* 46 (July 1976): 271–289. I interpret Childers' discussion of information and referral service objectives in the cities surveyed to mean that the systematic offering of advice is not one of the objectives; as to whether it is asked for, Childers reports, disappointedly, that "very little is known about the nature of the demands on public library I & R services" (p. 287).

11

Information Management in Large Organisations

Lynda Woodman

Information management is all about getting the right information, in the right form, to the right person, at the right cost, at the right time, in the right place, to take the right action.

That might sound simple enough but most large organisations are a long way from that ideal. This chapter looks at the factors which constrain the development of information management in most large organisations, and the progress different organisations are making towards ideal information management and the implications for society as a whole.

FACTORS WHICH CONSTRAIN INFORMATION MANAGEMENT IN MOST LARGE ORGANISATIONS

Information is created from the associations between logic and raw data. The biggest constraints on information management are the limitations of computer software in representing these associations. The 'fifth generation' promises to be better than the fourth but the complexity of representing these associations may require totally new concepts of programming and may not be truly available for many more generations of software.

A number of other factors also constrain organisations from progressing towards the ideal, and some of these are described below. They include: people not knowing what information they need; lack of accessibility; frequency of misinterpretation; the 'overload' resulting from multiple copies and massive reports; the association between information, politics and power; organisational inertia; ambiguous ownership of information; information 'float'; legislation and external pressures; intangible business value of information; and users with variable cognitive styles.

People Do Not Know What They Need

The more senior the person in a large organisation, the less predictable are his/her information needs. Commonly, people do not know what information they need until a particular set of circumstances arises—and then they want very specific information instantly.

The implication of this for information management is the storage of every element of data relevant to the organisation and all the logical associations. The costs of acquiring and storing such a large amount of information would almost certainly not be commercially viable. But, by synthesising business strategy with the capabilities of information technology, pragmatic decisions about the most likely information needs can be taken. Adaptive design techniques can also help people focus on requirements in a practical way.

Information Is Not Readily Accessible

Information tends to be held in different degrees of updatedness; at different levels of aggregation; with differing accuracy; with differing degrees of secrecy; in different languages; in different media (e.g., paper, microfilm, magnetic tape, optical disks, in people's heads); in different locations (e.g., desk drawers, filing cabinets, archives, on window sills, people's homes); in different forms (e.g., graphs, pictures, words, numbers); and so on.

This lack of order and discipline means that people have to depend on human memory and ingenuity to pull together all the relevant elements of raw data to provide the information required.

Data is being held increasingly in machine-readable form and networks are increasingly linking together various sources of information. But the reports produced are often too detailed to enable the reader to spot trends, or too aggregated to pinpoint key details.

Increasingly, systems are being designed to produce parameter-driven exception reports, which escalate issues up the management hierarchy automatically. Fourth-generation languages are making it easier to interrogate databases. Expert system dialogues, although in their infancy, are helping even further. All of these are beginning to overcome the problems of lack of accessibility.

Information Is Frequently Misinterpreted

The language used to describe information is often ambiguous. For example, in an insurance context the words 'date of risk' can have many different meanings, such as 'the date a risk starts' or 'the date from which time underwriters are liable for losses' or 'the date the premium is due' and so on.

Ambiguities are bad enough when they arise in conversations between people and when they can be readily resolved from their context. But information held in computers generally lacks context, and can be easily misinterpreted. For example, an insurance broker who looks up a client's ledger sees that a particular premium is shown as an outstanding debt and chases his client for the money, only to find out from the irate client that he paid two months ago and the cash has been posted to some other ledger because the client did not quote the broker's reference number.

'Pseudo officialdom' is a problem. That is, people who receive computer printouts tend to believe the information just because it has come from a computer; but with easy access to microcomputers, virtually anyone can produce an official-looking report, and the recipient often does not realise the context in which the report was produced.

Information 'Overload' Is Common

Information 'overload' occurs in most large organisations. Ever since the advent of the photocopier, people have tended to make extra copies just in case someone might like one. A major multinational surveyed the duplication of paper in its organisation a few years ago, and found that, on average, 40 copies were made of each piece of paper, of which 15 were kept indefinitely.

Most large organisations suffer from paper proliferation and it is often made worse by massive computer reports. One large organisation worked out that it printed 500 sheets of paper per employee per day.

Of all the copies and all the print-out, how much is acted upon? How much notice do people take of massive computer reports? How easy is it to find the information needed amidst so much other information? How often do users feel they are 'drowning in a sea of meaningless numbers'?

What are the true costs? Not just the costs of producing, filing, storing, and retrieving information, but the costs of people's time: time to create it; time to move it from one place to another; the recipient's time in reading it; time spent disposing of it; time in filing it; time spent indexing it. What are the storage costs in keeping it? Of retrieving it? And the costs of eventually getting rid of it? Few organisations know the total costs of their paper.

Information Is Associated with Politics and Power

Many people gain status or recognition within an organisation as a direct result of their knowledge and sources of information. Quite naturally, they guard that information jealously. They are reluctant to share it with others for fear of personal loss, and tend to surround their knowledge with mystique and folklore.

The individual thus creates a perception of his being indispensable and maintains the status quo.

People grow accustomed to information flows in large organisations. Everyone has a place entitling them to certain information and this information establishes the 'pecking order'. These and similar political situations are common. Breaking them open is one of the most difficult jobs systems analysts face.

Organisational Inertia Exists

Change is always uncomfortable. It means recognising obsolescence of old skills and old habits, and learning new ones. People need to see something 'in it for them' to make it worthwhile going through the discomfort of change.

A prerequisite to changing any information flow is a genuine 'felt need' for change shared by all the people affected by the old and the proposed information flows. Without 'felt need' people will resist and possibly counter-implement the proposed changes.[1]

Another (often overlooked) aspect of organisational inertia is the DP department itself. Systems professionals who learnt their trade in the sixties and seventies are often reluctant to face up to their own skill obsolescence. They prefer to stick with the design techniques they know rather than take the risk of exploring new ways to exploit state-of-the-art information technologies.

Ownership of Information Is Often Ambiguous

Where information is shared between a number of people, the rights of ownership are often ambiguous. It is common for different people from different parts of an organisation to claim exclusively the same rights to the same information: i.e., rights to create it, to update it and to determine who else in the organisation has the right to access or to use it. Without amiable resolution of these ambiguities, conflicts arise.

There is a danger that systems will be designed as a compromise between the contenders. The compromise will depend on politics, power, and organisational inertia. It extends information management beyond the association of logic and data to include behavioural factors as well. This is unlikely to be in the best interest of the organisation as a whole.

Information 'Float' Is Common

Information 'float' is the time-lag between an event occurring and the information that it has occurred reaching the person who needs to know about it in order to take some action.

Telecommunications is having a radical impact on organisations by drastically reducing information 'float'. For example: organisations which send mail across the Atlantic electronically can reduce their 'float' from a week by airmail to a minute by electronic mail; foreign exchange dealers and commodity dealers around the world now operate on a second-by-second, twenty-four-hour basis, due to virtually instantaneous telecommunications service; electronic funds transfer at point of sale (this is payment for goods by an instantaneous deduction from a bank account, rather than by cash) is made possible by telecommunications; so too, is home banking.

Legislation and External Pressures

Legislation of various aspects of information is being increasingly introduced by governments and regulatory bodies.

For example, privacy legislation is in various stages of introduction in various degrees of restriction in various countries. It defines the rights of organisations to hold information about individuals on computers, and the rights of those individuals to access and ensure the validity of that information. In Britain, the Data Protection Act has recently come into effect, but Sweden has had much tougher legislation for several years.

Another example of legislation is that of transborder data flows. A number of countries, notably Canada and the Scandinavian countries, recognise the value of data to be similar to the value of goods that they can tax when those goods pass across their boundaries.

These countries want to prevent the free flow of data across their boundaries.

Yet another example is the degree of regulation by the PTTs. America and Britain are fast deregulating telecommunications, whereas Germany and France have very tight regulation.

Business Value May Be Intangible

The value of information lies in the value of the actions a person takes as a result of having it. For example, consider an insurance broker who gets information that a potential client wants to insure a particular risk. The value of information management varies from the easily quantifiable (i.e., the broker's commission less the costs of processing the risks, negotiating any claims that may arise and processing any related transactions) to the intangible (i.e., getting the information that insurance is required in the first place, acquiring supplementary information to provide the most competitive quote, and possibly getting subsequent orders as a result of getting the order in the first place).

Unless business value can be clearly demonstrated, then business leaders are unlikely to invest in the funding of information management systems. Very often

the intangible benefits have far greater business value than the quantifiable benefits, and so business judgement is needed to value them, rather than traditional,
quantified, cost/benefit justification.

The value of information may not always be positive. Information that has
been misunderstood has a negative value, as shown in the example of misinterpreted information above. Trying to collect money which had already been paid
might damage the relationship between the broker and the client.

Users Have Variable Cognitive Styles

Individual people have different preferences for the form in which information is
presented. For example, some people can more readily understand pictures, graphs and
icons; some prefer numerical analyses; and others prefer descriptive text.

Information systems rarely provide individual users with choice of form so
that when people change jobs they can tailor the systems to suit their own personal preferences.

These and many other factors constrain us from achieving ideal information
management.

Some factors are more complex to overcome than others, but always the
process of overcoming them is one of evolution by gradually creating increasing
discipline and order.

PROGRESS TOWARDS IDEAL INFORMATION MANAGEMENT

Looking back, we have come a long way since the decimal classification system was published in 1876. Librarians were the first people to bring some discipline and order to information management with their classification and
cataloguing schemes. Although there are similarities between library classification
and modern database management systems, the major differences are the level of
detail and the interpretation of meaning.

Unlike librarians, who use their judgement to classify subject material as a
whole, computers deal with the precise content of the individual elements of that
subject material. Computers add value by interpreting the logical relationships between the specific elements of data and by being able to derive new information
from existing data.

This section looks at the role of computers and information technology in
making progress towards ideal information management. It considers the past,
present and future, i.e.,

- where have we come from? (the historical perspective)
- where we are now? (the current state-of-the-art)
- where are we heading? (trends)

Where We Have Come from—the Historical Perspective

Information management has come a long way since the first computer, the Eniac, was built in 1943 for the US Army to speed up the calculations of ballistics tables; it was later diverted for calculations associated with nuclear bomb theories. In those early days computers were not considered to be of great business significance. An apocryphal story has it that Thomas J. Watson Sr. (founder of IBM) once predicted 'the world will only need a dozen computers'. He evidently considered the potential market too small for IBM to enter. Last year IBM sold more than half a million computers in varying shapes and sizes all over the world.

However, until the 1950s the main use of computers was for scientific calculations and for the storage and retrieval of scientific information. Each decade since those early beginnings has seen a separate group of people pushing forward the frontiers of information management in business and commerce. The people of each era were seen as the 'upstarts' of their time.

Era	Upstarts	Focus
1950s	Organisation and Methods	Procedures
1960s	Mainframe computers	Technology
1970s	Decision support systems	Business
1980s	?	?

Each had a separate focus and tended to disdain that of the previous era.

1950s—Organisation and Methods

In the 1950s people using Organisation and Methods (O&M) techniques began bringing discipline and order to information management in business operations by measuring office work, improving clerical procedures, and introducing early technology such as comptometers into office jobs.

The O&M experts were seen as the 'upstarts' of their time, but they were overtaken by the mainframe computer experts who in turn became the 'upstarts' of the 1960s.

1960s—Mainframe Computers

Commercial batch processing applications became common in the 1960s. The late 1960s saw the formation of the Codasyl committees and the emergence of database management. The mainframe computer 'upstarts' of the 1960s were technology-focused and highly disciplined. They developed standard methodologies and formalised the Systems Development Life Cycle.

1970s—Decision Support Systems

The 1970s saw the development and growth of teleprocessing, decision support systems,[2] end-user computing, graphics, word processing, microcomputers, spreadsheet generators, more and more packaged software, and increasingly higher-level languages. Whereas scientific users had always been able to get their 'hands on' computers, these tools of the 1970s brought computer power out of the 'DP ivory towers' and into the hands of business people for the first time.[3]

The 1970s saw the maturing of the mainframe computer 'upstarts' of the 1960s, the maturing of professional bodies like the British Computer Society, the maturing of techniques such as the database,[4] and the maturing of data processing departments.

In 1974, when Gibson and Nolan wrote in the *Harvard Business Review* about 'Managing the four stages of EDP growth',[5] most data processing departments were still struggling up the learning curve, bringing discipline and order to a technology that in the 1960s often seemed untameable.

The 'upstarts' of the 1970s were business-focused, innovative and flexible, using decision support systems to achieve high visibility from minimum effort.

1980s—?

In the 1980s we are seeing computers in the hands of school children, the emergence of digital telecommunications, cheap mass storage, icon-driven systems, and a whole range of exciting diversified new technologies. So who will be the 'upstarts' of the 1980s?

The office automation experts? — Probably not.
The behavioural scientists? — Unlikely.
The telecommunications experts? — Most likely.

Office Automation Some six years ago in the early days of office automation, Zisman[6] predicted: 'office automation will evolve and mature from a focus on task mechanisation to one on process automation'. Yet today, the term 'office automation' is synonymous with the tools of the office, such as word processing, electronic mail, diary management systems, spreadsheet generators, and the like. Office automation experts focus on tools to improve office efficiency, rather than on ways to improve the effectiveness of office work.

To increase effectiveness we need to focus on the process of office work, rather than on the separate components. Examples include Matteus[7] and Woodman.[8] Matteus describes the paperwork production line of processing letters of credit in Citibank and how that process has been streamlined and integrated by capturing data at source for subsequent re-use. Woodman describes a similar process in Willis Faber, a large firm of international insurance brokers and underwriting agents.

Hammer[9] summed up the situation in *The OA mirage:* 'The key to success is ensuring that individual solutions to immediate problems adhere to an overall architectural vision, so that the end product is consistent rather than fragmented'. Keen describes vision and architecture in depth in his chapter in Otway and Peltu.[10]

Behavioural Science   Study of the human issues around computerised systems is becoming increasingly fashionable, particularly as people realise that any computer system is only as good as the people who use it. The most superb technical system in the world is worthless if the people who have to use it don't like it, because they have the power to make it fail.

There is much substantive work being done in this field such as Beckhard[11] on managing complex change; Keen[1] on the politics of change and the role of the change agent; Zuboff[12] on computer mediated work; or Bronsema and Keen[13] who analyse the strategic role of education in successful implementation of management information systems.

There are few practitioners. At their best, they are brilliant facilitators. At their worst, they focus on the form of work rather than on its content, or they indulge in 'psycho-babble'. They have little to say about how to manage information and much to say about how not to.

Telecommunications   Focusing on the process of office work requires linking together the components. Telecommunications provides the 'hub' and the 'glue' to do just that; see Keen's chart of an 'ideal' information capability (Figure 11-1).

Telecommunications are creating new trade routes and an electronic marketplace. They are enabling businesses to erode historical demarcations between separate market sectors, such as banking, insurance, building societies, stockbroking. Keen[14] describes the role of telecommunications in creating new market and

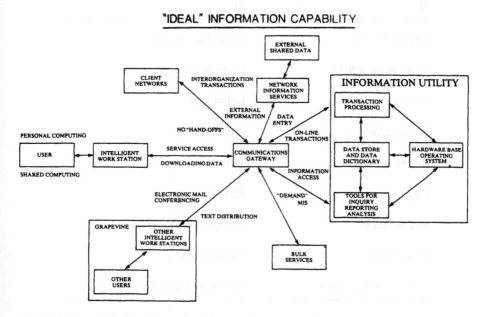

FIGURE 11-1   "Ideal" Information Capability

product niches, and the human and technical implications of these business opportunities.

As we move towards ideal information management, we will need to mesh the skills of all the 'upstarts'. The leaders in the 1990s will probably be those who have developed the skills of each generation and never stopped being 'upstarts'.

Where We Are Now—the Current State-of-the-Art

We are currently in a period of immense transition. Data processing (DP), with its roots in the centralised systems of the 1960s, is being replaced by the increasingly diversified technologies of the 1980s, commonly referred to as information technology (IT). Characteristics of information systems, styles of management, attitudes and skills of staff, are changing rapidly in the shift from DP to IT. Some of the key areas of change are listed in Figure 11-2, and described below.

Organisational Spread of Technology Is Increasing

The early computer systems only affected small groups of people in an organisation. For example, only the salaries department was affected by the payroll system. Technology is now spreading into every nook and cranny of firms' own

DP	IT
Departmental	Organisation wide
Structured tightly	Loosely coupled
Uniform	Individual
Predictable	Spontaneous
Repetitive	Variable
Logical	Human
Simple data	Complex data
Precedents	Green fields
Technical specialists	Technical generalists

FIGURE 11-2   Information Management Transitions

organisations and beyond to the organisations of their clients and markets. For example, airline reservation systems have extended their systems into travel agents' offices around the world; Homelink banking has spread its terminals into people's homes; and so on.

Structure Is Becoming Less Tight

Scientific calculations have a very precise structure, as do the accounting systems where computers were first used. However, as technology has spread throughout organisations, so the systems structure has needed to become more flexible and loosely coupled to be responsive to the needs of business.

Uniformity Existed in the 1960s

The only way to make systems work in those days was to force the users into a common mould; everything was standardised. But business does not fit nicely into such a mould—it is individualistic. Systems design needs to centre around uniformity only where it makes sense in business terms (e.g., payroll and ledgers), allowing systems to be tailored to suit individual business requirements, and change with changes in business needs.

Predictability Is Decreasing

With reduced structure, less uniform systems and more variable applications, users are demanding systems which can respond spontaneously to their needs, rather than accepting systems that make them specify their needs in advance. It is often difficult or impossible for users to specify in advance their precise requirements because of the unpredictability of their business environment.

Repetitive Labour-Intensive Work Was Computerised First

With telecommunications and diversified technologies spreading throughout organisations, less repetitive and more varied work can and is being supported by information technologies.

Logical Skills Were Sufficient for Developing DP Systems

However, the success of information technology depends increasingly on developers' skills in understanding, educating, and training people.[15]

Data Used to Be Simple

But variations in types, different media, massive increases in volumes and increasingly intricate relationships between the various elements of data are making data management more and more complex. The shift is from simple file structures to fully comprehensive information utilities.

Precedents Exist in DP

They have been accumulated from knowledge and experience gained over the last twenty-five years. Much IT requires development of totally new techniques, such as adaptive design, user-managed projects, user/technologist job swapping, and so on.

Specialist Technical Skills

These were needed to develop DP systems. A broad spectrum of technical skills is required to keep pace with the ever-increasing range and capabilities of information technologies.

Each organisation is in different stages of these transitions. The degree to which they are exploiting the power of information technology depends on the leadership of the information systems resource and the business leadership. Keen's chart[16] (Figure 11-3) categorises them.

Where Are We Heading? Trends

There are two major trends. These are towards: information executives; better price/performance.

Information Executives

Business leaders are becoming more and more innovative in order to survive in an increasingly competitive world. They recognise the value of information management to their business and seek out information executives (Figure 11-3) to deal with the key business, management, technical, and human issues.

Business Issues   What is our vision of our business in five to ten years' time? And what is the role of information technology in that vision, i.e., how can

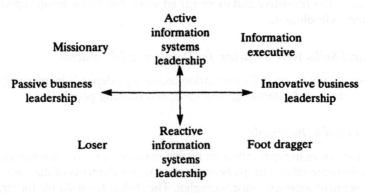

FIGURE 11-3   Categories of Information Systems Resource

we use IT to gain an edge on our competitors; raise the base-line level of service for our industry; run our business better; improve productivity; exploit new market niches; create new products; create barriers to entry; and so on?

Long gone are the days of cost-justifying data processing projects. Today's business leaders and information executives are not interested in saving half a secretary—they want information technology to contribute real profits to the bottom-line. They are interested in business value for money. They regard investment in improved systems like any other investment.

They look for ways to shift out their cost-base (for example, collecting data at source by getting their customers to do their data entry). They look for hidden assets (for example, selling their software, or their data). They look for natural extensions to their existing product range (for example, piggy-backing extra services on the back of an existing telecommunications network). They are prepared to look at anything that makes good commercial sense.

Management Issues   Information executives understand the new styles of management needed to exploit the business opportunities of information technology. They focus on the policies needed to make their vision happen, i.e., where will the funding come from, who will have what responsibilities, and with what accountability? And so on.

They translate those policies into practical methods. For example, what standards and codes of good practice do we need to establish? How do we manage the transition process? What risks are we exposed to and how can we minimise them? How do we manage our suppliers? What technical and organisational infrastructures do we need? Which people should we educate, with what awareness, knowledge, attitudes, and skills? What statutory issues may constrain our use of technology (e.g., regulation of PTTs, data protection legislation, border data flows) and what might the effects of those constraints be? Etc., etc. The list is almost endless; with new technologies emerging all the time, new management issues keep surfacing.

Technical Issues   Management issues mesh with technical ones. For example, which diversified technologies can help our business, and what is the most effective timing of their introduction? What degrees of flexibility do we need and what are they worth in business terms? What are the business/technical trade-offs? And so on.

Then there are the more technical issues, such as what database structures do we need to underlie our information utilities, and how should they be organised? What professional expertise could we embed into information technologies and how would we use it? What are our predicted capacity needs? What operating systems software and telecommunications infrastructures will we need? What are our design criteria variables? What adaptive design techniques should we use? How can we establish a systems invention life cycle to precede the traditional systems development life cycle? And so on.

At the individual device level, all issues are purely technical in terms of performance and functionality. But machines are only machines—they need people to make them work.

Human Issues   Information management is completely dependent on people: people to design the systems, people to run the operations, people to input the data, people to act on the outputs. Information executives recognise the importance of the massive range of human issues, such as changing career patterns, new job and skill profiles, personnel obsolescence, strategic computing education, learning-by-doing training programmes, behavioural dynamics of change, meshing personal and corporate objectives, and so on.

They recognise people always find change uncomfortable and they seek out incentives to speed up the organisation's readiness for change. They focus on user ownership of systems; getting user management to run development projects; or job swapping, i.e., getting systems analysts to do work experience in the user department and teaching analysis skills to users.

Above all they see the significance of organisation development, of changing the work content of jobs to maintain a balanced workload and realise job savings.

This has only given a flavour of the issues information executives are facing. For further and more detailed debate see Otway,[16] Maister,[17] Synott and Gruber,[18] and Woodman.[19]

Better Price Performance

Information technology is getting cheaper, smaller, and more powerful every year. The trends are shown in Figure 11-4. These trends have been predicted to continue until the end of the century.

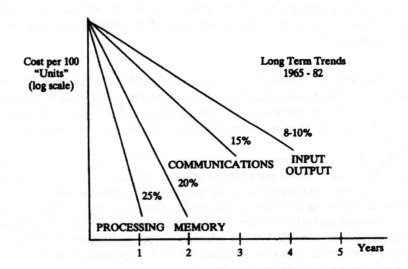

FIGURE 11-4   Cost Trends

IMPLICATIONS FOR SOCIETY AS A WHOLE

Many views have been taken of ideal information management, from the optimistic to the pessimistic.

There is Toffler,[20] who sees us entering a third wave of civilisation (the first wave being the agricultural revolution, the second the industrial revolution, and now the third wave the information revolution). Then there are people like Jenkins,[21] who see the collapse of work. And there are people in between, such as Valee,[22] who discuss choices such as: the digitised society or the grapevine alternative?

It is true that information technology displaces jobs. But that is equally true of all new technology; for example, the candlestick-makers lost their jobs to the gaslight-makers, who lost their jobs to the electric light people, and so on. But technology does not just displace jobs, it creates new ones. For example, how many new jobs have been created by the television or electrical appliance industry in the last fifty years?

However, the new jobs require new skills. In 1985, with unemployment running at 13 percent, there are many job vacancies in the fields of the new technologies; not just information technology, but all the other new technologies as well.

Supply and demand of skills has got out of balance. There is excessive supply of old skills and insufficient supply of new skills. Society needs supply and demand of skills kept in balance, so we can all look forward to ideal information management with optimism.

The world is moving at an increasing pace towards the ideal information management described at the start of this chapter. At the same time, there are many constraints, traditions, and problems holding back progress. The field of information management can seem very bewildering, but we do have a fairly clear idea of where we want to get to. This chapter has identified some of the major constraints and shown that they are being overcome, albeit slowly.

REFERENCES

1. Keen, P. G. W. *The Politics of change and the role of the change agent. (Forthcoming).*
2. Keen, P. G. W. and Michael, S. C. *Decision support systems: an organisational perspective.* Reading, MA: Addison-Wesley, 1978.
3. Rockart, J. F. Chief executives define their own data needs. *Harvard Business Review,* March/April 1979.
4. Nolan, R. Computer databases: the time is now. *Harvard Business Review,* September/October 1973.
5. Gibson, C. F. and Richard, L. N. Managing the four stages of EDP growth. *Harvard Business Review,* January/February 1974.
6. Zisman, M. D. Office automation: revolution or evolution? *Sloan Management Review,* Spring 1978 19(3), 1–16.
7. Matteus, R. The new back office focuses on customer service. *Harvard Business Review,* 57(2). March/April 1979 146–159.

8. Woodman, L. Broker driven systems: integrated processing to support the business. Paper presented to the AFIPS OA Conference, 1982.

9. Hammer, M. The OA mirage. *Datamation*. 30(2), February 1984, 36–46.

10. Otway, H. J. and Peltu, M., eds. *New office technology: human and organisational aspects*. London: Frances Pinter, 1983.

11. Beckhard, R. *Organisational transitions—managing complex change*. Reading, MA: Addison-Wesley, 1977.

12. Zuboff, S. New worlds of computer-mediated work. *Harvard Business Review*, 60(5), September/October 1982, 142–152.

13. Bronsema, G., and Keen, P. G. W. Education intervention and implementation in MIS. *Sloan Management Review*, Summer 1983.

14. Keen, P. G. W. *Telecommunications and business policy: the coming impacts of communication on management*. Massachusetts: Centre for Information Systems Research (Sloan School, MIT), 1981.

15. Woodman, L. Humanising office automation. Paper presented to the IEE conference, June 1982.

16. Otway, H. J. and Peltu, M., eds. *New office technology: managerial aspects*. London: Frances Pinter, 1983.

17. Maister, D. H. Balancing the profession service firm. *Sloan Management Review*, 24(1), Fall, 1982, 15–29.

18. Synnott, W. R. and Gruber, W. H. *Information resource management opportunities and strategies for the 1980s*. New York: Wiley, 1981.

19. Woodman, L. Telecommunications from the MIS manager's perspective. (To be published in *Datamation*.)

20. Toffler, A. *A third wave*. London: Collins, 1980.

21. Jenkins, C. and Barrie, S. *The collapse of work*. London: Eyre Methuen, 1979.

22. Valee, J. The network revolution. Paper presented to the IEE Conference, June 1982.

Part Three

A New Model for
Special Libraries

12

Post Information Age Positioning for Special Librarians: Is Knowledge Management the Answer?

Stephen Abram

Knowledge is power, not information. Information is power only if you can take action with it.

—Daniel Burris

In this article, I will take a few heretical positions that will challenge some of the sacred cows of our profession. Unlike most heretics, though, I've suggest a replacement for these views that I hope will steer us on to a better course to the future of special librarianship and, at the very least, initiate a debate on the best positioning for SLA and special librarianship.

HERESY NUMBER ONE: "SPECIAL LIBRARIANS ARE *NOT* IN THE INFORMATION BUSINESS"

We, as special librarians, made a potentially disastrous error, those many years ago when we decided to position ourselves in the "information business." Information businesses are marked by their ability to create information and disseminate it widely—often for a profit. Generally, special librarians do not, as part of our core mandate—create information. While we do create information about

Reprinted from *Information Outlook* 1, no. 6 (1997), pp. 18–25 by Special Libraries Association. Web address (www.sla.org). Stephen Abram is director, Corporate & News Information at Micromedia Limited in Toronto, Ontario, Canada. He is a member of SLA's Board of Directors and sits on the Association Finance and Strategic Planning Committees. He can be reached via e-mail at sabram@ micromedia.on.ca.

information (metadata), I believe this is a higher level calling in the knowledge continuum. The drive to stake out territory by positioning special librarianship as being in the information business has produced a number of negative behaviors that have, in my opinion, limited our ability to make as much forward progress in our profession, as we might desire.

Examples of this behavior include:

1. The growth of data professionals and technology experts into information roles has been perceived as a threat by many of our members. This has driven behaviors that mitigate against making a partnership with the very group that has access to the advanced technology and data skills we seek for success. We lose the ability to display our complementary skill set and are forced into a competitive positioning.

2. We view the natural progression of our traditional partners and supporter in formation suppliers and publisher as a threat, too. Their strategies to access the information end-user at the desktop is the next, most logical step for them to survive. Suppliers and publishers must protect and expand their traditional professional end-user markets as their old retail, library, and direct mail channels are disintermediated by the Internet and WWW.

3. We view the entrance of new players into the information field as a threat. Indeed, we've seen some library associations putting forward position papers to the traditional suppliers asking them to slow the pace of change and adoption of new technologies! Of course, we would all like the pace of change to be a little more leisurely—but asking for traditional suppliers to ignore the threat of the new players to their real information businesses is not a viable request. Indeed, a number of these new players present opportunities for major future alliances for both our profession and our association.

HERESY NUMBER TWO: "SPECIAL LIBRARIANS *CANNOT* MANAGE KNOWLEDGE"

Currently, we are running the risk of lurching headlong into a new positioning of our profession and our role as knowledge managers. The plain fact is that knowledge, per se, *cannot* be managed. In fact, capturing knowledge in any form other than into a human being's brain, reduces it to mere information, or worse, data. *Only the knowledge environment can be managed.*

The reality is that special librarians—possibly all librarians—have operated at a level superior to mere knowledge management. We play a role in the "knowledge environment" as key catalysts in the knowledge continuum. Information systems technology professionals will have grown from their data roots into information management and the systems to support information—including delivery, integration, search interfaces, etc. Our success as a profession has historically been when we are associated with knowledge-based enterprises (universities, media, engineering, accounting, consulting firms, etc.) or with the knowledge intensive portions of corporations (research and development, sales and marketing, strategic planning, etc.). This is primarily because our contribution to the knowledge environment of our organizations is a tangible one directly related to successful decision-making.

THE KNOWLEDGE CONTINUUM

To understand how I have come to believe the heresies above, it is necessary to relieve some of our language and assumptions about the building blocks of information, knowledge, and organizations. The process for knowledge creation and use flows through a continuum [see table next page] where data transforms into information, information transforms into knowledge, and knowledge drives and underpins behavior and decision-making. So bear with me while we move through some definitions.

BUILDING BLOCK #1: WHAT ARE DATA?

Data are raw facts that have no context or meaning on their own. The key success factors in data management are implementing standards and quality control procedures [that] allow the data to be used effectively and confidently. It rarely has value to end-users except in the context of turning it into information.

The transformations that take place during the creation of data include the application of standards, such as SGML, HLML, Fields, Tags, MARC. normalizing currencies, or applying rules like GAAP, Z3.9.50, etc. It is possible to practice special librarianship in a data environment. Indeed, in many respects the librarian's predominant and historical role in cataloging, indexing, and creating metadata systems is a good example of where the foundation is for roles in the knowledge economy. We see many emerging roles in the data environment and often these resulting positions revolve around the use and organization of data and its relationship to information.

BUILDING BLOCK #2: WHAT IS INFORMATION?

Information is a tangible representation of data or knowledge within a specific context—usually in some end-user oriented product like a book, magazine article, or study. The key success factor is the effectiveness of the representation in communicating the information. The same data can be represented many ways in order to meet the needs of different types of users. It only has value to the end-user if it meets their specific needs at the time they need it. Information is created by

Transitions	Data	Information	Knowledge	Behaviors
Selected Verbs	Collect Database Management Computer Record Records Management	Display Chart Format Graph Represent Publish Picture	Knowing Learning Filtering Evaluating Balancing	Do Decide Choose Apply Enact Act
Transformation by Information Professionals	Standardize Field Tag Organize Aggregate Format	Index Catalogue Select Organize Deliver Format Enhance Improve	Serve Interpret Educate Train Find Lead Direct Improve	Authority Endorsement Confidence Satisfaction Contribute
Technological Interventions	Electronic Conversations from print SGML or HTML conversions Electronic Aggregation Image/Text Formatting	BPR—Business Process Re-engineering Network Electronic Layout Electronic Distribution	Groupware Intranets Search Tools World Wide Web Decision Support Systems	No Technology—just Intelligent, Informed, Impactful behavior—the 3 "I's"
Questions for the Future	By moving towards information aimed at the needs of an individual, does the role and importance of large databases aimed at mass markets decline?	*Does increasing the number of information transactions make an organization more successful? Or should we focus on the quality of the transaction?*	If we accept that knowledge can only be stored effectively in an individual human brain, how do we store information so that it can be absorbed as knowledge faster?	What are the roles of special librarians in having material and measurable impacts on the behaviors within their organizations or upon their clients?

databases designed for specific outputs or by authors turning their knowledge into information for others.

The kind of transformations that occur in the creation of information are in the representation of data: display, chart, format, publish, aggregate, picture, graph, sort, rank, highlight, etc. A lot of special librarians practice in the information industries, as we do in all industries. One of the key components of the information business is the creation of information from knowledge and data. This requires both the librarian's research and technical skills. For instance, news and media librarians will often manage the research library but also enhance the newspaper with additional access points for the published electronic version.

BUILDING BLOCK #3: WHAT IS KNOWLEDGE?

Knowledge is information in context of an individual's role, learning behavior, and experiences. The key success factors include the congruity between the information and the individual's perspective. It only has value in the context of the situations where it is being applied.

The major steps that occur in the transforming of information into knowledge are learning, knowing, filtering, evaluating, and balancing. Hence, we are allied here with teachers, trainers, publishers, and other knowledge professionals in ensuring that knowledge transformations occur effectively. A great number of special librarians practice in the portion of the knowledge environment where information is provided to end-users who transform it into knowledge. For example, we see special librarians in academic settings where the product is knowledge as well as in integrated research teams within successful organizations.

BUILDING BLOCK #4: WHAT IS BEHAVIOR?

The most important behavior to special librarians, in the context of knowledge and information, is *decision-making*. We must focus on those decisions that result in action, even if that action is non-action. The goal of a good decision is for it to have **intelligent, informed**, and **impactful** results.

The value of the decisions in an enterprise or organization is in direct proportion to its results in the context of the individual or social organization.

Although knowledge—by its very definition cannot be managed, the *process* can. This transformational process is nicely summed up in the SLA slogan: *putting knowledge to work* and turning information into knowledge.

Perhaps some examples would assist here. The process is (A) moving information into knowledge and back and (B) creating and enhancing knowledge environments to have a material impact on the decision-making behaviors and results of our organizations and the individuals therein. I call this process "transformational librarianship."

MOVING INFORMATION INTO KNOWLEDGE AND BACK AGAIN—BUILDING KNOWLEDGE ENVIRONMENTS

Review the [table] provided with this article. In many cases this process has been represented as one where, by moving through the data-information-knowledge continuum, one can become wise. We all know by personal experience this is not necessarily true. So what creates a wise individual or organization? How does one develop "wisdom"? I believe wisdom is situational. One can be a wise accountant or a wise oil patch reference librarian. This wisdom comes from not only working through the data-information-knowledge continuum but in basing present and future behavior on the learning developed through repeated trips through the process. In the English language there are not separate words to define knowledge concepts. There is only the verb "to know." In French, however. there are two verbs, "savoir" and "connaitre," roughly "know how" and "know that" respectively. Thus, in the past, we have run the perception risk of being positioned as fact keepers ("know that") rather than for our true talents as an extremely information literate profession ("know how"). For success in the knowledge economy we need to play up our "know how" and the key role it will play in this new age.

WHAT ARE THE KEYS TO SUCCESSFUL *TRANSFORMATIONAL* LIBRARIANSHIP?

The keys to our future success lie in the following strategies.

1. Focusing on Where the *Transformations* Occur

Instead of thinking of our professional skills as being informational skills, we should look at what we do as transformational. Sometimes this is called "adding value." But, most of the time our added value is in the transformation and not in the products and tools we use. When we organize information, we are taking data, books, and bookmark files and making them more accessible and useful to the end-user. When we create indexes and catalogs we are creating tools and services to ensure less time is spent in the hunt for information and more time is available to turn it into knowledge. Indeed these skills have now become so important they have been renamed "metadata" skills or competencies in the development of information about information. One has only to search AltaVista a few times and get 200,000 hits to powerfully understand the importance of metadata skills to the knowledge economy!

2. Focusing on the *Learning Organization:*

The key activity that happens when users interact with us, our libraries and services, is "learning." Organizations that encourage learning and focus on learning in its broadest context will, I believe, be all the more successful. Strategist Peter M. Senge's works—including the book, *The Fifth Discipline: The Art and Practice of the Learning Organization*—contain many methods and theories for developing learning organizations.

3. Turning Information into Knowledge and *Putting Knowledge to Work*

Here is perhaps the biggest opportunity for us as special librarians. We have no primary need to look backward and see the growth of emerging professions into the information world. We must look forward into the knowledge economy and carve out a strategic niche for ourselves that allows our profession to have an impact in the new economy. The role for us in the new world is to be the guides and navigators for the exploration of the information ocean. We must develop new services and products while enhancing our skills to underpin meaningful social and economic development. Remember the three "I's": we will form the base for informed, intelligent, and impactful decision-making in our society and enterprises. Special librarianship will be one of the catalysts in this development—if we focus our skills, knowledge, and energies in this direction.

4. Learning the Tools of *Transformational Librarianship*

We know technology is vitally important to the emerging knowledge economy. We will NEVER forget that technology is just a tool, an enabler to the creation of the new age, a focus for opportunity, and not the *driver* of the change. The drivers of change are the people who adopt the enabling technologies and use them to promote improvements to knowledge creation and the management of the knowledge environment.

When we think about these tools it might be useful to divide them up into three types.

KNOWLEDGE TOOLS OR "K" TOOLS:

Knowledge tools are those tools that encourage data and information to flow more quickly into knowledge. Examples of these types of tools are the metadata tools or new search engines, indexing, filtering tools, and just-in-time information, or just an old-fashioned card catalog.

DECISION TOOLS OR "D" TOOLS:

Decision tools supply knowledge and information in a format or environment that allow for quicker, better, more effective or more informed decisions. Examples of these are decision support systems software, push technologies that provide information only at the point of need, the emerging communication tools that allow for conferencing so knowledge workers can interact for decision-making combined with the needed information, just-in-time filters, etc.

INFORMATION ARCHITECTURE FOR KNOWLEDGE ENVIRONMENTS

A new architecture is emerging for the creation of these knowledge environments—which recognizes decisions can be better when humans interact easily. Some of the emerging building blocks of this new architecture are client/server, net computers, standard networking protocols like TCP/IP, groupware such as Lotus Notes, and the new offerings coming from Netscape and Microsoft that emulate some of the Macintosh and Lotus models. One of the most exciting things about this emerging architecture is that it can be global, borderless, and open.

CONCLUSION

The Information Age ended sometime in 1995. It was an abject failure—not because information wasn't hugely important, but because the society of the old era continued to view and measure the Information Age with tools, paradigms, and strategies suited to that time. It's fascinating to watch the economists for the old economy furiously trying to apply supply and demand models to the information economy! Especially since supply/demand economics presumes a limited supply of something and that success accrues to those who harness the limited supply for wealth creation. Information, of course, is in unlimited supply and the emergence of the commercial Internet and WWW in 1995 destroyed an age! Future success will not go to those enterprises that corner or manage limited supplies or serve a manageable demand, but to those enterprises and professions that can effectively manage this unlimited supply of key and vital information through filtering, organizing, and improving accessibility.

TAKING THE KNOWLEDGE POSITIONING

My belief about using the knowledge environment as the paradigm for viewing our professional challenges at the dawn of this new age causes me to ask four key questions:

1. By moving toward information aimed at the needs of an individual as opposed to a group, does the role and importance of large databases aimed at mass markets decline?
2. Does increasing the number of information transactions make an organization more successful? Or should we focus on the quality of the transaction?
3. If we accept that knowledge can only be stored effectively in an individual human brain, how do we store data and provide services so that information can be absorbed as knowledge faster?

4. What are the roles of special librarian in having material and measurable impacts on the behaviors within their organizations or upon their clients?

Largely because it continues to be useful in understanding the changes that our society is undergoing, we still see the popular press trumpeting the arrival of an Information Age—an era that ended years ago. We know better—and we have the skills, in alliance with information technology professionals and emerging or traditional information businesses, to transform our enterprises in preparation for enormous success. Grasping the opportunity now to position ourselves and our organizations for the knowledge-based economy is vital. As part of this repositioning. I propose we think seriously about taking the knowledge positioning for SLA in support of its members.

As Nike (and, past SLA president Didi Pancake) said, "Just Do It!" "When I hear the mantra 'anything, anywhere, anytime', I try not to choke. My goal is to have 'nothing, nowhere, never', unless it is timely, important, relevant, or engaging." Nicholas Negroponte, *Wired,* Aug. 1994.

SELECTED KNOWLEDGE MANAGEMENT WEB SITES

Some Principles of Knowledge Management by Thomas H. Davenport, Ph.D. *http://knowman.bus.utexas.edu/pubs/kmprin.htm*
The Clemmer Group *http://www.clemmer-group.com/*
The Knowledge Management Forum *http:// revolution.3-cities.com/ bonewman/*
ENTOVATION International Knowledge Innovation (sm) Strategies for the Millennium *http:www.entovation.com/*
A Business Researcher's Interests: At the Crossroads of Business, Management & Information Technology *http://www.brint.com/interest.html*
CIO Magazine: *http://www.cio.com/CIO/*
Knowledge, Inc.: The Executive Report on Knowledge, Technology and Performance *http://www.webcom.com/quantera*
Knowledge Management: From Information into Knowledge *http://www. knowledge.stjohns.co.uk/Km/Default.htm*
The Official Intellectual Capital Homepage *http://www.business.uwo. ca/~nbontis/ichome.html*
Knowledge Management: Refining Roles in Scientific Communication *http://www.ckm.ucsf.edu/Papers/RefiningRoles/*
An Architecture for Information in Digital Libraries *http://www.dlib.org/dlib/february97/cnri/02arms1.html*
American Productivity and Quality Center *http://www.apqc.org*

13
Future Librarians

Robert C. Berring

The paradigm of information is changing. Western culture is shifting from a paradigm built around the icon of the book to one built around digital information. As one change breeds another, with the change in the source of information comes a change in the paradigm of libraries and the functions of librarians, who have long fulfilled the role of being the primary custodians of information.

While any librarian's experience is limited by the specialty in which they work, I have had the opportunity to view the profession from a variety of perspectives. For three years I served as Dean of the School of Library and Information Studies at the University of California, Berkeley, a position that offered insight into the nature of professional training in library education. During 1986 and 1987 I served as President of the American Association of Law Libraries, which allowed me to see professional organizations and the role such bodies have played in helping librarians react to the changes in the information environment. Nevertheless, because I hold a position as a law professor as well as that of a law librarian, my views may be skewed.

THE PARADIGM CHANGE

This essay is premised on the idea that the advent of digital information is bringing about a shift in the paradigm of information. While it may take a generation for all of the implications of this change to work themselves out, the battle is largely over. The paradigm has shifted.

Whenever a paradigm changes, there are prices to be paid. Paradigm shifts occur when patterns that sorted the old world into recognizable, manageable categories become obstacles preventing an understanding of the new world. The new pattern is difficult to perceive, and the irony is that the tools that aided in understanding the old pattern may obstruct the new. There may be considerable groping

toward understanding the nature of the change, which can bring about dislocation, unrest, and fear. Librarians are no different than any other group caught in
the midst of such change. The foundations of librarianship are shaken by the current shift in the information environment, and, indeed, the change is revolutionary. It is not a matter of new forces taking over an existing power structure; this is
a real revolution in which the entire structure is rebuilt.

Revolutions often produce predictable varieties of reactions as different
camps rise to meet the challenges produced by the advent of a new paradigm. Regardless of the type of revolution, the camps can be classified into three groups—
conservatives, reformers, and radicals—and librarians' reactions to the change of
the information paradigm is no exception.

In revolutionary times it is the conservatives who plead the truth and beauty
of the old system. They see in the old way a power that will be lost in the face of
change. In the change of the information paradigm, the conservatives are the book
people, the people who see digital information as part of a general decline in
intellectual culture. Information not contained in a book is somehow at best mid-
dlebrow, the stuff of mechanics and popular culture. Librarians who are conservatives see themselves as identified with the book, so deeply enmeshed in the world
of the book that leaving it destroys the very core of what they do. They resist
change in the profession and cling to old explanations of the world. The conservatives view the exponents of change as barbarians pounding upon the gates of the
sacred keep.

The reformers, who are often caught in the cross fire of the conservatives
and the radicals, are those who believe that some of the old can sensibly be
blended with some of the new to reach the best end. Reformers often share the
conservatives' belief that there is some precious kernel in the old way, some style
or value that can and must be saved. Yet the reformer also recognizes that the
paradigm is changing and that while it is important to save the crucial parts of the
heritage, it is also necessary to improve upon it with tools drawn from the changing pattern. In the information revolution these reformers put forth what Geoffrey
Nunberg calls "reassuring ecumenism." Specifically, they feel that society will use
both books and digital information in the future.[1]

Among librarians, the reformers are the people who are attempting to
evolve the profession into a new role. They advocate changing the names of Library Schools to Schools of Library and Information Science or Library and Information Studies.[2] They believe that the precious kernel for librarianship lies in the
ideals of the profession and its traditional concern with the equitable distribution
of information. For them the new technology can and must be used to enhance the
old model. They see a gradual change, an evolution, taking place.

The radicals are the true believers in total change. They see the old system as
a problem in and of itself. For them it is time to shed the skin of the old system
and charge forward into the new. They see the reformers as especially feckless; for
the radical, half measures have no place. In the shifting paradigm of information,
Raymond Kurzweil predicts the end of the culture of the book in his *Library Journal* article. His views can stand as a fair statement of the radical creed.[3] In the

radical's view, every element of the old system must change and conciliatory maneuvers are not feasible. Attempting to cling to a "kernel," a radical would say, will doom the enterprise. For librarians, the radicals are represented by those who feel that the entire template of librarianship must be discarded, the old stereotypes being too encrusted with the detritus of the old system to ever be changed. Indeed, radicals may see themselves as no longer associated with librarianship at all as they attempt to create a new reality for the profession.

The profession of librarianship is at a crucial juncture. The facts of the crisis are clear enough, including the closure of quality library schools. Within the last decade the two symbolic flagship institutions of library education have been closed by their universities: the Graduate School of Library Science at Columbia, the first library school founded by Melvyl Dewey, and the Graduate School of the University of Chicago, which was long viewed as the most rigorous of library schools. When this essay was written, in 1993, the School of Library and Information Studies at Berkeley was no longer accepting students, and the School of Library and Information Science at UCLA is in the process of losing its independence and being merged into the School of Education. Both of these schools were listed among the premier library schools until the very end. In a speech in New York City in October 1993 Richard Budd, the dean of Rutgers's library school, contended that librarianship should no longer be taught in a professional school but rather offered as an undergraduate major.[4] Revolutionary change is afoot.

As information is becoming a more central topic in society, the profession of librarianship, the information profession, is in decline. At the very moment when librarianship should be striding forward it is in full retreat. What has happened?

Some of the causes of this professional crisis may not relate to digitalization per se. They may relate to the internal problems that face the profession of librarianship, or to the elitism inherent in academic communities where the professors are the aristocracy, the graduate students are the knights, and the librarians are loyal retainers. In a time of dwindling resources, budget cuts are first dealt to the loyal staff. Librarianship has always been a service profession, and great librarians have been devoted to the institutions that they served. This identification is shown by the fact that librarians designate their profession by the names of the institutions in which they labor. It is the American Library Association, not the American Librarians Associations, the American Association of Law Libraries, not the American Association of Law Librarians. Librarians have always viewed themselves as part of a larger entity. In these days of bottom lines and downsizing, such an attitude can be fatal.

But for all this, it is digitalization that has occasioned the largest changes. In 1986, when the Provost of Professional Schools of the University of California called me and asked me to serve as Dean of the School of Library and Information Studies at Berkeley, she told me that the Library School had toddled along quite adequately, safe in its relatively quiet niche for many years, but that now it was coming upon some valuable turf. This turf promised great opportunity but also brought great danger. Others would want it, and they would fight for it. The Business School might want to fill this role, the Computer Sciences Department might try to claim this turf. The Library School, she assured me, would be in for a battle and they needed a dean. She was right. The change in the nature of information created opportunity and danger, and the result is being played out today, at places like Berkeley and elsewhere across the country.

Many librarians have written concerning the crisis and the paradigm change. But by looking at what librarians do, and how the move to digital information will change what librarians do, we may be able to gain insight without a dogmatic battle. While such a functional approach may not resolve the larger arguments among the conservatives, reformers, and radicals, it may offer a glimpse into the future.

Throughout history, librarians have carried out three basic functions.[5] First, they have gathered and protected data; second, they have organized and stored that data according to some system; third, they have distributed that data to users. Each of these functions deserves to be addressed, both as the function has been performed until now and as digital information might change it.

THE FUNCTIONS OF LIBRARIANS UNDER THE BOOK PARADIGM

Gathering and Protecting Data

Gathering and protecting data was the greatest challenge to librarians until the modern era. The word "data" may sound prejudicially modern, but it is meant to encompass books, papers, manuscripts, really any artifact. The physical act of gathering these items was once an inordinate challenge. Books and manuscripts were relatively rare and precious. Such items represented power and wealth, and they might be perceived as a threat by those who did not have or use them.[6] Books and manuscripts allowed for the growth and spread of ideas, representing an almost magical power in a largely illiterate world.[7] When I taught "Introduction to Information," a course then required of all graduate students in the School of Library and Information Studies at Berkeley, I assigned my students a short story by T. Corraghesen Boyle, "We Are Norsemen." Boyle writes this story in first person as a Viking poet, someone from the oral tradition who is accompanying a group of Vikings on a raid. In the final act this band of almost subhuman specimens attacks a monastery. After destroying everything in sight they head for the last stronghold. At the top of the last stairway, behind the last door, they find the library. The Vikings confront the monk librarian who attempts to protect his books. In the words of the narrator:

> *The book. What in Frigg's name was a book anyway? Scratchings on a sheet of cowhide. Could you fasten a cloak with it, carry mead in it, impress women with it, wear it in your hair? There was gold and silver scattered round the room, and yet he sat over the book as if it could glow or talk or*

something. The idiot. The pale, puny, unhardy unbold idiot. A rage came over me at the thought of it—I shoved him aside and snatched up the book, thick pages, dark characters, the mystery and the magic. Snatched it up and watched the old monk's suffering features as I fed it, page by filthy page, into the fire. Ha![8]

I told my students to keep in mind that though things may look bleak—their budgets might be cut and their salaries might seem low—it is unlikely that a ship of Vikings would attack them. But at one time it *could* have been that bad. Boyle's fiction reveals the visceral hatred that the book can inspire. The emotions that Boyle shows us are sparked by an earlier paradigm shift, when the oral culture, "natural" and "real," was changing to a threatening written tradition. Boyle's Viking skald provides a glimpse of the deep antipathy of the old for the new, and it may serve us well to recall this scene as we sail into an age where we may be taking books off the shelves.[9]

The culture of the book won out over the forces that despised it, but the book is still a powerful symbol, representing culture and power in the current paradigm. Bookishness is a symbol of intellectual attainment, a library a place of calm and learning. Individuals may collect their own small libraries in their homes and take the often bulky collections with them when they move from place to place. The book is a powerful force in most traditional religions, often symbolizing divine knowledge. How better to empower a means of communicating information than to conceptualize it as divine utterance made tangible?

Books can also inspire fear, perhaps akin to that felt by Boyle's Viking. The book is still subject to frequent attack. In today's world it is still a criminal act in some societies to retain heterodox or offensive books, with the nature of heterodoxy being defined by those in power. Repressive authority fears the power of the book. On the opposite side of the language of censorship is the language of books. People use the phrase "book burning" as an emotional description of any form of censorship, whether or not it involves books. There is repression of other media—movies are banned, pictures are condemned—but books are still special. The American legal system accords decidedly different standards to books; compared to other media, books receive special protection.10 The welter of issues surrounding these questions thus remains vital, and librarians continue to be on the front line of the battle. Courageous librarians continue to fight to keep certain titles on the shelf.

But the challenge of just *getting* the information is now largely gone. Modern industrial printing has changed this. Books appear in great numbers and voluminous editions. What cannot be bought can be photocopied or microfilmed. The great explorer librarians who traveled the world searching out rare collections and finding odd titles are now a tiny band indeed. Each year there is a river of new books. No library can own it all. The function of gathering has been transformed into the challenge of choosing. Given the development of interlibrary loan, the photocopier, and, in recent years, the fax machine, one can still gain relatively easy access to information one chooses not to obtain in its original form. Information is pouring down upon us. Even specialists are hard-pressed to keep up with everything published in their area, let alone read it all. The problem is no longer finding information, but sorting it, filtering it.

Preserving and protecting information is an important aspect of this function. A book is a physical object; it occupies a particular space. Once obtained it has to be protected. Formerly librarians assumed the roles of guardians of books, first gathering the books together, then protecting them by controlling both the books and access to them. This issue of *control* has been key for librarians throughout the ages. There were always physical threats to books. William Blades, in his charming series *The Enemies of Books,* listed the whole catalog of challenges to books: vermin, fire, water, even librarians. The great Zen koan of librarianship was the drive to find and protect material and the inevitable need to give people access to it.

The American system of open-stack libraries in part answered this challenge by declaring that the user's need to access materials was more important than the need to protect the books. Such a decision leads to wonderful freedom for the library user but exacts an inevitable toll from the books. Despite innovations like open stacks, librarians came to be identified with the guardian function. The stereotype of the librarian standing ferocious guard over materials that she would rather not see touched is etched in popular consciousness.

There is another element to the preservation function. The dirty secret of anyone who works with the collections of books in great research libraries is that the books are rotting on the shelves. While we know how to preserve them, we cannot afford to do so. The acid content of most paper produced in the last 150 years has doomed the books printed on it to slow, inevitable deterioration.

Lastly, it is worth noting that the sheer number of books now held by research libraries has become a problem in and of itself. Libraries are warehouses of information, but the inventory is out of control. Most great research libraries have been forced to consign parts of their collections to remote storage, sometimes to places where retrieval presents a major challenge. But under the old paradigm, the guardian librarian had a duty to hold onto the books. Discarding the books was not an option.

Each of these aspects of the old prototype of the librarian is based on the function of guarding and protecting. But today's librarian is actually someone who is filtering a flood of information, most likely with no real ability to control or preserve what they already have. The modern librarian may still be called upon to show courage to retain certain titles in the face of political pressure, but they will face the problem of finding the necessary resources to purchase all the information desired, not the problem of finding the information itself.

Organizing Information

The modern profession of librarianship has emphasized developing methods for organizing information. As the problem of gathering waned, the problem of organizing the data grew. The way in which this challenge was met can be split into two parts: physically organizing the data and cataloging it.

The first is the most basic; how should one organize the data? The data here was largely books. As physical objects, the books needed to be put somewhere. What methods should be used to shelve them? Of course one could simply shelve them in the order in which they arrived. This system, constructed around an "accessions book" recording each arrival, might serve in certain situations. In a closed-stack library, where a library employee retrieved each book as it was requested by inventory number, the system worked fine. In a small collection the librarian might not even need a record of what had arrived; she might know where each book resided, and with a small enough collection and the right set of users, each user might know as well.

But even small collections soon developed classifications systems. Systems could be quite basic, perhaps an alphabetic arrangement of titles, or the books could be grouped into large categories. Recall, for example, the important role classification systems play in Umberto Eco's *The Name of the Rose*.[11] In the novel, the solution to the murder, indeed the crucial piece in the whole puzzle, lies in the organization of the books in the monastery library. Primitive classification systems soon gave way to the pressure of growing numbers of books. As more and more books on more and more subjects appeared, libraries that collected general materials were forced to turn to universal systems of classification. The large libraries were holding first hundreds of thousands and then millions of books. More precise means for classifying the books were needed so that the books could be reshelved after each use in a predictable manner.

This need led to the development of the pre-coordinated index, an index designed before having access to the information. It is the opposite, for example, of indexing a book, where the information is already there for the indexer to describe. A pre-coordinated index provides a systematic description of every possible topic into which books will be regrouped.

The challenge of creating a system that provides a topical universe covering every possibility is not trivial. Melvyl Dewey supplied his Dewey Decimal System, a broadly based but comprehensive system that worked well enough with fairly general collections, and one still used in some smaller collections. But the size of many libraries outstripped the organizational specificity of the Dewey system. As the great libraries grew, more precision was needed. Smaller specialized libraries too needed more depth of description for the collections they housed. It was useless to a library to have all its books carry the same classification designation. Some libraries opted to create their own classification systems, each of which represented the intellectual effort of a librarian grappling with information.

In the U.S. the Library of Congress undertook the challenge of developing a system that was precise enough to allow meaningful classification of large numbers of books while also providing the depth of description needed by small specialty collections. The Library of Congress has been in the process of constructing such a system over the course of recent decades—indeed is still being constructed—that, when complete, will offer a universal system for putting books on the shelf in the most effective order. The Library of Congress's collection dwarfs all others in the country, so its needs were the most pressing. The system created to serve the purposes of this enormous number of books had to be universal—no book can be denied a place—and the attempt is made not just to shelve the books into a universal system, but in fact to place them in a compelling arrangement. Debates have long raged as to how to divide up the world of ideas into the most useful arrangement. A professional librarian is always amused to hear a researcher talk about how they often work based on serendipity, going to the library shelf looking for one book and then, incredibly, find an even better one by miraculous chance. Of course, legions of librarians have spent their lives trying to create arrangements that would allow just this kind of miracle to take place. Think of it as prearranged serendipity.

This is not the place to retell the stories of the development of these kinds of classification systems, but it is important to recognize that it was the fact that each book within the library had one unique location that compelled librarians to create the system. Many books cover more than one topic, but the book could only be put in one place. The library user needed a way to find a book without having to puzzle out the classification system. It was to meet this need that the other great intellectual effort of descriptive cataloging and subject analysis was undertaken.

Subject and descriptive cataloging is the process of precisely describing each book and creating a separate set of records reflecting those descriptions. These records describe the books according to a standard protocol, thus enabling the library user to find a specific book by any one of a number of access routes.

Card catalogs were an enormous improvement in organizing information. They allowed the librarian to describe a single book in several distinct ways. Unlike the shelving of the book, where the book had to be placed in one specific location, a whole set of catalog cards could be made. While the description of the book might be the same on each card in the set, each card could also carry a designation reflecting a different element of its description. For example, one might first create a catalog card that reflected the "main entry" for the book. (Main entry represents the primary access to the book by the user. At its most effective, main entry is the way to find a book by its most logical access point.)

The beauty of the card catalog was that it provided multiple points of entry to a static set of books. But it too possessed some of the problematic traits inherent in any tangible representation of information. It was bulky, and as collections grew, card catalogs grew to be huge. Also, since most cards were filed in alphabetical order, there was a limited range of options for organizing the information. As the numbers of cards swelled, new algorithms for organizing the cards had to be devised. Librarians responded by developing increasingly intricate schemes for putting the cards in order, schemes that were often difficult for library employees to understand and almost completely impenetrable to the average library user.

Another inherent limitation was that each card still existed in only one place. Thus, one could search by author, but not by author and by subject at the same time. Furthermore, since the cards were not cross-filed against each other, even a skilled searcher had to shuttle back and forth between cards. There was also the inevitable problem of how to manipulate such a large number of physical objects. To allow for the filing rules to be served, very precise forms of description were developed. These guidelines were created for professional catalogers, and even among this group, the rules were and are a constant matter of debate. The old chestnut that the same cataloger would describe a book differently if they did it twice on consecutive days was probably correct; with such complicated rule systems, it could hardly be otherwise.

These systems of classifying and cataloging information were necessitated by the physical nature of the book. Librarians devoted themselves to perfecting these systems. As the database of books grew larger and larger, the systems became more and more stressed. Librarians developed increasingly detailed rules for filing catalog cards and describing books. Indeed, these rules became so complex that many librarians had trouble following them. Great research libraries took enormous pride in the specificity and precision of the descriptions in their catalogs. Of course, as the complexity of such systems grew, their opacity to the user grew apace. The typical user had no chance of understanding the algorithm that guided the construction of the catalog.

Librarians took on the stereotype of cataloger and classifier. The image of the librarian laboring to describe a book in painstaking detail and creating drawers of catalog cards, which were zealously guarded as the written record of the library's holdings, is one that is a part of many a person's consciousness. The librarian as organizer, as creator of precise systems of control, is intertwined with the paradigm of the book.

Distributing Information

This third function of librarians has been increasingly emphasized in recent years. At the most basic level, distributing information in the form of books is simply a matter of allowing physical access to them. This is the flip side of protecting the books. The American movement toward open-stack libraries in which the user is allowed to walk directly to the shelves to retrieve their own book rather than asking to have it paged was the first major step. Paging a book involved having the library employee retrieve the book while the patron waited. This system afforded librarians great control over the books, indeed, it allowed shelving arrangements to be based on nothing more than convenience, but it made the users completely dependent on the library's finding tools. As library collections grew and the variety of materials grew more complex, such restricted access was hardly sufficient. Library users were puzzled by the size of the collection, or incapable of using the finding tools provided. Indeed, some users had problems understanding how to use the books once they found them.

Librarians created two solutions for this problem. One was an increased level of reference assistance. This concept included more aggressive forms of outreach to the library patrons and the development of pathfinders, handouts, library guides, and other reference tools. Reference librarians debated the ethics of how much to involve themselves in the library patrons' reference questions. The dynamics of the reference interview and the best strategies for helping the user find what they needed were explored in professional literature and in the library schools as librarianship became increasingly concerned with issues of communication.

A second solution to the problem was called bibliographic instruction. Librarians were cast as teachers whose mission was to guide the users by teaching them research skills. This form of instruction placed the librarian in a proactive position. Rather than serving only as a guardian and organizer of information, the librarian became one to assist in its interpretation and use. This is not to say that a librarian had not previously played a role as adviser and helper, but the role of teacher grew in importance.

As the image of librarians shifted toward one of distributing information, new challenges were posed. How far could and should librarians go? In some ways the librarian's legacy as guardian data gatherer and supremely precise information organizer made it hard to think about these issues creatively. Straying too far toward training the user led one right out of the profession of librarianship. The logical extension of this movement is the involvement of public librarians in literacy training. The librarian actually assists the user in learning to read. No longer is it enough to get the books, organize them, and hold them open for use; now the librarian must teach the user to read them as well.

It is important to note that each of these distributive functions, with the exception of literacy training, is driven by the physical nature of books. The dilemma of whether to allow the public access to them relates to the properties of the unique physical object that is the book. If it is stolen, or its pages torn, it is removed from the information base. The problem of finding the book on the shelf, as well as many of the issues related to using the book once found, is tied to the limitations of the book as a physical object.

A Word on the User

There are many types of library users. For the purposes of this essay it is especially vital to note two large divisions. The first is the average user. This person, in whatever library setting they might be found, is a non-expert user of the information systems. They may know how to perform some basic searching functions, but they do not really understand the larger systems. They may be completely intimidated and incompetent, or they may be able to stumble along, but their most important characteristic is that of being a non-expert. They are not capable of fully exploiting the traditional tools of information organization and categorization. They have neither the time nor the interest even to try. They simply want the data they seek.

The second kind of library user is the expert. This is a person who grasps the operative principles of the library's organization. They understand precisely what the librarians are doing, and, indeed, since so much of what librarians do is subjective, they may well disagree with the way the librarians work. I will always recall the late Professor Richard Baxter of Harvard Law School. When I was Acting Director of the Law Library there he would leave notes attached to books telling me how the cataloging and classification of each volume could be improved. To Professor Baxter, a book assigned to the wrong classification or given an improper subject heading was an intellectual affront. Such an expert user is both the joy and the bane of librarians.

Traditional research libraries were designed to be used by experts. The intricacies of the great organizational schemes—indeed, the depth of data gathered in the great research collections—were only truly appreciated by a knowledgeable few. As the user population expanded and the number of books increased into the millions, reference librarians embarked on rehabilitative projects designed to assist the average user in gaining some measure of expertise, but the library systems continued to be designed for the expert user, and the systems continued to become more filigreed. However, with the digital revolution, this set of traditional functions has been changed completely.

THE FUNCTIONS OF LIBRARIANS UNDER THE NEW DIGITAL PARADIGM

The paradigm for the use of information has changed. Barring some worldwide economic catastrophe, the change to the widespread use of digital information is inevitable. This fact, so apparent to those willing to look and so incredible to those entrenched in the old book paradigm, will be assumed for the purposes of this essay. In light of this change, what will happen to the traditional functions of librarians? Will they be preserved, reformed, or destroyed?

Gathering Data

The old model of the library was based on a conception deeply rooted in the idea of the book. Indeed, librarians, the profession that served the information needs of society, named itself after the buildings that housed the books. Librarians went forth into the world to gather information and bring it back to the library, where they guarded it. If it was a rare item, because it was scarce or had a special quality of binding or illustration, it was placed in special storage. But every item that was brought back to the library was *owned* in a physical sense by the library. It might be borrowed by a user, but when it was taken, careful records were maintained of who had it and where. Each physical entity, no matter how banal its information, was physically unique. Once again, many of the common stereotypes of librarians grew out of this monitoring function. The library card was one's ticket to privilege, allowing a person to use the books, to remove them. The systems for monitoring the book's use, especially the systems of enforcement like the library fine, became a fixture in comedic literature. Librarians were seen as the book police.

Some materials were so costly, so large, or so likely to be needed by large numbers of people that they could never be allowed to leave the library building. These items were not necessarily rare, but they were valuable and thus had to be controlled. Once again, it is the physical nature of the book that makes this action necessary. The book can only exist in one place at a time, and only one user at a time can comfortably use a single volume.

The new paradigm of digital information completely changes this set of relationships. Digital information does not exist in one tangible place. It cannot be stored in an edifice, nor can it be owned and controlled like a book. It lacks all of the attributes of physicality. The data is stored in electronic form and may be scattered throughout the memory of the storage vehicle. When one wishes to use it one can take a copy away while leaving the original in place. Use by one patron in no way precludes use by others. Nor does the information have to be returned; it can be retained by the user. There is no need for guarding it and monitoring its use, at least no need related to the librarian's function.[12] The digital information beginning to flood the information marketplace is infinitely elastic and uncontrollable. The entire concept of ownership will have to be rethought. But regardless of the shape that the new conceptualization takes, it will not replicate the library model.

If individuals who need information can gain access to it via a home computer and a modem, they will not have to come to the library at all. While some information may continue to be restricted due to its content, or have its access limited by being priced on a per-use basis, there will be no rationale for screening users from information since the information no longer possesses physical attributes. If a library user wants to use an electronic reference work over a modem on their home computer, there is no need to move an object to them or them to the object. She can use, perhaps even copy, the object without prejudicing the ability of others to use it as well. Whereas one user hunched over the unabridged dictionary excluded all others by their ownership of the physical aspects of the book, in the digital paradigm it will be possible for a number of users to all have access to the electronic version of the same dictionary at the same time.

For librarianship this will be most unsettling. No longer will librarians be curators or caretakers of information. There will be no need. Librarians will have to choose what data to purchase or lease and how to structure its availability, but most of the rest of the basic tenets of the old paradigm are gone. At the Research Libraries Group Symposium on Electronic Libraries held in Menlo Park in August 1993, Douglas Van Howeeling of the University of Michigan stated that librarians must realize that in the new information age they are retailers of information, discount retailers, in fact.[13] In the old world of information warehouses, librarians guarded the information and protected it from a sometimes hostile world (remember the Boyle quotation). In the new world librarians will be facilitating patrons' use of information: moving information out, packaging it, marketing it.

This is a deep and serious shift in the profession's image and role. There is a great danger facing librarians if they do not perceive the change and become retailers of the information they own. The database vendors may decide to distribute information directly to the users without using librarians, or even libraries, as intermediaries. The full-text databases LEXIS and WESTLAW, that are now so important in law, have already effectively achieved this end. When LEXIS and WESTLAW were first introduced the systems were made available through the use of dedicated terminals, each terminal having a unique number. The user went to the appointed terminal to conduct their search. Law students came to the school law library because that's where these terminals were located. Lawyers went to the law firm library for the same reason. The terminal was physical, like a book, and subject to all of the custodial and guardian functions that defined the relationship between librarians and books.

But as the technology advanced and user sophistication and demand shifted, LEXIS and WESTLAW moved to a new system that did not require dedicated terminals. Under the new arrangement, each user received an identification number. This number could be used on any standard terminal equipped with a modem, thus freeing the user to work at their desk, home, or other location of their choice; they no longer had to come to the library to access LEXIS and WESTLAW. LEXIS and WESTLAW developed a large number of support tools, designed to make the systems easy to use (they even offer a toll-free 800 number to assist beleaguered researchers). When the user entered the LEXIS system, they found all of the databases ready for use, and theoretically needed no librarian at all. As the change to digital materials continues, with more information originating in digital format, the appeal of using these systems will increase. For law students—and there are 120,000 students currently enrolled in accredited law schools—the shift is easy. As law schools move into the digital age, there will be less and less need for the law student, or the lawyer, to go to the physical place called the library at all.[14]

If such a scenario, or any variant of it, spins out in the future, there will be no place for the librarian as gatherer and guardian. There is nothing to defend. If the conservatives do choose to defend this turf, they will die upon it. Nor can the reformers do much here, except to serve as discount retailers of information through public libraries, the least well-funded sector of the profession. In the digital shift, the gatherer and guardian functions are going to be vestigial at best.

Organizing Information

It was the tangible nature of the book, its property of occupying one particular space, that led to all the efforts to describe it and categorize it. Once the book was assigned to a location, no matter how well thought-out that location, systems had to be designed to lead users to the book from various starting points. It was never apparent that the physical nature of the book dictated these decisions until digital information demonstrated that the tangible form of the book was inherently limiting. Such limited vision is natural in any paradigm because one cannot see beyond one's environment—indeed, it is hard to see one's environment as an environment at all. The essence of a paradigm is that one sees it as a reality. And digital information allows us to see just how limiting the book's physical form was.

Digital information does not occupy a physical space in the same sense that a book does. The electrons that make up a body of digital information do not sit on a shelf; they may be scattered throughout the storage mechanism used and only reconfigured as needed. In a full-text digital on-line system, the finding tool does not lead one to the single specific location of a physical manifestation of information; instead the tools recreate the information. In other words, one formulates the parameters of the search for information and is then given appropriate results. In a very real sense, full-text on-line systems create a customized result for each search. This obviates the need for classification systems since one does not use the results of the search to go somewhere else. Now instead of the user going to a shelf, the information is recreated according to the needs of the user and brought directly to them, almost instantaneously.

Since the information is not limited to one location, and since it does not have to be "found" in the old sense, it does not have to be classified. But does it have to be described and cataloged? Naturally the proper paths for finding information have to be embedded within it to allow for its retrieval for later use. But this function of creating pathways for retrieval is usually the work of the database creator, not the librarian. Just as librarians do not prepare the index or table of contents in books, they do not prepare the search engines for most databases. But where the patron had to find the book to use the index, the index can now leap out at their command. All of the indexes can become one enormous index, made manageable by the search engines replacing the old organizational systems. Once again the mediating function of the information-gatherer librarian is rendered unnecessary by the nature of digital information and by electronic publishers' development of their own user-friendly search systems.

These search engines, which allow the user to search databases by hooks embedded in the data, or by Boolean search connectors,[15] and to penetrate the full text of documents, are rendering any form of catalog less and less useful for most users. The original LEXIS and WESTLAW systems were touted as paragons of Boolean searching, in which the user can search the whole document for particular words or phrases, even specifying the joint occurrence or proximity of terms in the document. Since the legal databases included each word of each document, this offered enormous power. Unfortunately Boolean searching is hard to do.[16] Although it is very good at locating unique terms (one can quickly and easily find every case where the word "Twinkie" was used), there are searches where Boolean techniques do not work well, such as subject searches, where conceptual thinking is involved.

But Boolean searching was not the final step. The search engines for LEXIS and WESTLAW continue to improve. Research and development departments are working on front-end systems designed to assist the user in finding what they need. These are systems that will transform the user's inept search into a dynamic effort. The first big step was taken when WESTLAW introduced the WIN system. The WIN system allows a user to type a sentence in natural language into the computer, relying on the computer to parse it out, interpret it, and retrieve results. The user doesn't need to know any protocols at all. WIN is still far from perfect, and at the time this essay was written, LEXIS was rolling out a competing system. These systems are only the first step—the search engines will get better and better, but they are a far cry from the old methods librarians used to organize information.

Librarians have long known that most people had trouble using card catalogs. Most library users are just not good subject searchers. Being precise and complete in describing each book called for a level of detail and a complexity of organization that rendered the systems of information location produced counterproductive for everyone but the expert. When I instructed graduate students in Library and Information Studies at Berkeley, I would spend two full classes teaching them how to use the Library of Congress subject headings for finding books. It struck me as odd that nascent experts, graduate students, were struggling to master systems that librarians asked the average patron to use successfully.

Now the point is moot. If one can search for information through a modem on-line bibliographic system using a "words in title" search that does not require precision or the use of protocols, one seldom will resort to any subject system that, by its nature, requires protocols and hierarchical judgments. The next step is to turn to a full-text system and, using the embedded search hooks and the power of full-text Boolean searching, go straight to the information itself. Such systems already exist in the field of law. The commercial databases offered by LEXIS and WESTLAW, which compete for the soul of legal researchers in a ferocious marketplace, have the full text of American primary legal materials: cases, statutes, administrative rules and regulations, and constitutions. They also contain legal periodicals, loose-leaf services, and other tools. Each also offers access to stunning reservoirs of non-legal information. And all of this is in full text. When the American law student, equipped with a free home-use LEXIS or WESTLAW identification number, signs on via their home-computer modem, they have full-text access to more information than any law library contains. And they need no library catalog to search it. All of the necessary tools are built in, and the system is designed for simplicity, not for the appreciation of expert users.

These legal systems are the Rolls Royces of research, and it is fair to contend that the average person could never hope to afford to use them. But the systems are proof that the idea works. The price will come down as the market grows. Other vendors will learn.

As such systems develop, they will be applied to the information that exists in digital form. Thus, as more and more information is converted to that form, these systems will replace any intermediary engine developed by librarians. One could debate at length the speed with which existing information will be put in digital form via imaging or some related technology, but one must assume that where there is a market for such conversion, it will occur. As it does, the role of librarians and the systems of organizing and classifying information that they have so carefully developed will grow less and less relevant.

The intangible nature of digital information, and the systems to format and retrieve it that are coming to the fore, have potential that cannot be matched by any traditional system. Those trained in the old ways may remain more comfortable using them, may in fact regard the new systems with the same visceral hatred that Boyle's Viking felt for the printed word, but it will be the comfort of familiarity and emotional attachment, not logic, that maintains them.

Distributing Information

The most puzzling part of the paradigm shift is its impact on the distribution of information by librarians. Digital information raises a host of distribution-related questions that are moving to the center of the stage of societal debate. Federal policy on information is now getting increased coverage, and the related intellectual property issues are rising to the fore.[17] Jane Ginsburg's article in [the volume this article was taken from] outlines many of these concerns in arresting detail. But legal issues aside, what will be the role of librarians in the new systems of information distribution?

The conservatives see the librarians as attached to the old tradition: librarians as the protectors of the book. The book stands as an icon in need of defense from the computer-hacker barbarians who pound upon the gate. There will be a new entry in William Blades's *The Enemies of Books* series: Digital Information. In part this defense will relate to the essence of the function that librarians have performed for millennia. It is hard to abandon the old ways. But the defense also partly relates to the deep cultural association between intellectual legitimacy and books. Someone who grew up in the old paradigm might use a computer if it can provide some especially useful or efficient service, but it will still lead them to a print source in the end. Information received on a screen is inevitably regarded as second-class or lowbrow. It can never be viewed as substantive.

There is a marvelous example of this in the world of legal research. Although law schools have been turning out ardent users of on-line systems for the past few years, most senior legal professionals were trained in one of the most book-intensive environments possible. They remain skeptical of the usefulness of on-line systems and view LEXIS and WESTLAW as gimmicks or expensive toys, or, at best, as case finding tools that point one toward the right book. Some would resist viewing a case printed out from one of the databases as valid information, preferring to wait until a "real" version of the case appeared.

Someone at WESTLAW realized that it helped to format WESTLAW printers to make them produce printed pages that looked just like the pages in printed case reporters, complete with double columns of type. It was a marvelous triumph in recognizing the importance of form over content in information consumption. Senior faculty members who had scorned the printouts looked at the new pages, nodded approvingly, and said, "Well, this is real." They accepted it because the format was close to what they will always view as legitimate information—books.

The conservatives in the library profession will side with these book people. In doing so they will define the purpose of librarianship as guarding and distributing books. They may suffer the introduction of computer terminals into the library, but it is permitted with tolerance at best. The computers are not really a part of the "library," but rather something alien introduced into it. They will never abandon the book distribution paradigm; indeed, they will fight to defend it. There will be enough demand by other members of the book generation, users who wish to remain in the old paradigm, to sustain some functioning of the old model for years to come, but it will be an increasingly small business. Younger users and users who must be conscious of economics will abandon them. If librarianship allies itself with these conservatives, it will become a vestigial profession. Of course, to the true conservative, it will be more fitting, more glorious, to perish than to convert.

The radicals in the library world are already abandoning the profession. The world is in the midst of an information obsession. When Jay McInerny, a symbol of everything trendy in American letters, began a recent essay in the *New Yorker*, that citadel of the old literate culture, with an account of "infosurfing" on the Internet, no one could any longer deny that digital thinking had truly arrived.[18] The potential of the Internet and the information superhighway are everywhere among us. The fiction of William Gibson paints a picture of a new world,[19] and the radicals wish to be a part of it. They see the traditional library paradigm as wrongheaded. Indeed, to the radicals the game of distributing information, at least premium information, is lost to librarianship already. For them the mergers of telephone companies and cable television operations have more to say about the use of information than anything associated with the concept of shelving books.

Business schools are training management information systems specialists, computer science departments are training database managers, and undergraduate programs are beginning to offer majors in information. These people see information as a commodity. It is the new preferred product and its distribution will become the business at which the U.S. excels. The new corporate heroes are figures like Bill Gates at Microsoft, the symbol of information manipulation and the new paradigm.

This puts librarianship's old model for the distribution of information in jeopardy. The radicals within the profession do not want to be called librarians; they want to cut loose the old heritage and move on. They can point to the fact that the two most prestigious library schools in the country have closed and that those at both Berkeley and UCLA are severely threatened. They can contend that, in any case, the life and energy of information is not found in the halls of any library school. Those halls are filled with librarians; the wrong horses are in place. There may continue to be library schools, but they will train information workers who will be clerical and who will never hope to aspire to the humanitarian goal of public enlightenment.

There is a bundle of complex issues present here, issues that relate to the long-term undervaluing of librarianship as a women's profession and the service ideal of librarianship and its relation to entrepreneurship. Without disentangling those issues, it is nonetheless important to recognize that what has brought about this particular crisis, and what needs to be addressed now, is a problem created by the changing paradigm of information distribution. Each of the old challenges that the profession faced pales in comparison to the magnitude of this crisis. The radicals are correct: librarians cannot distribute information the old way without limiting themselves. But the radicals' solution is to abandon the profession of librarianship and move on to new careers. In doing this, they may find answers for themselves, but they offer no rescue to the profession in its crisis.

There are still the reformers. The reformers see several roles for a revitalized librarianship. They see a place for those who want librarianship to help users committed to or trapped in the old paradigm move to the new, or at least to understand the new. They also wish to transfer the values of service and integrity, which have been the defining virtues of librarianship, to the new paradigm of information. The reformers understand that information has become a commodity and that the world demands bottom-line accounting of every action, but they remain committed to the fact that people need information and that a librarian's role is to help them find it.

The central dilemma is caused by the fact that librarianship has retained its ideals, its commitment to service. Other professions, like law and medicine, long ago opted for systems designed to yield hefty remuneration for their members, but librarianship has retained a sense of service at its core. This central ethos is part of what the reformers want to save, and they seek a way to protect it while keeping the profession vital.

The reformers also recognize that librarians have always understood how people use information and that librarians have always served as the medium for introducing new information vehicles. Librarians are the people who understand how information works, how it fits together. The reformers see the power of this strength but they also realize they have no natural allies. The conservatives have a visceral dislike of any change—temporizing does not help—so they scorn the reformers. The radicals see the reformers as pathetic accommodationists. Worse still for the reformers, there is little in the way of resources to support them. The organizations in which librarians work, whether academic, public, or private, are currently caught in a dangerously shortsighted cycle of cost centering. It is more likely that an organization will cut the library's budget to realize short-term savings than support the reformers' efforts to bring about logical change for long-term gains. Through bitter experience librarians have learned that the organizations they serve will not be of help. The only path available is to work with vendors.

Vendors of information are also caught in the paradigm switch. They too are unsure how to manage the change. For vendors, just as for librarians, there is danger in the air. To refuse to change is fatal, but to change too quickly is equally deadly. Many information vendors have recognized the need for the understanding of information and its use that is exactly what librarians can provide.

In the field of law librarianship one can currently observe a fascinating phenomenon. The annual meeting of the American Association of Law Libraries is now attended by the presidents and chief executives of the major publishers. These decision-makers come seeking advice. They know that librarians still have contact with the patrons, and they believe that librarians can see which configuration of information works and which does not. Librarians can help train people in using the new systems. They have credibility with the users.

These executives are asking for help. Some traditional librarians view such overtures as illegitimate. For them the idea of dealing with the vendors as partners smacks of selling one's soul to the devil of commercial enterprise. Librarians have always viewed the distribution of information as a neutral activity, one where information producers were to be held at arm's length. The vendors, with their focus on profit, were always the enemy. But now, with information being organized by information producers and the old warehousing function gone, the librarians must see that their best hope is to work with vendors to structure tools for distributing information. Librarians can help design and implement the new systems. Librarians can be the intermediaries. The information producers are the librarians' natural allies. Librarianship must become entrepreneurial. It must help put together systems and introduce them into organizations.

Yet it remains crucial to remember the role of the user. Expert users of the new information, the techno-cowboys of the new generation, will need little help. But the vast majority of users in any library will be average and they will need to be taught how to navigate the increasingly digitized library. Some believed that as digital systems proliferated, typical users would grow more and more sophisticated until they no longer needed librarians. This theory is demonstrably wrong. As the systems have developed, users have grown used to icon-based, menu-driven systems that are extremely easy to use. The average user today expects to be prompted by systems that call for no training and operate intuitively. Large-scale database systems have yet to meet these expectations, so, in fact, users need more help than ever. The librarian's role can be to provide that help.

Librarians must recognize that the modern distribution function consists of holding the digital hand of a database user, serving as the neutral expert who can credibly advise users on what they are using. To do this librarians must insert themselves in the process of creating, organizing, and introducing these databases. This is new and it is intimidating, but it is the profession's last hope.

Someone will have to fill the helping function. Librarians would be the best choice since the profession is already in place, but it will have to show that it is ready and it will have to move quickly. In four or five years the executives of the large database companies will not be coming to library meetings asking for help. They either will have received help from librarians or they will have gone elsewhere, but whatever the source, the boat will have sailed. Librarianship should do everything that it can to be on that boat.

Will the reformers be capable of capitalizing on this new opportunity? Will they be able to retain the ideals of service that have been part of the library profession while also forging alliances with the private sector? It will not take long to discover an answer. This scenario will spin out over the next few years. If librarianship cannot change dramatically and quickly, it will become a vestigial profession. Such apocryphal statements are safely made. Librarians will wither away as the functions they filled for so long become unnecessary in an age when digital information is plentiful, self-sorted, distributed directly to the user. But if librarians can recognize the change and work with vendors to become the mediators of the digital revolution for the average user, there is hope.

NOTES

1. See Geoffrey Nunberg's essay in [the volume this article was taken from].
2. The evolution of the University of California's School of Librarianship to the School of Library and Information Studies and then to the School of Information Studies is instructive.
3. Raymond Kurzweil. "The Future of Libraries, Part 2: The End of Books," *Library Journal,* 15 February 1992.
4. This speech was recorded on audiotape and will be available in the near future, though I do not yet have publication information.
5. This particular functional breakdown is my own, although many have produced similar and dissimilar categorizations.
6. Book burning and censorship have been part of many regimes. This pattern is not limited to Western culture. The famous "Burning of the Books" in which the Emperor Chin Shih Huang Di attempted to destroy all heterodox writings in 212 B.C. is one of the most famous events in Chinese history. It was repeated in the destruction of all non-Maoist literature during the Cultural Revolution of 1966-76.
7. It is interesting to note that as the paradigm moves away from printed information toward digital information, scholarship on the change from the manuscript and oral traditions to the paradigm of the book is blossoming.
8. Coraghessan Boyle, *Descent of Man: Stories* (Boston, 1979).
9. It is worth noting that Boyle chooses a skald, a poet of the oral tradition, as narrator. Who would find books more threatening?
10. Books are treated differently than other forms of expression with the doctrine of prior restraint, which prevents the banning of books coming into play.
11. Umberto Eco, *The Name of the Rose,* trans. William Weaver (San Diego, 1983).
12. Jane Ginsburg's essay in [the volume this article was taken from] discusses some of the ways in which the ownership of information and its distribution may change. Monitoring use of materials for some future compensation system may introduce a new kind of control function for librarians.
13. These proceedings are in the process of being published, though no publication information is currently available.
14. The recent report issued by the University of Dayton Law School is an interesting and balanced projection of how this transformation may take place. (Interim Report of the University of Dayton School of Law and the Mead Data Central Joint Committee to Study Computer Technology, Mead Data Central, Dayton, 1993.)
15. If one is unfamiliar with Boolean searching, see Robert Berring, "Full-text Databases and Legal Research: Backing into the Future," *High Technology Law Journal* 1 (spring 1986), especially note 31.
16. The best summary of the problems of full-text Boolean searching is still Daniel Dabney, "The Curse of Thamus: An Analysis of Full-Text Legal Document Retrieval," *Law Library Journal* 78 (winter 1986): 5-40. It also explains indexing theory with startling clarity.
17. The questions of federal information policy, especially given Vice President Al Gore's interest in the information superhighway and the recent pressures brought to bear on the Government Printing Office, will be complex. It is difficult to predict how impor-

tant the federal government's role will be, but it is safe to assume that it will be a key factor.

18. Jay McInerney, "The Way of All Text," *The New Yorker*, September 20, 1993, 128.

19. If one wishes an introduction to the culture of information, try William Gibson's *Neuromancer* or *Count Zero*, which were foundation stones of the culture and literature known as cyberpunk. Gibson introduced terms and phrases that are now found throughout popular culture.

14

Blow up the Corporate Library

T.H. Davenport and L. Prusak

This article seeks to examine why the many corporate libraries play such a marginal role in today's corporation. This is especially vexing since we are constantly told how we are living in the 'information age' and librarians rightly perceive themselves as information professionals. We feel that librarians often operate under the wrong conceptual model of what an information service should be in the 1990s. This outmoded concept, we call the 'warehouse' model. Alternatives are needed which are better suited to today's corporate needs and constraints. The two alternatives are the 'expertise centre' and the 'network'. These concepts are all fully developed in the text, as are the reasons (with accompanying research findings) for this situation.

INTRODUCTION

The information age is clearly upon us. Academics, consultants, and managers state that information is a critical competitive weapon, that information can transform organisational structures and processes, and that we are all now in the information business. By every measure, including the proliferation of informa-

Reprinted from *International Journal of Information Management* 16, no. 6 (December 1993), pp. 405–412, with permission from Elsevier Science. Tom Davenport is a Partner in Ernst & Young's Center for Information Technology and Strategy in Boston, MA. He is responsible for the research and multiclient program activities of the Center and also participates in selected consulting engagements. His primary research and consulting interests include the role of IT in the redesign of business process, planning for future IT and its applications, and assessing the organizational impacts of IT initiatives. Larry Prusak is a Principal at Ernst & Young's Center for Information Technology and Strategy. He is responsible for managing the center's information resources, working on center research programs, as well as selected consulting to clients. His primary research and consulting interests focus on information management. His areas of specialized expertise include designing and implementing executive information systems, competitive and environmental scanning services, and working with corporate centres and libraries.

tion sources and expenditures for information, the generation and use of information is growing. Management experts such as Peter Drucker and Tom Peters, and Kodama and Nonaka in Japan, consistently trumpet the importance of information use and effective information management.

These, then, should be halcyon days for libraries as the keepers and distributors of information. What function would be better positioned to understand information requirements, distribute information to the right employees and locations, and determine the structure of the 'corporate memory'? Surely not information systems functions; they are still largely concerned with technology, despite the presumptuous title of chief information officer.

Libraries do play an important role in some firms, particularly in research and information-intensive organisations such as pharmaceuticals, investment banks, and consulting. They are significant cost centres at many large firms. There are at least 20,000 professional librarians working in corporate or government libraries, as well as another 50,000 non-professionals. Almost all major (and many smaller) corporations have a library, or library-like functions, as do most major government agencies. Several very large firms have library organisations with as many as 50 distinct units. While it is difficult to determine what information is specifically bought by libraries, it is estimated that corporate libraries collectively spend 1.7 billion dollars annually.

Yet corporate libraries in the USA have largely been left behind by the information revolution. They have performed relatively narrow functions, mainly associated with identifying and acquiring information, and have not become integrated into the major organisational processes for managing information. Most of them operate on obsolete storage-based models of information management. They have little influence and their employees are often in dead-end careers. Though in many organisations the head of information technology reports to the chief executive officer, to argue that a librarian should do so would be unprecedented. Even though librarians often know more about 'information' than any other staff professionals, few if any have received the title of chief information officer.

It would be easy to say, "blow up the library", and indeed library budgets are often among the first to be cut during hard times.[1] But libraries and librarians have a high degree of potential value. They often know, better than anyone else in the firm, what information is needed for specific projects, and how to facilitate the effective delivery of that information. Unlike their counterparts in the information systems function, they have chosen to focus on information, rather than technology. Finally, some of the 'library' functions we have studied in other parts of the world—particularly in Japan—provide a valuable model for how libraries can fully achieve their potential.[2] We are therefore arguing that libraries should be blown up in a positive sense—that their mission, function, and scope should be significantly expanded, and perhaps combined with other information functions in the firm. All that needs to be detonated is the physical library, the low-level box on the organisational chart, and the stereotypes of librarians more concerned with books than business needs.

WHAT'S WRONG WITH LIBRARIES TODAY

Despite their potential key role in the 'information age', corporate libraries today have many problems. They are poorly understood even by their own managers, and are based on an obsolete model of information provision. They are usually not well integrated with either the businesses they serve or other information-oriented functions. As a result, the value they deliver is often unclear, and in any case less than what is possible.

Libraries are not well understood by those who manage them. About 40 percent report to general administration functions whose managers rarely know, or care much about, information provisioning. Out of 165 corporate libraries surveyed in a previous study, only three reported to a person who had any professional experience in running library.[3] Libraries that report to specific functions such as marketing, planning, or R&D are better represented with management; however, they usually serve only their host functions well, developing materials primarily relevant to single functions. And while this has obvious value for these functions, there is no leveraging of sources.

The corporate library developed and grew in the 1920s and 1930s, when print-based resources were predominant, and was based on the model of the public library. The goal was to obtain as many physical volumes—books—as possible on the assumption that someday someone would want to use each one ('a book for every patron' was a common library mission statement). Library policies focused not on how to ensure that information resources were used, but rather on ensuring that they did not leave the premises illicitly. Librarian skill development focused on acquisition, storage, and classification of printed materials, and distribution of them on request. This is essentially a *warehouse* model of information provision. Yet potential users of the information not only had little idea what was in the information warehouse; they also frequently lacked an understanding of why they should even take a look.

As books began to be supplemented by a panoply of less voluminous and structured sources, in more sophisticated organisations the model of information provision did change somewhat. Instead of warehousing books, this new model of the library warehoused people—specifically subject matter experts. Such an *expertise centre* model assumed that employees requiring information on a topic would simply seek out a content expert in a library unit dedicated to a particular topic, e.g., competitive information or information about microelectronics. But this model neglected the fact that most of the people in an organisation with subject-matter expertise are not information professionals. Expertise centres are clearly an improvement over the warehouse model, but they do not go far enough in distributing information around an organisation.

Furthermore, no real rethinking of either the warehouse or expertise centre models took place when computers entered the library, or when users got access to desktop computers and all-pervasive networks. The improvement from storing CD-ROMs in the warehouse rather than books is one of marginal efficiency, not effectiveness. Though schools of librarianship, or information science, have taught computer skills and advocated more active roles for many years, actual practice in most firms has not changed significantly.

There has also been little integration or even co-operation between libraries and other information-oriented functions. Librarians collect, categorise and store largely textual information; information systems groups focus on largely quantitative or transactional information, and rarely do the twain meet. If an executive wanted to find out more about a customer or competitor who shows up in the latest weekly printout or terminal display, he or she must go to an entirely different source for the information, using different protocols for expressing the information requirement and accessing the source. Only in precious few organisations, such as some universities, firms with strong R&D functions, and financial service firms, for example, have librarians and information technology executives begun to seriously collaborate. Other information-oriented groups, e.g., market researchers, executive assistants, and finance, have also not generally been closely aligned with libraries.

A focus on information content is of great potential value to any organisation. Yet librarians have focused on functional efficiency and the profession of being corporate librarians. They often know little beyond the information content needs about the businesses they serve, and are thus unable to suggest ways to make more effective use of information within those businesses. They spend their time not living with information users, but maintaining the stacks. It should also be pointed out that information systems professionals are also often as poorly integrated into the businesses they serve, but they are making faster strides in the right direction than librarians are.

Without this intimate knowledge of the business, neither librarians nor most of their information systems counterparts have been able to focus on actively determining the broad information needs of managers and employees and providing that information in a useful format. As a result, librarians and IS managers are often hard pressed to prove or demonstrate the value of their functions. Because of their distance from the usage of information, putting a value on the information itself is virtually impossible.

Librarians have also declined to try to influence or shape information behaviour, or how employees identify, use, and share information. Attempts at outreach programmes often involve teaching employees how to best use the facilities rather than how to solve information problems, or how information can create product and service value. This absence of focus forms a critical gap for many firms, since no other information-oriented function has assumed it either.

As is perhaps obvious by now, the problems of libraries are not only structural and historical. They are also at least partially attributable to librarians themselves. Though there are many exceptions, the typical library professional does not relish the hurly-burly of business. As several librarians have told us, 'we librarians prefer books to people'. Few students would enter library schools in order to get on 'the fast track'. Though such reticence has its attractions, it hinders the effective use of information by business people who sorely need it.

Of course, the fault lies not only with librarians, but also with managers who do not value information in the first place, and who are proud of their ability to act on uninformed intuition. We would argue more generally that the American business culture does not place a high value on acquiring and using information. An indication of this problem is the guilt many managers feel when they are seen reading a book or a journal at their desks. This behaviour is much more the norm in Europe and Japan, where we have observed senior executives actually *reading* at their desks or in the library, with no apparent shame. Perhaps this cultural problem will be eased by the growth of computerised information sources; our culture's love for technology generally attaches much less of a stigma to staring at a cathode ray tube.

OUT OF THE WAREHOUSE

It is time for a new model of the corporate library and the librarian. The warehouse concept must be blown up; librarians, or rather information managers, must view themselves not as warehouse custodians, or even as providers of centralised expertise, but rather as overseers of a multi-media network (see Table 14-1). They must be concerned with the structure and quality of the content that goes out over the network (programming), in what format it is distributed (media selection), to what audience it is directed (broadcasting vs. narrowcasting), and how the receiver's behaviour changes in response to the content (advertising response). However, just as television networks do not produce all of the programmes they broadcast, the role of the information network executive in firms should be to encourage wide participation in information creation and dissemination. Broadly speaking, the role of the information professional becomes the establishment of connections between those who have information, and those who want it.

The library itself must be viewed as a virtual information network. The network should be multinodal, with eventually more nodes than there are employees. Several Japanese firms, including Mitsubishi, Nomura, and Dai-Ichi Pharmaceuti-

TABLE 14-1 Models of Information Provision

Model	Primary objective	Mode of operation
Warehouse	Control and storage of printed matter	Limited information distribution; establishment of formal systems
Expertise centre	Provide access to human experts and their information sources	Reliance on information professionals; some value added to information
Network	Connect providers and users of information	Computer-based multi-media networks with pointers to human sources

cals, already have substantial technical and business information networks in place. These well-designed networks provide access to internal and external textual and quantitative information, and will eventually allow access by virtually all employees. In the USA several firms have developed, or are developing, broad networks for employee conferencing and information access. The firms include Barclays and Chemical Bank,[4] IBM, American Airlines,[5] and several professional services firms. These networks serve both a communications and an information function; some percentage of the materials on them will eventually become part of the 'corporate memory'.

For the technical and employee networks to be effectively combined, someone must devote considerable effort to structuring the information, deciding what should be discarded or saved, and educating the organisation on how to use them. Some of the new technologies for information exchange, including Lotus Notes and NCR's Cooperation, are much more amenable to the provision of document-oriented information than previous technologies. However, no technologies currently available can decide what information should go onto the network, how different information bases should be structured, and what information is worth keeping around. We are likely to need humans for such activities over the next few decades. Librarians are the most likely candidates for these roles, if they take up the challenge. If no one accepts the roles, the technical networks firms build for information exchange are likely to be severely underleveraged, as was the case at one professional services firm where only information systems people were involved in implementation.[6]

This is not to imply that computer networks are the only vehicle for information networking. Librarians must be creative about the media used to help employees achieve 'current awareness', as it is called in the profession. This might involve arranging seminars, broadcasts over corporate video networks, or disseminating audio tapes for drive-time listening. At NEC, a large Japanese firm, researchers are asked to create posters about their research work, which are then hung on corridor walls for passers-by to study. Finally, there will probably always be a role for the human 'information assistant', who knows what information is needed by an executive, how to get it, and how to summarise and interpret it. These positions are expensive, but as long as senior managers have a greater need for information than they have time to obtain and digest it, they will continue to be valuable. Due to budget cuts, many of these information assistants are no longer around. In the September MIE meeting, Bob Eccles said he had to either teach 20 percent more or lose his business analysts. Ed Hann of NCR said they have already lost their analysts. Those people not adept, at gathering information take time away from their job to collect information.

Under the network model, book-banning, never an activity favoured by librarians, must come into vogue. Though we love books as much as anyone, they are often inefficient vehicles for the dissemination of information in corporations. They have more information than most managers need for *ad hoc* requests and they are difficult to copy and distribute. Even technical journals contain much information that is not useful to an individual reader, and also have copyright problems. On the other hand, on-line databases and CD-ROM already contain most of the information that managers need day-to-day. Many publishers of books and journals are experimenting with unbundling of printed materials and with publishing them in electronic form. Even periodicals' clearinghouses, which manage lists of magazine and journal subscriptions for corporate libraries, are also addressing this issue. Information managers should work with these firms to try to speed their development efforts. The token copy of Michael Porter's *Competitive Strategy* can remain on managerial bookshelves, but the real use of information awaits new media and new approaches.

With a decreasing emphasis on books and shelves, there should be much less of a need for the library as a place. While having a physical location for printed materials can be logistically beneficial, it does more harm than good. Librarians should attempt to place printed materials on credenzas and in briefcases, not in the stacks. Browsing, which happens rarely anyway in our book-averse culture, should be facilitated over networks. When we visit the new firms who do maintain attractive reading rooms, we rarely find people using them. And librarians themselves should be found not among books, but among users (either actual or potential) of information. At one contract research firm, for example, there is a kiosk equipped with an information professional and an array of printed and electronic sources in each technical area.

Corporate librarians and information systems managers should align more closely. Better yet, those employees who are skilled at information content issues—not only librarians but also some information systems professionals, business analysts, and functional specialists—should align with each other, and providers of technological infrastructure in both camps can join together in a separate organisation. The problem with folding them all into one information organisation is two-fold. First, librarians and data centre operators have little in common in terms of knowledge and responsibility. Secondly, many organisations might fear the idea of a single functional entity with responsibility for all aspects of information management. If information is truly power, a united information function might prove to be powerful. Perhaps the appropriate model is similar to that in the current US telecommunications industry, in which some firms (e.g., regional Bell operating companies, AT&T) have concentrated on network infrastructure, and others (Dun & Bradstreet, McGraw-Hill, Dow Jones) have focused on content. Alliances between these two worlds are desirable and becoming common, but no one firm seems able to master both.

As Peter Drucker has noted, we have only begun to understand how managers and organisations use information. There is a great need for understanding of how people use and value information—how they gather it, share it, act (or not act) on it, and dispose of it—and under what conditions it should be supplied, including preferred medium and source. The combination of all of this detail would yield a true information architecture, with flows, nodes, inputs, outputs, transformations, and usage patterns. Previous versions of information architecture have been much too granular, technical, and detailed to be of much use; future versions should be created not at the data element or entity level, but at the level of bounded information—often in the form of a document. Again, no one is better positioned than librarians to pursue and act on these issues; they deal frequently with information requirements and documents.

The librarians or information managers in tomorrow's organisation must realise that people, not printed or electronic sources, are the most valuable information asset in any organisation. Legions of annual reports say that 'the experience and knowledge of our people is our most valuable asset', yet firms do little or nothing to capitalise on or provide access to this asset. The modern librarian will catalogue not only printed materials or even knowledgeable information professionals, but also that Jane Smith is working on a sales force compensation project, and that Joe Bloggs knows a lot about the metallurgical properties of wheel bearings. When another division or a customer calls to find out this sort of information, they will finally have a place to go. Several of the firms we have worked with already feel that this is a valid role for librarians; at one telecommunications firm, for example, librarians were referred to as 'human PBXs' because of their ability to make connections between people requiring information and people possessing it.

All these changes will undoubtedly seem daunting to information professionals (they are summarised in Table 14-2). They do comprise a radical shift in how people provide information throughout organisations. Better, however, to transform these information jobs than to lose them entirely. The old model of librarians guarding the stacks from information users, or of researchers and executives browsing in comfortable reading rooms, will never be appropriate again.

IMPLICATIONS AND CONCLUSION

As we can see, librarians have their work cut out for them. There are many potential roles to be performed for which they are well-suited. All the more shameful that they continue working in the passive, low-status environment that characterises most corporate libraries today. Some of today's librarians may find it difficult to make the transition to network executives, and for virtually all this is

TABLE 14-2   Requirements for Tomorrow's Information Professionals

1. Get out of the library, and into the business
2. Actively assess who needs information, and who has it—then help them to connect
3. Focus on multiple media, and how they can be exploited using tomorrow's technologies
4. Develop an alliance with the more user-oriented IS personnel
5. Don't assume that technology will replace humans in information provision
6. Develop an architecture of information
7. Work with external providers to develop more useful vehicles for information
8. Emphasize usage of information materials over control

a transition that will take a number of years. The combination of information functions, and the blending of different types of information skills, will make the necessary cultural changes more possible.

Of course, the issues described here are bigger than the library. What we are talking about is, in fact, a larger set of issues around information management. Whether computer people, librarians, market researchers, or outsourcers provide these services is not really important. That they are ultimately provided in an effective form is what really matters.

It may also be clear that the ideas presented here, because they represent incremental functionality, will require incremental resources. Some current information-oriented activities, such as purchasing the same information multiple times across the organisation, spending time in searching for information (about 11 percent of total work time, according to one recent study of 200 executives),[7] and buying information for the warehouse that never gets used, can be streamlined or eliminated through better information management. But the information revolution won't come for free. We must be willing to invest in the management of information that helps us make better products, decisions, and customer relationships. What makes this even more expensive is that once someone has been provided with good information, he or she often just wants more. When the information is germane and well-packaged, there is no such thing as information overload.[8]

The library was created at a time when formation access and usage was a more leisurely activity. We might want to return to those days, but they have not been present for a long time in the corporations we study and work with. To adapt to current and future information environments, radical changes must be undertaken in corporate libraries. Ironically, if they are not begun soon, libraries, and those who focus on content rather than computers, may become extinct in the information age.

NOTES

1. Matarazzo, J. (1981). *Closing The Corporate Library: Case Studies on the Decision-Making Process.* Special Library Association, New York.

2. Matarazzo, J. and Prusak, L. (1992). *Information Management and Japanese Success.* Special Report, Ernst & Young's Center for Information Technology and Strategy, Boston, MA.

3. Prusak, L., Matarazzo, J., and Gauthier, M. (1990). *Valuing Corporate Libraries: A Survey of Senior Managers.* Special Libraries Association, Washington, DC.

4. Rothstein, P., Stoddard, D., and Applegate, L. (1992). *Chemical Banking Corporation—Developing a Communications Infrastructure for the Corporate Systems Division.* Harvard Business School Report No. N1-192-103, Boston, MA.

5. Anderson, E. and Mckenney, J. (1992). *American Airlines: The InterAAct Project (A) & (B).* Harvard Business School Report No. N9-193-013/4, Boston, MA.

6. Orlikowski, W. (1992). *Learning from Notes: Organizational Issues in Groupware Implementation.* CISR working paper 241, MIT Center for Information Systems Research.
7. Accountemps (1992). Survey conducted by Accountemps and reported in *Information Week*, p. 47.
8. Bruns, W. and Mckinnon, S. (1992). *The Information Mosaic.* Harvard Business School Press, Boston, MA; the authors find little evidence of information overload among manufacturing executives, even though the information received is often of poor quality.

15

Our Profession Is Changing: Whether We Like It or Not

Betty Eddison

Outsourcing came like a clap of thunder to the attention of information professionals in the U.S. in the summer of 1995. That's when General Electric Co. decided to outsource the operation of its headquarters' information service to Teltech. One result of that contract is that some information professionals perceive that they are threatened. Thoreau said, "why the hurry to succeed?" One response might be—because we must protect our jobs.

The practice of contracting for the provision of specific services by people outside of an organization has been around for a long time, even in libraries. What appeared new to many of us in 1995 was the outsourcing of the management of complete special libraries.

In this article, I explore some of the ways in which contracting for outside services has been used over time. I also identify some companies started by librarians to provide outsourced services for other librarians. These companies began because the founding librarians perceived a need and a market for their services, and they continued because they acquired and kept customers. Although the NIH syndrome (Not Invented Here) was a reasonably popular industrial attitude some 20 years ago, it has become increasingly unpopular. Now companies understand that it is better to bring in services from the outside to achieve quality services than to do everything on their own.

The same is true of librarians in many corporations. Librarians who realize that they can provide better service to their clients within the organization if someone else does the cataloging, or delivers the documents, or puts labels on books, or even does searching of databases for a subject in which the library staff is not experienced, are librarians with vision. The point is that it is the librarian

Reprinted by permission of *Online Magazine,* "Our Profession Is Changing: Whether We Like It or Not" by Betty Eddison (January–February 1997): 72–81. Communications to the author should be addressed to *Betty Eddison,* Chairman, Inmagic Inc., 800 West Cummings Park, Woburn, MA. 01801; 617/938-4442; Fax 617/ 938-6393; beddison@inmagic.com.

who is in charge, who finds the source of assistance, and who manages the whole operation.

THE EARLIEST OUTSOURCING

Outsourcing has been around for several centuries. Perhaps the first—certainly one of the first—instances of outsourcing occurred when "The monks employed the services of several printers in their press and nuns were employed in the composition and illumination. . . ".[1] It looks as though this printing press was established in the Convent of San Iacopo di Ripoli in 1476 under the leadership of two monks. They knew they needed help.

OUTSOURCING AND U.S. INDUSTRY

In more recent years, contracting for services has become increasingly popular in U.S. corporations and organizations as a tool to help organizations to focus. "Companies are in mid-passage, shifting from management evolved during the Industrial Revolution to models suited for the information age. Not yet settled into new organizational paradigms, they are refocusing on the core activities of the business. All units, and particularly those providing internal services, are being examined in a new light and must show explicitly how they contribute to the economic performance of the corporation."[2] How does your special library or information center contribute to the economic performance of your organization?

The most widely outsourced area today is the management of computer services (MIS, data processing, etc.). This is a large industry in itself. In 1996, that industry in the U.S. exceeded $10 billion annually and was growing at a rate of 16 percent a year.[3]

Outsourcing in U.S. industry is increasing in other fields as well: records management, planning, healthcare, strategic planning, human resources, accounting services, transportation, copying and fax services, mailroom operation, travel, auto fleet maintenance, procurement, construction, manufacturing, distribution, telemarketing, training, and more.

Corporations have moved from thinking that they can do everything better and less expensively than others, to thinking that they must focus on the things that they really know how to do well. As a result, they increasingly contract with other companies to carry out the services that are needed by companies whose focus is that service. They are beginning to adopt the notion, as defined in the August 26, 1996 issue of *Business Week,* that "by working with direct competitors, customers, and suppliers, a company can create new businesses, markets, and industries."

This is corporate America's current mantra.

OUTSOURCING AND INFORMATION TECHNOLOGY

An article in *Information Week* quotes a CEO as saying, "I wanted a strategic partnership relationship, someone with a vested interest in my success." The articles continues: "These efforts make the contracting of IS services, as well as business-process services, more effective. *The ultimate goal: to build virtual corporations, in which companies work together to perform the functions previously carried out by the hierarchical corporate structure* . . . What we outsource is not our organization's core business, but it *is* that of the vendor, who is in a better position to deliver a quality product" [emphasis added].[4]

To support this growing corporate interest in outsourcing, an Outsourcing Institute has been formed. The Outsourcing Institute, "a professional association for objective, independent information on the strategic use of outside resources," was founded in the spring of 1993 and provides products and services to the outsourcing community—those who engage in outsourcing and those who use outsourcing services. The Outsourcing Institute offers its members (and non-members for a larger fee) the *Annual Buyers Guide* which lists companies which provide outsourcing services.[5]

Paul Strassman has reported on research he has done, which shows that strategy is not driving outsourcing. His statistics demonstrate that the real reason companies outsource management of information technologies is simple: they're in financial trouble. Strassman concludes by saying that "I am in favor of outsourcing for any of the good reasons that would take advantage of somebody else's capacity to accumulate know-how faster than it remains home-grown. It should not be applied as an emetic. I will be especially encouraged about the prospects for outsourcing services when I get a large list of prosperous and growing organizations that have picked this option as a way of enhancing their mastery of information management."[6] However, not many people appear to agree with him at the moment.

OUTSOURCING AND SPECIAL LIBRARIANS

Special librarian-targeted outsourcing services (to use current terminology, but not that in vogue then) began in the 1970s. These services include specialized cataloging, thesaurus development, document delivery, online searching, temporary or permanent staffing, loose-leaf filing, subscription management, bindery services, table of contents services, database design and data entry services, moving services, plus library management.

Contracting for cataloging services started more than two decades ago with the development of systems now known as OCLC, MARCIVE, WLN, RLN, and others. Special librarians often contracted with others for cataloging because they didn't have and couldn't justify or afford full-time technical services people, or because they needed special kinds of cataloging services. Sometimes they were with organizations that required the use of locally developed classification systems or specialized subject headings, neither of which was in use at the Library of Congress, then the primary source of cataloging information. For example, services provided by Warner-Eddison Associates, Inc., WEA, a company which Alice Sizer Warner and I began in 1973, included cataloging as well as printing catalog cards for special librarians with special needs.[7]

Outsourcing the *management* of special libraries really began when the Federal Government began to think of ways to reduce the numbers on its payroll. Government libraries have contracted for services for more than 15 years, and several companies have participated in the running or management of special libraries within the Federal Government.

Labat-Anderson Inc. has operated a number of the EPA libraries in several regions for a long time. They also have had contracts to run other government libraries. As they are growing, they are preparing themselves to run libraries in the private sector, as well as government libraries.

Australian Librarians Look at Outsourcing

Synergy in Sydney, a 1995 conference in Sydney, Australia, included a number of programs about outsourcing and special librarians. These papers indicate that special librarians in Australia feel much the same way that special librarians in the United States and Canada feel about outsourcing—and that they are dealing creatively with the issues raised.

> Paul, Meg, Director, Freelance Library & Information Services Pty Ltd. "Coping with Contracting Out." *Synergy in Sydney 1995*, pp. 183–191.
>
> Meg Paul begins by writing "Management techniques come and go as organisations look for new ways to become more efficient. In Australia following the lead from England and the United States, 'outsourcing' or 'contracting out' is now becoming an accepted way for organisations to downsize and cut overheads" (p. 183).

> Butler, Yvonne, Managing Director, The Information Source. "Survival in Special Libraries: The Current Issues." *Synergy in Sydney 1995*, pp. 1–13.
>
> Yvonne Butler supports, strongly, the use of business planning in special libraries. "If you have worked in the same organisation for more than a year, it is time to commence learning again about your organisation. Many things will have changed in the year, and whilst you may think you have picked up on most things, you most likely will be surprised . . . Talk to other managers and find out what they have done during the year. Read their annual reports. See their business plans. Ask to see the organisation's business plan. Understand where the organisation is headed and the constraints under which it is operating" (p. 8).

Dean, Ione. "The 7 Habits of Highly Effective Information Professionals." *Synergy in Sydney 1995,* pp. 33–42.

> Ione Dean takes Steven Covey's *The 7 Habits of Highly Effective People* (1990) and applies them to information professionals.

Gaebler, Jan, BankSA. "When the Going Gets Tough . . . We Need Our Libraries More Than Ever!" *Synergy in Sydney 1995,* pp. 27–32.

> Jan Gaebler's paper discusses how a very negative situation at the State Bank of South Australia resulted over time in a positive outcome "by capitalising on lean times to demonstrate the economic efficiencies of a special library. The importance of productivity measures, service quality, promotion and 'irrefutable' facts in putting the case for the library are emphasised" (p. 1).

Aguado, Patricia, Gardiner Library Service. "Insourcing—Creating Work and Diversity in Special Libraries." *Synergy in Sydney 1995,* pp. 171–182.

> Patricia Aguado describes how a library service was created in one part of Australia to help health-related organizations after an earthquake destroyed the original organization. "We were forced to refocus our thinking, and reconsider the direction we would take, in terms of which services to develop, and which to drop; and which services to implement on a fee-for-service basis, and whether these would be on a cost-recovery or profit basis" (p. 172). "Insourcing allows librarians to redefine their expertise and their services in terms of core business, and then to reposition themselves in the market place. As well as staying in business, they are thus able to create further business" (p. 174).

McConchie, Brenda, AIMI Training and Consultancy Services. "Insourcing-Outsourcing: Making the Right Decision." *Synergy in Sydney 1995,* pp. 193–196.

> Brenda McConchie tells us that ". . . the librarian needs to ensure that the library can address the queries when they are raised and in particular deal with the strategic value of performing the function internally. One way to handle this is to introduce a planning cycle which not only plans for what is ahead but also looks at what has been done and how well it was done. It is one thing to have a forward focussed strategic plan and it is another to have in place ways of monitoring progress and performance as a matter of routine . . . Evaluation is essentially about checking whether what was intended was achieved and if not, why not. In order for evaluation to be effective, the achievement criteria or performance indicators must be determined and then measured for compliance" (p. 194).

It is good to know that our colleagues in Australia are contributing leadership which applies to all of us.

The proceedings are out of print; information about document availability from beddison@inmagic.com.

For Further Reading

The General Electric information center management award to Teltech made outsourcing a frequent program topic in regional and national meetings of library and information professionals (SLA, AALL, National Online Meeting) throughout 1995 and 1996. The issue prompted headlines and concerned reporting in many media sources, including these:

DiMattia, Susan, "Outsourcing, Ongoing Concern." *Corporate Library Update* 4, No. 11 (August 15, 1995): p. 4.

"Outsourcing Promotes Value, Teltech Executive Asserts." *Corporate Library Update* 4, No. 12 (September 1, 1995): p. 4.

"Minority Position in Teltech Announced by Knight-Ridder." *Corporate Library Update* 4, No. 12 (September 1, 1995): p. 1.

"Outsource in 1995? Teltech's Take on the Benefits." *Corporate Library Update* 4, No. 13 (September 15, 1995): p. 4.

"The Path Toward Outsourcing, Inevitable in GE Atmosphere?" *Corporate Library Update* 4, No. 14 (October 1, 1995): p. 4.

"Teltech Purchases CHR, Online Search Specialists." *Corporate Library Update* 4, No. 17 (November 15, 1995): p. 1.

Quint, Barbara. "Teltech: Tool or Rival?" [interviews with Teltech executives] *Searcher* 4, No. 2 (February 1996): pp. 22–26. This article was the first in "The O Word: Issues in Outsourcing," a continuing series that ran monthly in *Searcher* throughout 1996 and examined several aspects of the practice.

Two recent articles provide case studies of libraries responding to management challenges.

Lemon, Nancy. "Climbing the Value Chain: A Case Study in Rethinking the Corporate Library Function." *Online* 20, No. 6 (November 1996): pp. 50–57. The former library supervisor at Owens Corning, now Leader of Knowledge Resource Services, describes how she turned her library, her job, and her future around by recognizing what needed to be changed.

Katz, Trudy. "How to Prove Your Worth to Your Management." *Marketing Library Services* 10, No. 3, (April/May 1996): pp. 4–5. Katz describes the role of Mary Ann Kalambay at Rothschild North America. The President of Rothschild announced that Kalambay had just been promoted to Vice President, and went on to say "The library is the nerve center of Rothschild" (p. 4).

The School of Information and Library Science, University of North Carolina, Chapel Hill, has a contract to provide library and information support for the EPA library in Research Triangle Park, North Carolina. NOAA and a number of other government libraries have been under contract to the Scientific and Commercial Systems Corporation for some time.

Nevertheless, government libraries outsourcing has not made special library press headlines in the same manner as the award of the General Electric outsourcing contract did. That may be because government contract awards are usually handled pretty quietly, or it may be because no new contracts have been awarded recently. As indicated above, the GE award was certainly both recent and newsworthy.

OUTSOURCING AND PUBLIC LIBRARIANS

The trend toward outsourcing library services has even spread to public libraries. A classified advertisement in *Library Hotline,* June 17, 1996, p. 10, indicates that the Public Library of Charlotte & Mecklenburg County, North Carolina, was looking for a database manager who would manage the outsourcing contract and database that would be the result of outsourcing their Technical Services Department.

Hawaii State Librarian Bart Kane told the library community in May 1996 that "the organization that can shave delivery and turnaround time, provide better quality, and tailor its products and services to a customer's precise needs is an organization that will succeed in the 21st century." He made this statement when discussing the five year contract that the Hawaii State Library has signed with Baker & Taylor for choosing the books to be cataloged, labeled, and delivered to the 49 public libraries in Hawaii. "Under the new agreement, Baker & Taylor will provide new books in ten days, compared to the 47 it takes the Hawaii State Library under previous ordering and processing arrangements. Customer service has driven the entire reengineering process for Hawaii this past year. In the public library world, without customer service and without lower cost, half of the public libraries in the United States will be out of business in ten years," Kane declared. "Staff should be on the floor 99 percent of the time, not the 40 to 50 percent average in American libraries," in Kane's view.[8]

OUTSOURCING—COMPANIES MANAGED BY LIBRARIANS

Over the last 15 or 20 years, increasing numbers of smaller companies, started and managed by librarians, have aimed at providing services to special librarians. A look at their marketing brochures or a brief telephone interview reveals that, in addition to spreading the word about the importance of library services, they are usually ready to work with librarians to provide information services to the library's clientele.

Representative Outsourcing Information Service Companies and Organizations

Note: This listing is not exhaustive.

Advanced Information Consultants (AIC)—Corporate Headquarters: Canton, Michigan; 313/459-9090 or 800/929-3789; Fax 313/459-8990; info@AdvinfoC.com; Peggy Hull, Manager, Library Services for AIC; 1200 Broad Street, Suite 202, Durham, NC 27705; 919/286-3715; Fax 919/286-9583; hullp@nando.net. Quotation from a letter from Peggy Hull, June 18, 1996.

Association of Independent Information Professionals (AIIP)—Headquarters, Suite 2103, 245 Fifth Avenue, New York, NY 10016; 212/779-1855; 73263.34@compuserve.com; http://www.aiip.org. Mary Ellen Bates, Bates Information Services in Washington, DC, is the 1996–97 president. AIIP publishes a directory of its members' businesses.

Burwell Enterprises, Inc.—3724 F.M. 1960 W, Suite 214, Houston, Texas 77068; 713/537-9051; Fax 713/537-8332; http://www.lpn.net/net/lpl. html. Burwell Enterprises publishes *The Burwell World Directory of Information Brokers* annually, now with listings of over 1,800 information brokers around the world.

Carr Research Group—Baltimore, MD; 410/719-8630; Fax 410/719-0482; carres@ix.netcom.com; http://www. carr-research.com.

C. Berger and Company—327 East Gunderson Drive, Carol Stream, IL 60188; 708/653-1115 or 800/382-4CBC; Fax 708/653-1691.

FIND/SVP—625 Avenue of the Americas, New York, NY 10011; 212/645-4500; Fax 212/645-7681; postmaster@findsvp.com; http://www. findsvp.com.

Gossage-Regan Associates, Inc.—25 West 43d Street, New York, NY 10036; 212/869-3348; Fax 212/997-1127.

Labat-Anderson, Inc.—8000 W. Park Drive, Suite 400, McLean, VA 22102; 703/506-9600; Fax 703/506-4646; http://www/labat.com. This is the headquarters office. There are other offices around the U.S.

The Library Co-op, Inc.—Library and Information Specialists. Gloria Dinerman, President, 3840 Park Avenue, Suite 107, Edison, NJ 08820; 908/906-1777 or 800/654-6275; Fax 908/906-3562.

Library Management Systems—400 Corporate Pointe, Suite 755, Culver City, CA 90230; 310/216-6436 or 800/567-4669; Fax 310/649-6388.

NERAC, Inc.—One Technology Drive, Tolland, CT 06084; 203/872-7000; Fax 860/875-1749; NERAC@NERAC.COM.

Savage Information Services—2510 W. 237th Street, Suite 200, Torrance, CA 90505; 310/530-4747; Fax 310/530-0049.

Scientific and Commercial Systems Corporation—7600 Leesburg Pike, Suite 400, Falls Church, VA 22043; 703/917-9171: Fax 703/917-9797; mlee@scsycorp.com.

TeleSec Library Services—Mary Jo Detweiler, Library Division Manager; 301/949-2303; telesec@ix.netcom.com.

Teltech Resource Network Corporation—2850 Metro Drive, Minneapolis, MN 55425-1566; 612/851-7500 or 800/833-8330; Fax 612/851-7766. Andy Michuda, President, Knowledge Management Services Division, Teltech Resource Network Corp.; 612/851-7577.

What follows does not pretend to be a complete list; rather it is an illustrative one. The above gives location information for some of the companies excerpted as follows and others that are also active. They are all possible places to turn to for help in carrying out your varied responsibilities.

"TeleSec has been providing staffing solutions to the libraries of metropolitan Washington since 1972. Each day, TeleSec library personnel are working in over 100 area libraries, including the major federal, academic and special libraries, on a temporary or long-term contract basis . . . Four out of five of the Washington Post's top 100 companies rely on TeleSec . . . TeleSec has the largest registry of experienced librarians and library technicians in the Washington area . . . TeleSec is managed by experienced librarians with MLS degrees and we employ a wide range of professional and paraprofessional workers." There are several firms that specialize in staffing—both for permanent placements and for projects—including Gossage-Regan Associates, Inc. in New York City and C. Berger and Company in the Chicago area.

Benchmarking: A Tool for Regular Use

Benchmarking is one of the current management tools considered important in business circles. Therefore, it is important to learn about the process of benchmarking and total quality control, and to practice benchmarking on a regular basis, so that we can demonstrate from year to year just where we are in terms of quality management.

A benchmark is a point of reference from which measurements can be made. In other words, you measure the services provided by your library or information center against those of other peer organizations. This helps you determine whether the services you provide are too expensive, less costly, or of comparable value. This is a useful annual exercise.

Resources for Benchmarking Assistance

Library Benchmarking Newsletter
Library Benchmarking International
P.O. Box 2593
Universal City, TX 78148-1593

Fax and Voice 800/659-1914
lbi@world-net.net.
http://www.world-net.net/users/lbi
"The mission of Library Benchmarking International is to help librarians and information professionals achieve library excellence." The same publishers also publish a series of Benchmarking Notebooks, such as *Identifying Benchmarking Partners: Special Libraries*.

Benchmarking for Quality Management & Technology

MCB University Press Ltd.
60/62 Toller Lane
Bradford, West Yorkshire
BD8 9BY England
http://www.mcb.co.uk
This company also sponsors Internet conferences.

The American Productivity & Quality Center
123 N. Post Oak Lane
Houston, TX 77024
713/681-4020
Fax 713/681-8780

Market Data, Inc.
5 Tanglewood Drive
Branford, CT 06405-3335
203/488-7457
Fax 203/488-7459
keitheri@mktdta.com
Denise Lipkvich, President, offers training workshops in benchmarking and other topics.

The Quality Network, Inc.
110 Linden Oaks Street,
Rochester, NY 14625
800/836-0325
This is a consulting firm that specializes in benchmarking for corporations.

There are companies in many other geographic areas which offer similar services. Advanced Information Consultants (AIC), established in 1982, has offices in Michigan, Minnesota, North Carolina, Indiana, and New York, and a staff of over 100. AIC is made up of "librarians who work with librarians, not against them, to offer high quality services that can extend their capabilities or allow them to pursue other goals."

On the West Coast, Library Management Systems "has been providing library and records management consulting and personnel services to the Los Angeles, San Diego and Orange County communities since 1983." Staffing, document delivery, database building, cataloging, and research services are among the collection of services offered. Savage Information Services, Inc., in Torrance, California, finds that they are increasingly involved in records management contracts.

The Carr Research Group, based in Baltimore, Maryland, emphasizes doing research for its customers. Their brochure says, "when you call upon the services of the Carr Research Group, you tap the expertise of graduate-degreed professionals with extensive experience in all aspects of information retrieval, organization, and analysis. They know the latest information resources and research techniques . . . "

Asking your colleagues is probably the best way to identify independent information services firms that work for librarians, but if you don't know anyone who is outsourcing, or don't want to ask, there are two directories that offer a substantial starting place.

Helen Burwell started Burwell Enterprises in 1983 in Houston, Texas, as a publishing and consulting company focusing on providing information research and retrieval for a fee. Now she publishes *The Burwell World Directory of Information Brokers* in print and CD-ROM format. Burwell was also the first president, in 1987–88, of the fast growing Association of Independent Information Professionals.

Outsourcing: Competitive Threat or Technology Trend?

Outsourcing companies are knocking at the door. Are they an ally, an enemy, or a decoy? More importantly, why are they here? How librarians and information professionals answer the second question will determine the answer to the first question. Outsourcing is an emotional lightning rod for Information Resource Center managers. For some IRCs, the trend toward outsourcing is a competitive threat. For others, it's access to additional manpower or expertise during times of need. What many IRC managers fail to understand is that outsourcing is really another manifestation of the continuing and inevitable impact of information technology in the workplace. Just as the Industrial Revolution replaced skilled craftsmen with machines, the Information Revolution is creating technologies which simplify tasks. Simplified tasks do not demand the expertise or expense of highly trained information professionals.

Behind the Outsourcing Headlines: What's Really Going on Here?

According to the 1995, study *The Value of Corporate Libraries* by Prusak and Matarazzo,[9] the corporate library service most valued by senior managers was searching of electronic databases. This service was cited by 48 percent of the respondents. But in a similar study undertaken by the same authors five years earlier, 78 percent of survey respondents placed electronic database searching as the most highly valued corporate library service![10] If this trend continues downward, Gartner Group analysts predict that by the year 2001, electronic database searching will have become the *least* valued of all corporate library services [Figure 15-1].

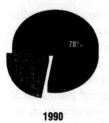  

1990   **1995**   **2001**

FIGURE 15-1 Value of Librarian Electronic Database Searching to Management: 1990–2001 (*Sources: 1990/1995-Matarazzo and Prusak • 2001-Gartner Group*)

The value placed on electronic database searching has been and continues to be in a deep decline. Has outsourcing been the catalyst for this trend? Is outsourcing the real competitive threat? I think not.

There are several significant trends creating evolutionary changes in corporate libraries and information centers. Chief among them are ubiquitous connectivity and a focus on the development of end-user interfaces by the information industry. End-users have been given the keys to the world of content; the manual shift has been replaced by the automatic transmission.

If senior management believes that corporate libraries' greatest value resides in its ability to serve as intermediary searchers of electronic databases, the biggest competitive threat to the IRC is not the outsourcing community. It is information technology.

Shifting Gears: Where Do Corporate Librarians Go from Here?

A revolution both destroys and creates. During the Industrial Revolution, machines replaced craftsmen by simplifying a process, allowing less skilled individuals to perform the same task. We are now observing the same phenomenon during the Information Revolution—and it is no less inevitable. The need for librarian-mediated searching is diminishing. Its value to senior management is eroding.

Librarians have two choices:

1. *Manage the change* created by the Information Revolution. Move from the role of processor to become a process *manager.*
2. *Resist change* if you believe that your skill as an intermediary searcher is invaluable. Stand your ground if you can be the lowest cost provider of this service. There are still some highly skilled craftsmen who can repair typewriters.

Edward B. Stear is Senior Research Analyst, Information Resource Center Management, Gartner Group, Inc., a leading provider of IT advisory and market research services. Founded in 1979 and headquartered in Stamford, Connecticut,

Gartner Group serves approximately 6,600 client organizations worldwide. Additional information about Gartner Group is available at http://www.gartner.com. Communications to the author should be sent to Edward B. Stear. Gartner Group, Inc., P.O. Box 10212, Stamford, CT 06904-2212: 203/316-6913; Fax 203/316-6480: estear@gartner.com.

Outsourcing Online Searching: What and How?

Although corporate information center outsourcing of at least some online searching activity is not yet mainstream, it appears to be the future for many organizations. There are already several successful companies engaged in online searching as an outsourced service, and in increasing numbers, we are hearing about information centers that are outsourcing their "transactional" or "commodity" searches so that they can devote staff time to other activities.

But what exactly is being outsourced? I made a few phone calls to investigate. For most companies doing any outsourcing of searching, I've heard that "continuing" and "very large" projects are what is contracted out. For some, current awareness searching is outsourced; for others, this search activity is done in-house by support personnel or by users at their own desktops. One company told me that they outsource all large-scale investigations into competitor products or companies; another said they wouldn't dream of allowing outsiders to do a competitive intelligence assignment.

Do librarians have a sense of the relative costs of outsourcing versus doing these searches themselves? Does it matter if one is more expensive than the other? Who chooses the service provider, who may contact the provider directly, how is quality ascertained and maintained? Are there advantages to contracting with a company instead of using a stable of suppliers? What are the factors to consider in choosing an outsourcer? How often are contracts re-negotiated? Are there advantages with smaller companies as opposed to larger ones? From a practical standpoint, how are requests relayed and results delivered? Is confidentiality a problem? Is anyone within the company tracking the topics and results of projects, or is that corporate knowledge going out the door? Most important, is it worth it? What are corporate librarians doing *instead* of searching?

Obviously, I still have questions. I think the issues of online search management are going to occupy us for several years to come, and I am afraid that we may well form a bit of scar tissue of our own as we work through various answers. Since its inception, *Online* has served as a forum for the discussion of online search practices, management, and evaluation. We intend to continue that role. If you have experiences to share as a user or supplier of online search outsourcing, please contact me at SusanneBj@aol.com or 203/263-4195. Your name and affiliation will remain private, but the information you share may help colleagues as we all face this new development in online. —*Suzanne Bjørner*

Currently, the Association of Independent Information Professionals (AIIP) has more than 800 members in over 15 countries. Members of this trade association of information businesses provide a variety of information services: "online database searching, market and industry surveys, document delivery, library services, general research services, public records research, thesaurus building, indexing and abstracting services, digital library development, competitive intelligence, and specialized research in specific subject areas." AIIP publishes a membership directory and will provide referrals to potential clients.

OUTSOURCING—COMPANIES NOT RUN BY LIBRARIANS

Not all information service companies are run by librarians. Widely known FIND/SVP in New York City has been providing business research services for many years, including supplying research reports from a number of investment organizations. Librarians are part of their customer base. When asked if they were planning to offer outsourced corporate library management, Andy Garvin, president, replied that "when that is recognized as a widespread need, FIND will certainly consider it."[11]

NERAC, a non-profit corporation in Connecticut, offers a variety of services to U.S. companies to help them stay abreast of new developments to enhance productivity and global competitiveness. NERAC does research for many customers, including librarians, in technical and business areas. In business for many years, NERAC has built its staff of information specialists, scientists, and engineers into a functioning team. Dan Wilde, president of NERAC, is a longterm supporter of special librarians, and NERAC regularly exhibits at SLA.

Teltech Resource Network Corporation, the winner of the contract for General Electric's RFP, is based in Minneapolis, Minnesota. Teltech's brochure says that "Technology-driven companies rely on Teltech for help in gathering, analyzing and managing the critical information they need to compete in today's global marketplace."[12] Teltech began as a provider of access to people, experts in various technical, scientific, and engineering fields. Then the company grew to searching online databases in those fields.

The most recent service offered by Teltech is what they call Knowledge Management Services (KMS). KMS is "designed to help organizations optimize the use of internal and external knowledge sources for competitive advantage . . . KMS services include information benchmarking, creation of internal knowledge-sharing networks and training that encourages desired knowledge-sharing and knowledge-application behaviors." Teltech hires and contracts with librarians and information specialists to assist in database searching, and many librarians are among their customers. In 1995, they bought Cooper Hydock Rugge, Inc., a business and technical research firm and operator of Knight-Ridder Information. Inc.'s DialSearch research service. Former CHR president Linda Cooper, who has been active as a librarian and business owner, has been asked to represent the world of librarianship to Teltech as Director of Information Professionals Market Development.

WHAT NEXT?

Now that the clap of thunder has diminished in volume, has the storm passed? Is it reasonable for librarians to continue to perceive outsourcing as a threat? There is no doubt that outsourcing is within the GE corporate culture and that the company issued the RFP and awarded the contract as a way of cutting costs. It has been said that, since the General Electric corporate library was practically "a virtual library" it was not necessary to have an extensive library on site.

I think it is time to move beyond fear, but we must acknowledge that our profession is changing, whether we like it or not. Following are some things you can do now and regularly thereafter to meet the challenge.

- Keep up-to-date with the literature of managing information services and organizational change.
- Build bridges to the Product Development Group; sit in on their planning meetings and tell them how you can support their efforts with information. Be proactive, innovative, and wide-ranging. Help the Marketing Department with information about the market for new products; assist the Planning Department with in-depth information about possible acquisition candidates; deliver background information to the CEO on possible new members of the Board of Directors.
- Carry out an Information Audit. Interview senior, middle, and junior staff members to find out what they perceive as their information needs today, and find out how they are meeting those needs. Tell them about the new information tools you can introduce them to, and work with them to bring those tools to their desktop.
- Decide with your staff what the priority items are in terms of activities performed by library staff. Is cataloging or database building a top priority? If so, can you get what you need from an outside vendor?
- Read the most recent five years of your organization's annual reports. Memorize the goals of your organization for next year and for the following year.
- Identify and keep current files on each of your company's top competitors.
- Identify the power centers in your organization and get yourself aligned with them.
- Prepare an Information Center Annual Report. Make sure that copies go to the CEO, the Board of Directors, and all department heads. Use good graphics and layout (get help if needed) to make sure it gets read! Don't report on how many research projects you undertook or how many books circulated. No one cares—not even you! Instead, tell which departments, groups, and divisions the Information Center has assisted over the last year; include how much money the Information Center has saved or made for the organization. *If you can't do that this year because you haven't collected the information, figure out right now how you can achieve that next year.*

- Identify peer organizations and information centers and conduct bench-marking studies.
- Promise yourself that you will learn something new every year. Look around for places that teach the skill you have decided you need. Keep on learning; every new skill makes you better able to lead and to stay ahead.

Change is not easy, but there is no doubt that change is required. The ostrich approach won't work. If we don't initiate a change process ourselves, we risk having it done to us. Cement your library or information center to the goals of your organization. Test regularly to make sure the glue is still holding.

Cisco Systems used an advertisement in 1996 that includes a picture of a highway, with these words: "The Information Highway Is Paved with Rhetoric, Metaphors, and the Scar Tissue of Misinformed Executives." Our challenge is to prevent that kind of scar tissue from ever forming.

REFERENCES

1. Pettas, William A. *The Giunti of Florence: Merchant Publishers in the Sixteenth Century.* San Francisco, CA: Bernard M. Oriental, 1980, p. 5. Kindness of Therese A. De Vet, classics scholar.

2. Farkas-Conn. Irene. "Linking Information Services to Business Strategies." *Bulletin of the American Society for Information Science* 22, No. 4 (April/May 1996): p. 9.

3. Gurbaxani, Vijay. "The World of Information: Technology Outsourcing." *Communications of the ACM* 39, No. 7 (July, 1996): p. 45.

4. Caldwell, Bruce. "The New Outsourcing Partnership." *Information Week,* Issue 585 (June 24, 1996). p. 50 ff.

5. Strassman, Paul A. "Outsourcing: A Gain for Losers." *Computerworld* 29, No. 34 (August 21, 1995).

6. The Outsourcing Institute, 45 Rockefeller Plaza, Suite 2000, New York NY 10111: 800/421-6767; Fax 800/421-1644: http://www.outsourcing.com.

7. WEA has not been operating since 1986.

8. "Bart Kane on Outsourcing, Role of Customer Service." *Library Hotline* 25, No. 20 (May 20, 1996): p. 2.

9. Matarazzo, James M. and Laurence Prusak *The Value of Corporate Libraries: Findings from a 1995 Survey of Senior Management, a Report of the Special Libraries Association in cooperation with Ernst & Young Center for Business Information,* 1995. James M. Matarazzo, Dean and Professor, GSLIS, Simmons College, Boston MA: jmatarazzo@vmsvax.simmons.edu.

10. Matarazzo, James M. and Laurence Prusak *Valuing Special Libraries, a Report of the Special Libraries Association,* 1990. James M. Matarazzo, Dean and Professor, GSLIS, Simmons College, Boston MA: jmatarazzo@vmsvax.simmons.edu

11. Personal communication, September 1996.

12. McCleary, Hunter and William J. Mayer. "Teltech . . . Expert Systems the Old Fashioned Way: Person to Person." *Online* 12, No. 4 (July 1988): pp. 15–24.

16

Special Libraries at Work: The Library Manager as Part of the Organization Team

Elizabeth Ferguson and Emily R. Mobley

The thrust of this section has been to point out the significance of the library's position as a part of the organization. The library manager has the responsibility of managing his department and therefore is an integral part of the organization's management team. The management responsibility for a library is akin to managerial responsibility for any other department. Management responsibility should be built upon a solid base of clearly formulated, officially accepted goals and objectives. The library's goals state its purpose or mission within the organization. The goals tend to be long-range. Helen Waldron has called this statement the library's charter. The term, objectives, is often misused interchangeably with goals, but we here consider objectives as short-range or the stepping stones to achieving the long-range goals. In some rare instances the officials responsible for establishing the library produce such a statement of purpose. This was true in the case of the library recently established by the Aluminum Association, Inc. Usually, however, the library manager must take the initiative for working a statement out, shaping it into final form with the collaboration and approval of the manager's superior. Objectives constitute checkpoints for planning, reporting, budgeting, and evaluating.

The special library manager not only has the responsibility of departmental management but has the added responsibility of bringing professional expertise to bear on solving company problems. This dual responsibility is one aspect of the situation any professional may encounter in a corporate position. The librarian is both a professional librarian and a company manager. It is a question of two allegiances—one to the organization and one to his/her profession. On the one hand, allegiance to the library profession is very much involved in a librarian's competence on the job; and this competence can only be maintained by strong professional connections and by keeping abreast of current developments in a fast-moving profession. On the other hand, allegiance to the organization is implicit in the library's mandate to provide information service that supports the company's work and furthers its goals. Identification with the company is in the nature of the job and, as we stated concerning the philosophy of this book, the librarian is first an employee and second a librarian.

The conflicts inherent in this situation have been discussed at length by William H. Whyte, Jr. in *The Organization Man* and by Peter Drucker in *The Practice of Management* and other titles. Alvin Toffler in *Future Shock* and *The Third Wave* has further highlighted the impact of professionalism and the trends toward crossing organizational lines by means of task forces, interdepartmental committees, and project teams, leading to a less centralized "matrix" type of corporate organization. To take this a step further, the recent comparisons of Japanese versus American corporate behavior point out that American managers retain an allegiance to their professions over and above their allegiance to their companies, whereas, with the Japanese manager the opposite is the case.

As an employee, the library manager has a specific slot in the corporate hierarchy. The level of that slot in relationship to other managers with similar responsibilities constitutes the "status" or "prestige" factor. Titles and designations of management levels vary from company to company. Titles may signify levels in the hierarchy but they do not necessarily signify authority. There is fairly general agreement on three levels: top management (corporate officers); middle management (in charge of professional-level personnel and/or departments); and supervisory management (in charge of primarily clerical-level personnel and operations). To give an idea of current practice in the placement of library managers in company hierarchies, Martha Bailey's 1979 study of 238 heads of libraries in 200 companies found that three heads of libraries classified themselves as top management, 85 as middle management, and 139 as supervisory management.[1]

Quite aside from the obvious personal status or prestige involved, a high position on the organization chart is advantageous to the work of the library in many ways. In order to plan and direct services accurately, the librarian needs to be intimately informed on the workings of the company—its trends, changes in policy, the political interaction of people and departments and the like. Easy access to key officials, attendance at high-level staff meetings, membership on corporate committees, and automatic inclusion in the distribution of official notices and memoranda assures a good flow of such information. The "trickle down" method of getting information on company matters is notoriously undependable. These formal and informal relationships often uncover opportunities for service or tips on future projects for which new material will be needed in the library.

The organization charts have shown that there are wide variations in the management levels at which libraries are placed. They also indicate the rank of the officer to whom the library reports. If the library serves the entire company, this superior officer or boss has responsibility for several departments, often for other staff departments as well. He may be a line officer. He might be a controller or a manager or a vice-president for administrative services or personnel. If the library is organized under a single department such as the research department, it may report to the head of that department or to a designated assistant. The library's official communications with top management funnel through the officer to whom the library reports, the library's designated boss. This person is responsible for seeing that the operation of the library is carried on in conformance with company policies, and is usually in a position to make some management decisions and serve as the liaison between the library and top management when higher authority is needed for matters like the budget, major expenditures, or policy decisions.

It is very rare that an officer in charge of a special library starts with any real knowledge of what goes on in a library. The library operation is indeed unlike other departmental operations, and looked on from the outside, it sometimes seems mysterious. Library operations do not fit into the pattern of other company operations. No other department has to reckon with such routines as checking in magazines, cataloging books, and charging out books; nor do other departments have the difficult task of trying to put a value on an intangible like information service. It is therefore incumbent on the librarian to explain and interpret library procedures and activities for the superior's understanding. As Shirley Echelman once said, "If the librarian wants his boss to understand and support the library, he had better be prepared to discuss his own work in his boss's terms."[2] The "boss's terms" means discussing and communicating library matters in business language without using library jargon.

Communicating with the library's superior is done both formally and informally. As in any business operation, formal communication is the bedrock. Many formal methods are dictated by corporate policies. An annual report is a very common requirement, with the format and type of information required often dictated by higher management. All libraries have trouble reporting the intangibles involved in information services, and doing it in business terms is even harder. Progress reports are another mechanism and are particularly effective in keeping management updated on the progress of new projects or services. They may or may not be a requirement. Other types of reports are possible such as reports of studies undertaken by the library. These not only inform the superior but through that level may reach a wider audience. Formal memoranda are used for good business procedure—"put it in writing." Departmental reviews are sometimes required on a periodic basis and provide an opportunity for direct communication with higher management. All these communications to the library superior provide and arm him/her with something tangible to use as a basis for upward communication.

Over and above the formal requirements, librarians use any number of individual ways and means to maintain informal contact. Notes on interesting happenings in the library, letters of commendation, or personalized information alerts may be used. Face-to-face communication provides that all-important human element.

Proposals and recommendations for new programs and services usually require even more specialized and detailed communications with the superior officer. Careful preparation and businesslike presentation are of the essence.

The downward flow of information to subordinates or the library staff is as important in its own way as the upward flow to library superiors. The library manager serves as the liaison between the staff and upper management. In this capacity, there is inherent responsibility for keeping staff informed on company policy and important decisions. As the departmental leader, the manager creates an atmosphere whereby decisions can be openly communicated. This is an atmosphere in which planning and implementing new programs and changes in job functions can take place smoothly. Cultivating staff participation in planning and implementing job functions, offering opportunities to develop and advance on the job, and the assurance of good personnel policies, are morale factors. Good staff morale is largely the result of proper communications.

The significant duty of a library manager is to run a businesslike operation. Ideally, the librarian has total responsibility for the conduct of the library. Total responsibility includes not only the professional aspects but the business aspects as well. The professional aspects are directed toward the product of the library—effective information service. The business aspects are directed toward the operations which are inherent in the librarian's role as a part of the company's management team—planning, organizing, staffing, directing, coordinating, reporting, and budgeting. Businesslike operation and accountability are expected of a department which is nonprofit making and exists as "overhead" expense.

NOTES

1. Martha J. Bailey, "Middle Managers Who Are Heads of Company Libraries/Information Services," *Special Libraries* 70 (December 1979): 509.
2. Shirley Echelman, "Libraries Are Businesses, Too!" *Special Libraries* 65 (October/November 1974): 409.

17

Information Management: A Process Review

James M. Matarazzo

A PROCESS VIEW

Many books and articles in this field have been produced to introduce us to and influence us in favor of a specific technology. Whether it is a cataloging module or a circulation system, the focus has been on the technology and not on the information. However, corporate information has many names and an equal number of access points. It is in people's heads and in their files. Information, valuable information, is often in their briefcases, phone books, or on the shelves of the corporate library. Managing information requires building bridges between sources of knowledge. These knowledge sources may or may not be in the existing computer system. It is important, then, for the manager of an information resource center to be familiar with the complex world of information sources, human or otherwise.

One way to gain the needed familiarity is to use a process module. A process model is helpful in identifying the key tasks by which information is acquired, stored and used. Figure 17-1 is a general model of these tasks within a process perspective.[1] The sequence of presentation is logical, but it may not be necessary for the tasks to be addressed in any order. Indeed, improving any of these process tasks will have a beneficial effect on the use of information in any organization.

This process model links activities that are otherwise separated by functional, managerial, or other boundaries. Since information management is cross functional, the expertise of others at an organization may be necessary and even desirable to produce new and more effective approaches and mechanisms to manage information.

Obviously, if the whole information management process is to be seriously studied and revised, a significant amount of resources and time will be necessary.

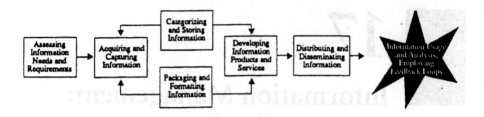

FIGURE 17-1 A Process Model of Information Management

Few firms make the opportunity available for a complete review of all of these processes. The following sections provide a review and offer approaches to their accomplishment.

INFORMATION NEEDS ASSESSMENT

From our own research and from years working as consultants, my colleagues and I have found that the tasks of identifying information needs is a real challenge for most information managers. As consultants, we often find information systems in place that are designed to meet expressed needs. The difficulty appears to be the tendency for changes in the business to make those needs obsolete, which should cause those systems to change. The reality is that the systems in the information center continue as if the business need is still present or is destined to return at some unknown time frame in the future.

Many of the processes put in place to meet perceived needs today will not be sufficient to provide solutions over the long-term. Thus, systems put in place must be modular and reviewed in light of business needs in a systematic way. If not, corporate information managers will continue to add system on top of system until none is capable of being executed in a competent fashion. The focus must shift from doing things right, to doing the right things.

Information professionals have an urgent need to become fully acquainted with the business they serve and the needs of their customers within their companies. This will require the information specialist to physically leave the borders of the library and become more accessible in the organization. Only when we leave the "lair" will we be able to understand the kind of information our customers need and how it is subsequently used.

In the Summer 1992 issue of *Special Libraries*,[2] Roger Jester, Manager of Management Communication at IBM's World Trade America Group, observed the following:

> *I find it strange that in my two decades of experience in a major American corporation, I have yet to see corporate librarians attending a business results or product review meeting. I have attended my fair share of business*

strategy sessions with colleagues from practically every corporate function but I cannot recall a single instance when a member of the librarian's staff was present.

In assessing user needs, information specialists need to know customer needs firsthand. These needs come to light when customers meet. Another method of assessing customer needs is a focused discussion on how information is used in a variety of business contexts. Participants in these discussions often express the requirements for information as well as the content of the information necessary. Then, and only then, will we be able to build systems to meet the needs of our customers.

ACQUIRING INFORMATION

Most corporate librarians cannot afford the luxury of building collections in the same sense as their counterparts in academic institutions. Even if the funds were available, the space in most corporate information centers will not allow for the classic collection development program to be in place. Instead, corporate libraries strive to have access to the appropriate information on a continuous and systematic basis.

A colleague and I visited the Business Information Center at Toshiba in Japan.[3] One of the functions this Center provides is systematic and continuous information on subjects of high interest to the staff of the Company. Each day a great deal of information arrives at the Center from databases, government reports, journal articles, reports from staff in the field and a whole host of other sources.

A team in the Business Information Center is trusted to know which sources should be briefly abstracted, translated, and made available to the system users. All of the information is read by the staff and those stories and reports with specific meaning to the firm are added to a system, called TOSFILE [see Figure 17-2]. All of this work is done by a team of librarians, systems managers, and library managers who understand the firm and the needs of their internal customers.

It would be technically possible at Toshiba to distribute all of the raw data to executives and managers. However, no one would have the time to read or even scan all of the material. The significance of the service is that a human intermediary is placed between the information and the customer. These individuals at the Business Information Center have the experience and knowledge *to filter the information* for those who will ultimately use it.

A high cost, in terms of staff and expense, is associated with this information capture system. The executives at this firm, however, feel it is worth the expense to receive the best available information. The staff of the Business Information Center are trusted employees who recognize quality and the relevance of the information they scan. In light of the time constraints faced by busy staff at Toshiba, the system is appreciated and used. And, use is a key factor in any

*Firm's Business Information Center acquires materials
and distributes information technology to 600 users daily
through TOSFILE.*

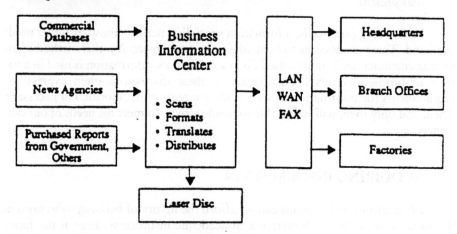

System has 600 daily users. Near-future plan calls for text and
image sent by satellite to non-Japan facilities.

FIGURE 17-2   Toshiba—Distributing Information Effectively

information system. At Toshiba, 30% of the staff of the Corporate Headquarters
make use of the system on a daily basis.

The technology that makes this system possible is important, to be sure, but
it is secondary to the information that is sent out over the system. Bud Mathaisel,
Director of Ernst & Young's Center for Information Technology and Strategy,
made the point about the pre-eminent value of information when he recently
wrote:

> *There are clear signs that information, per se, is finally becoming a full part-
> ner with technology. In recent long-range strategic planning studies we have
> witnessed a familiar theme once again re-emerging—executives are stressing
> timely and relevant information with which to manage their businesses and
> this theme is rising in prominence relative to others in the planning process.*

ORGANIZING AND STORING INFORMATION

It seems obvious that the only way to make appropriate decisions on how
information should be organized and stored is to view these plans in the light of
internal customers and the business to be served. Several basic questions must be
addressed:

- What business function will be advanced by the organization and storage of the material?
- How will the customers be better served by the proposed organization and storage scheme?
- What information is to be organized and stored?
- Does the information to be stored and organized have any vocabulary that is natural?

While the questions are closely related, the answers are important to the internal customers and to the designers of the system. It is also clear that the time and effort expended to find answers to these questions will be significant. Yet, the failure to do so will lead those who plan the systems to develop practices best applied to the organization and storage of data. Our efforts instead should be directed to organizing and storing only necessary information.

Recently a leading financial services firm asked me to assist a staff team in a review of their corporate library, specifically to help analyze the team's review of library operations. This strategic and operational review provides a good example of the application of the principles just reviewed. Our task in the review was to determine the key business functions at the firm and to determine how the library's services and products should support these functions.

Our analysis of a significant amount of data gathered at the firm has considerable relevance for information organization and storage. We found that the corporate library was committed to what we described as a storage model. Under this model, the staff collected, organized and stored a great deal of material on a wide range of subjects over long time frames just in case internal customers someday might need the journal, book, or report. Most of this material was on paper or microfiche, making access and storage expensive in terms of labor intensity for the library staff and an unnavigable ocean of data for the internal customers. While the library was staffed for longer than the normal week, the analysts and professional staff of this financial services firm worked many more hours than was practical to staff the corporate library.

An Information Needs Assessment of the behavior of the internal customers and their information seeking patterns revealed the following:

- The internal customer's needs were clustered around a core group of documents.
- The need for these documents was continuous and users requested these materials by document code.
- These documents were frequently ordered from a third-party vendor, even though the library had a complete set.

These findings led to a reorganization of how these documents were organized and stored, with a much stronger focus on how they were actually being used. For this area, the study team recommended the following:

- Purchase the required documents on CD-ROM.

- Make one set available for use 24 hours a day and locate it in the analysts' area.
- Make the document code the key to access the document to give the internal customers not only physical access to the material, but also a simple method of retrieval.

INFORMATION PACKAGING

This skill focuses on the actual form in which the information is presented to the internal client There is most certainly a substantial body of research to substantiate the claim that when information is conceived, the medium is an important part of the message. Others feel that the content of whatever is supplied is most important and that the format is not important Regardless of your feelings on this matter, you are urged to review the information presented in the chapter by Anne W. Talcott in the *SLA President's Task Force on the Value of the Information Professional.*[4]

Briefly, Talcott describes the work of an information professional who packages information for executives. These materials are taken by busy executives in preparation for visits to other companies. The material presented, impressive in itself, is very definitely packaged for ease of use, while representing a selection of the very best information available.

Another case worthy of note was seen in a visit to the Library of Nomura Research Company in Japan. The staff of the library were frequently called upon to provide government statistical information. Since the information in Japanese Government statistical compilations was so great, the library staff decided to gather all available government statistics, organize it, and package it in the form of a rather hefty monograph. This information package is now prepared and distributed within the Company. The packaged product proved so valuable that it is now offered for sale to others outside the firm.

What was developed, formatted, and packaged to meet the need of this firm has now become an information product produced entirely by the library staff. This package of information and its sale in fact produces an alignment between the Company and its sale of research and the library and its sale of information. The packaging of information also leads us to another core component for information specialists—that of developing information products and services.

INFORMATION PRODUCTS AND SERVICES

If it can be done, this process task has one of the highest returns for the information professional. This is, however, a turbulent time in business and it is difficult to secure funds for any project that will not have a short-term payback to the firm, especially to the firm's bottom line. Certainly the recent research report commissioned by KPMG Peat Marwick Management Consulting in the UK, confirms the focus on the short-term profit mentality in leading firms.

In spite of this, very successful models have come about from a more process-based approach to the management of information. The reward of use is that the internal customers of the company will find these products and services valuable and this value will be acknowledged by customers of the corporate library.

An excellent illustration of a successful project took place at the Sumitomo Insurance Company in Japan. The director of the library spoke to the sales manager at the firm and convinced him that the library staff could provide real time sales assistance to salesmen in the field. Using portable computers, sales agents prior to visiting clients, extract valuable information from the staff of the company library. This sales support system has been extremely successful and now consumes more than 90% of the library staff's time.

This project was funded by the sales department after the library director took the initiative to present the plan. This suggests that it is often easier to gain support for projects that serve the needs of other units at the firm. Projects done for research and development, marketing, and sales, can be justified, especially since their benefits, if successful, will be obvious to the sponsoring unit.

The library director at Sumitomo had a second guideline he used with this project It had been his feeling that the most important goal of his firm, the source of all that the firm stood for, and indeed its future, was sales. He felt, because he understood the business and what really mattered, that somehow he had to align the services of the library to the strategic thrust of the firm. His sales support system from the library was the method he chose.

In another case a large electronics firm's library sought to increase staff and budget, but was told repeatedly that the library would have to remain its present size and budget for the foreseeable future in the light of current budgetary restrictions. A number of the library staff in concert with the director of the library developed an alternative to growth—that of adding a second department to the library.

The staff of the library noticed that various departments they served were in need of unbiased research and analysis on various topics. Instead of contracting out for these services, a new unit of the library was contracted for the business previously outsourced. In order to do this without any increase to the library's budget, the unit pre-sold its work for one full year to internal units. The staff was hired after the work was sold.

This effort was so successful that work had to be turned away the first year. In the second year the staff was doubled as a result of the same system of pre-selling research and analysis to internal clients. By the third year of operation, the research and analysis unit staff was larger than that of the library.

It is worth noting that both the project at Sumitomo and the one at the electronics firm were initiated during difficult business cycles.

DISTRIBUTING AND DISSEMINATING INFORMATION

There is a common notion that the responsibility of the information professional ends with the delivery of a service or a product to the customer's desk or

PC. This implies that the nature of the delivery channel is well-known and deserves little attention. This is clearly not the case. Instead, there is a real need to build distribution channels for the products and services of corporate libraries.

In a series of research studies, a British researcher, John Blagden,[5] has demonstrated repeatedly that corporate libraries and information centers share twin problems which require both attention and resolution. Blagden has found first that the services available from corporate libraries *are known to few* at each of the firms studied. My work as consultant confirms his research . . . too few corporate staff members are aware of the capabilities and/or services available to them from this information resource. It is no wonder, then, that at the first sign of an internal review and/or an economic down trend, corporate library staffs and budgets are reduced, often to crippling levels.

One way to build strong and high value information channels to distribute information is to create a cost structure based on the value of service or product. While this may be counter to the strong service orientation of information professionals, a charging mechanism does place a quantifiable value on the service offerings from the corporate information center.

Charging for services also creates a distribution channel based on "mutual need" and it insures a feedback mechanism, since people are more likely to comment on a service for which they have paid. If the culture of your firm allows for charging, your services will be grounded legitimately within the context of a paid transaction and more likely to be accepted by corporate management. This subject of cost justifying information dissemination leads directly to Blagden's second finding.

Blagden also discovered that what we do in information provision for our customers has real value to our firm. The issue is for us to develop some sort of method to provide the concept of value in information provision. If we fail to demonstrate value to the firm we service, our future is tenuous at best.

EMPLOYING FEEDBACK LOOPS

There is *an extraordinary lack of knowledge and information surrounding information use.* A singular exception to this situation is a study completed by Joanne Marshall[6] under the financial sponsorship of the Special Libraries Association. In this study, Dr. Marshall has provided evidence that the products and services of the corporate library have an impact on its customers. Nearly 400 executives and managers in five firms indicated that the information supplied to them by the library staff: (1) made an impact on their decision-making and (2) had some impact in exploiting a new business opportunity, on deciding a course of action, or in improved client relations. In addition, these senior staff members ranked the library and library services highly as a source of information.

We do know, however, that for the institutions in her study and for the staff of these corporations, their corporate libraries make a difference. In fact, information supplied through the professional staff of the corporate library helped avoid the loss of time, the loss of funds and poor business decisions. And Marshall has provided full details so others can replicate the study.

This is exactly the kind of information needed today since all costs are carefully monitored. In today's corporation, functions that contribute will be retained; those that do not will likely lose corporate support.

It seems to me that a significant number of my colleagues believe that the application of information technology to what in the past has been done manually will solve many of the problems they face. While the library staff may be better off with these applications, no evidence has been provided to demonstrate that our customers have been better served.

The time has come to begin to prove that all we do in corporate libraries and information centers makes this unit more *effective*. If any of the possible IT applications are to really mean anything, one must absorb the messages in *Process Innovation: Redesigning Work through People and Technology*. The advice in this book is that all of us help change the manner in which the people in organizations work.

Many IT applications result in much more expensive operations with little bottom line justification, less the supposed "status" in the organization served. Yet, the visible and invisible costs to support these technological application are very large. To these costs must be added the acknowledged cost of time and training with little evidence that information is distributed more effectively.

Most firms document success with a very narrow view of short-term profits. In the light of this we must focus our efforts on viable and visible information tasks. A process orientation to information management can provide a guide for our efforts.

REFERENCES

1. The author wishes to acknowledge extensive discussions on this model with Laurence Prusak, Principal, Ernst & Young Center for Business Innovation, Boston, MA.

2. Roger E. Jester, "To the End of the Earth: Librarians and Information Management Needs," *Special Libraries*, v. 83, no. 3, 1992, p. 141.

3. For a full report on Toshiba and seven other Japanese firms see: Laurence Prusak and James M. Matarazzo, *Information Management and Japanese Success*, Washington, DC: Special Libraries Association, 1991.

4. Anne W. Talcott, "A Case Study in Adding Intellectual Value: The Executive Information Service," in the *SLA President's Task Force on the Value of the Information Professional*, edited by James M. Matarazzo, New York: Special Libraries Association, 1987, pp. 37–44.

5. John Blagden. *Do We Really Need Libraries: An Assessment of Approaches to the Evaluation of the Performance of Libraries*. London: Clive Bingley, 1980.

6. Joanne G. Marshall, *The Impact of the Special Library on Corporate Decision Making*. Washington, DC: Special Libraries Association, 1993.

Index

For Product Safety Concerns and Information please contact our
EU representative GPSR@taylorandfrancis.com Taylor & Francis
Verlag GmbH, Kaufingerstraße 24, 80331 München, Germany